THE LEAGUE OF
EXOTIC DANCERS

THE LEAGUE OF
EXOTIC DANCERS

Legends from American Burlesque

KAITLYN REGEHR &
MATILDA TEMPERLEY

OXFORD
UNIVERSITY PRESS

Oxford University Press is a department of the University of Oxford.
It furthers the University's objective of excellence in research, scholarship,
and education by publishing worldwide. Oxford is a registered trade mark of
Oxford University Press in the UK and certain other countries.

Published in the United States of America by Oxford University Press
198 Madison Avenue, New York, NY 10016, United States of America.

Library of Congress Cataloging-in-Publication Data
Names: Regehr, Kaitlyn, author. | Temperley, Matilda, photographer.
Title: The League of Exotic Dancers : legends from American burlesque /
Kaitlyn Regehr and Matilda Temperley.
Description: New York, NY : Oxford University Press, 2017. | Includes
bibliographical references and index.
Identifiers: LCCN 2016034963| ISBN 9780190457563 (hardback) |
ISBN 9780190457587 (epub)
Subjects: LCSH: Stripteasers—United States—Interviews. | Burlesque
(Theater)—United States. | League of Exotic Dancers (United States) |
BISAC: PERFORMING ARTS / General. | PERFORMING ARTS / Dance /
Popular. | SOCIAL SCIENCE / Women's Studies.
Classification: LCC PN1949.S7 R44 2017 | DDC 792.7092/273—dc23 LC
record available at https://lccn.loc.gov/2016034963

1 3 5 7 9 8 6 4 2
Printed by Sheridan Books, Inc., United States of America

For our mothers

CONTENTS

THE LEAGUE OF
EXOTIC DANCERS

Circus de Moccos performers compete in the Tournament of Tease at the Burlesque Hall of Fame, 2015

*Tammi True at the
Titans of Tease
Showcase, 2013*

GLITTER AND GRIT
AN INTRODUCTION

A T THE TITANS OF TEASE Legends of Burlesque Showcase at the Burlesque Hall of Fame Annual Weekender, seventy-five-year-old Tammi True glided onto the stage and performed one of her traditional striptease numbers. She beamed as she slowly caressed and swayed her hips from side to side. She then swiveled, turned her back to the audience, and attempted her signature move: bending over and looking between her legs[1] while shaking her beaded panties. Although True's range of motion and ability to actually get her head between her legs was simply a nod toward what the move used to be, the burlesque enthusiast audience of 800, mostly young women, cheered in anticipation of Tammi's big reveal. Finally, after removing her bra, Tammi stood with her arms in the air, belly out, joyously bouncing her pastie-clad, stage-veteran breasts and anything else that cared to bounce with them.

Perhaps out of gratitude for the expression of freedom and defiance of common preconceptions of women's bodies, particularly aging ones, or perhaps viewing the performance as a means to undermine the shaming that has been, or often still is, directed at sexually expressive women, or perhaps because they just really liked it, the crowd leaped to their feet in outright celebration. One woman beside me dabbed tears from her eyes; another, in front of me, pounded her fist in the air and exclaimed, "Fuck yah!"

The Burlesque Hall of Fame has its roots in the Exotic Dancers League (EDL), a group started by Jenny "The Bazoom Girl" Lee,[2] which was incorporated as the Exotique Dancers League in 1955.[3] Their first meeting, which the *Los Angeles Times* described as being "colorful but well-balanced" with "three redheads, three blonds, and three brunettes,"[4] was held in June of that year with the primary concern of raising the minimum wage for strippers in Los Angeles.[5] This early sex workers union employed a variety of unorthodox acts of protest to advance their cause, such as a "cover up" strike.[6] Eventually, however, the group took the form of a social group for dancers that included a

Fremont Street, 2015

softball team named the Barecats and an annual meeting that continues today as an annual reunion in Las Vegas.

Situated five miles and fifty years away from the tourist strip is downtown Las Vegas, or "Old Vegas." Iconized by its decrepit casinos and vintage neon signage, this once rundown and forgotten enclave is now home to both a hipster-driven rejuvenation and the current Exotic Dancers League headquarters—renamed the Burlesque Hall of Fame. The Burlesque Hall of Fame reunion now operates as a social gathering and support group, where these late-life dancers perform their now half-century-old routines from the golden age of burlesque to a rally of counterculture fans.

Five years ago photographer Matilda Temperley and I headed to Nevada to begin photographing and interviewing this community—a group that, like "Old Vegas" itself, continues to survive sixty years past its supposed prime. Here, in a smoky, off-strip casino, we found women, at times well into their eighties, subversively bumping and grinding away preconceptions about appropriate pensioner behavior and enjoying their young adoring burlesque enthusiast fans who lovingly refer to their burlesque elders as "legends"—a rare intergenerational support group and sisterhood.

*Kaitlyn Regehr and
Matilda Temperley
with Dirty Martini
at the Burlesque
Hall of Fame, 2015*

Over the past twenty years, burlesque—a mid-twentieth-century, working-class entertainment—has been embraced and reclaimed by a counterculture movement, known as neo-burlesque, for purposes of artistic, sexual, and personal expression. In the last ten years, burlesque dance or striptease has moved further into the mainstream in the form of women's fitness trends (even Oprah tried striptease aerobics), hen nights, and Hollywood blockbusters, staring at the likes of Cher and Christina Aguilera. The rhetoric that surrounds most of these striptease-themed entertainments and activities is often one of female empowerment and sexual liberation. This narrative positions dancers of the mid-twentieth century as feminist icons and situates burlesque as an inclusive, liberated safe space that—in contrast to (lowbrow) modern-day strip clubs—is (and always was) art.

From the time of the burlesque revival's inception, a common feature of it has been the concerted effort made by many individuals to dissociate burlesque from contemporary stripping. As Michelle Baldwin states:

> The question asked most in the early days of the new burlesque was "Are you a stripper?" to which many answered emphatically "No." They were dancers, striptease artists, burlesque performers, but many wanted nothing to do with the term stripper. Many still hold this position.[7]

From this perspective, the neo-burlesque movement has often positioned burlesque as nostalgic, feminist, and separate from claims of exploitation that sit at the heart of much of the discourse regarding contemporary exotic dance and the sexual entertainment industry at large.[8] A frequent narrative regarding the history of American burlesque posits its death at some point in the middle of the twentieth century (the 1930s,[9] the 1940s,[10] the 1950s,[11] the 1960s[12]), only to be succeeded by a rebirth or revival some fifty years later.[13] This death narrative places burlesque in a time capsule[14] and thus removes it from the evolution of the modern strip club as well as from the contemporary sex industry.

In this way, though the intergenerational relationships at the annual Weekender can be very positive for this aging community, glamorizing this history can at times trivialize some of the difficult realities experienced by some of these dancers. As noted in burlesque legend Bic Carrol's interview, "To glorify it [burlesque] is kind of silly. It was a way to make money, it was a job. It wasn't a hobby. To [the neo-burlesque community] it's a hobby. To us, it was survival."

The interviews in this project suggest that this history does not sit neatly in a mid-twentieth-century time capsule but rather lingers on, intersecting with other forms of sex work and erotic entertainments and complicating the common narrative surrounding theatrical burlesque. Furthermore, as the dancers in this project often cite the "death" of burlesque in relationship to their own careers (anywhere from the late 1940s to the mid-1990s), the interviews raise questions about whether burlesque ever actually "lived." It is possible that when viewed through the nostalgic lens of history, striptease and erotic entertainment more generally were always thought to be cleaner and "classier" in earlier incarnations. That is, in its contemporary form, striptease will always be viewed as sex work while in the "good old days" it was less messy—that is, more disconnected from social problems and stigma.

The discussions in this project indicate that although burlesque in its theatrical and variety format did indeed change over time, it did not "die." Rather, the dancers and acts themselves moved into and intersected with other forms of erotic entertainment such as nude go-go or the golden age of pornography in the 1970s. These mid-twentieth-century burlesquers collectively danced through (and at times between) many incarnations of striptease, from famed staged burlesque, into supper clubs, and further into lap dancing. With these developments, other issues arose as dancers were asked to step off the stage and into the laps of patrons. With this close contact, some dancers also found themselves "aged out" of the industry much earlier than a generation before.

In the spirit of embracing complexities and alternate tellings, we did not seek to shape interviews so that they might "fit" together. Rather, the interviews should stand as individual accounts, experiences and moments within the context of American burlesque history. Three expanded interviews with accompanying essays will be utilized to contextualize others. These accompanying essays each propose a theme or storyline that intersects with the predominant narrative surrounding burlesque and further disrupts common understanding of the performance form. Many of these disruptions center on change in the space where striptease was performed, or the frame through which striptease was viewed.

Drawing from my time assisting famed burlesque queen Tempest Storm at festivals across the United States, I examine intersections between striptease and fame. This discussion is influenced by Roland Barthes's work on striptease,[15] which proposes the concept of layers that exist between the staged striptease dancer and the audience, helping to frame the performer as a star. I investigate how these layers in theatrical burlesque, such as costuming and spectacle, allowed dancers to achieve celebrity status. However, I theorize that although contemporary understanding of burlesque history often states otherwise, Tempest Storm is a notable exception, as there were very few famed burlesque queens who were able to gain her mainstream status. Further, unlike celebrities who enter public consciousness by other means, the dancers who actually reached celebrity status in burlesque still always risked the possibility of falling into what Tempest defines as un-"classy" and, further, "slum" territory.

In my interview with Kitten Natividad, I explore the choice of one dancer who, dissatisfied with this change of frame from staged burlesque to nude go-go and more laterally lap dancing, left striptease for erotic film. This discussion disrupts the common telling of burlesque, which encapsulates the dance form away from other forms of erotic entertainment—in this case, modern lap dancing and erotic film. Tangible intersections between pornographic film and burlesque history during the golden age of porn, through shared theaters and performers, are highlighted in this interview, as the burlesque queen gives way to the porn star. In addition, this interview reveals issues of intimacy in nude go-go and, more substantially, hard-core pornography, and questions boundaries surrounding "real" versus "performed" sex.

Finally, drawing from my meetings with burlesque legend Marinka, I examine the narrative surrounding burlesque as a space of positive body image—that is, the common (often neo-burlesque) understanding that burlesque has always been accepting of bodily difference. Here I observe difference as it relates to age and specifically age and sexuality. Utilizing Marinka's interview as a case study, I discuss prejudices toward age and sexuality specifically in relationship to exotic dance as it evolved over the latter half of the twentieth century. I propose that lap dancing demands a much younger dancer than staged striptease, which, thanks to the aforementioned layers of theatrical frame, lights and costuming, is a much more forgiving form. However, though theatrical burlesque may have allowed for longer career spans for some dancers (particularly famed burlesque queens), this was not the reality for most of the legends in this project. Many dancers in this project were aged out of the industry, a harsh reality with serious consequences for both financial livelihood and identity.

By contrast, the Burlesque Hall of Fame has provided a new multigenerational space. These now-elderly dancers are reframed and given a new safe space away from the marginalization of ageism. However, I also argue that work in the sex industry is often accompanied by complicating factors surrounding issues of need, survival, and a question of free choice. As a result, I find that this framing of the Burlesque Hall of Fame event as an uncomplicated liberated, safe space is often an oversimplification.

Framing is a subtheme throughout this project. My thoughts on this topic have been influenced by Irving Goffman's *Frame Analysis*. In this work Goffman uses the analogy of a picture frame, which gives structure to content. The burlesque variety show format, along with its costuming, the props, and the stage itself, gave a physical frame to burlesque dance. In turn, this physical frame of the theatrical stage also enabled a social framework, which positioned the dancers as theatrical entertainers rather than sex workers. The historic physical and social framing of burlesque is similar in prevailing academic and popular narratives surrounding burlesque and its death. The death narrative removes mid-twentieth-century burlesque from the timeline of exotic dance and thus disconnects it from contemporary strip clubs. Regrettably, this framing ultimately contributes to the marginalization of some contemporary forms of sexual entertainment and subsequently the women who perform in those media.

However, in making this likely volatile statement, I wish to situate my own relationship to this community and subsequent potential bias. To a great extent, it was my role as a broadcaster on a documentary television series about burlesque that aired in Canada—and subsequently the United Kingdom and various countries across mainland Europe—that allowed me initial access to the community. This television program was ideologically allied with the positive body image movement that populated mainstream media in the early 2000s.

From this perspective, the program positioned burlesque dance as an empowerment tool. Though I now question the labeling of burlesque with the blanket term of "empowerment" a designation that was in vogue when I entered this community five years ago, it was my work on this "empowering" television series that facilitated my preliminary interviews for the project.

The importance placed on my own proximity to fame seemed to be of interest for some of the participants in this project. This fame factor (albeit Canadian C-list fame) created a notable dynamic—some women would speak to me solely out of interest in my supposed fame frame while I questioned them about their former fame frame provided by the burlesque house. It was in this space of arguably artificial or at least precarious frames of new and old C-list fame that I was first welcomed by a few early members of this community.

In addition, the role of "television personality" granted me another occupation outside the role of academic. Not uncommonly, individuals in this community express a general dislike of academics who have often attempted to enter the burlesque community and are viewed as expropriators as they patronizingly champion the liberated culture. As I was once told by Jo "Boobs" Weldon, headmistress of the New York School of Burlesque and pioneer of the neo-burlesque resurgence, strippers don't need the "approval of some PhD" to tell them whether they are empowered or not. Thus, as I navigated this project, I have tried to play three roles—all of which I made known to the community: (1) my role as an academic researcher; (2) my role as a television personality, which enabled me to obtain initial interviews; and most important, (3) my role as a member of the community. It was this latter role, which grew and strengthened over the years, that enabled me to be a part of and experience this social microcosm from within. The interviews in this project were conducted and transcribed over a five-year period. Due to the sensitive nature of the content, all participants were informed at the time of the interviews that they could choose to omit all or any portions they did not wish included in the publication. Most of the preliminary meetings required follow-up telephone interviews for clarity and expansion. Thus, some of the interviews presented in the project may have taken place at a different moment from the specific interaction described.

My hope is that this project will offer color and complexity to this relatively untold women's history. A sense of personal agency, independence, excitement, and sexual freedom is present in some interviews while physical, substance, and sexual abuse are also common threads. It is in this supposed death period that this project lives. The stories reflect a period of transition, when many dancers moved from decrepit burlesque theaters to tired traveling shows, to gaudy nightclubs, to sometimes soulless strip clubs, and at times back and forth again. With this project we do not put forward one correct answer but rather show these late-life exotic performances, and the burlesque history from which they come, in the multidimensional forms in which they were presented to us, with both their trials and triumphs—their grit and their glitter.

*Both images this page:
The Cheesecake
Burlesque Revue at the
Burlesque Hall of Fame,
2015*

Miss Exotic World, Queen of Burlesque 2013, Lou Lou D'vil watches the Tournament of Tease with fellow burlesque dancer Miss Red, 2015

Trixie Little is crowned the Queen of Burlesque, Miss Exotic World, 2015

AGING, STAGING, SPARKLE, AND STRUGGLE
FRAMES OF CONTEXT

Exotic World and Archiving Erotica

EXOTIC WORLD WAS FOUNDED BY tassel twirler Jenny Lee, who having collected "stripper droppings"[1]—an old pastie, a shoe, a G-string—"began tacking them up"[2] on the wall of her strip club the Sassy Lassy, in San Pedro, California.[3] Upon moving to a goat farm in Helendale, California, for health reasons, Jenny Lee brought the artifacts with her and encouraged dancers to make an annual reunion pilgrimage to the farm and bring their "stuff"[4] to add to the collection. The Helendale property has been described as "every cliché of the dirtiest part of the desert possible," complete with tumbleweeds, dust blows, Joshua trees, and a general void of vegetation.[5]

With the assistance of her friend and successor, Dixie Evans—known as the Marilyn Monroe of burlesque because she impersonated the star, allowing audiences to imagine Monroe without her clothes on—Jenny Lee wanted to build the property as a safe haven for ex-strippers. It was to be a place that could house and support former exotic dancers where they could live in mobile homes on the property and assist at the museum. In its envisioned idealized state, the museum would create revenue to support former

Opposite page: Pasties for sale at the Burlesque Bazaar, 2015

dancers who lived on the property while also providing a place of education for dancers entering the industry. As Big Fannie Annie explained in a July 2014 interview:

Dixie said they were going to open up by the motel there and make it for the legends who have nothing. That's what it was all about at one time, to help the legends.

World Famous *BoB* at the Burlesque Hall of Fame, 2015

Though the intended retirement community did not become a reality, the educational outreach component of the annual reunion did come to fruition with the addition of a competition element. It was the Exotic World pageant that motivated young burlesque enthusiasts from the emerging neo-burlesque resurgence to join the annual reunion and compete for the title of Miss Exotic World. Word of the reunion grew through the 1990s and, as comedian and neo-burlesque performer Margaret Cho has noted, by 2001 Exotic World had become "the Mecca for a generation of women who made the goat farm Ground Zero of the largest burlesque revival since the 1940s."[6]

Outfitted in a fantastically oversize, bubblegum-pink beehive wig and three-inch-long false silver lashes, and costumed in the hyperfeminized style of drag performers, self-proclaimed female-female impersonator, World Famous *BoB* explains that she began making the pilgrimage in the early 2000s: "You would have to fly into Las Vegas or L.A. and then you would have to find someone with a car, and you would drive through all these winding roads."[7] Eventually one would come to a sign that said, "Wild Road...appropriately named."[8] When arriving at the large, arching, wrought iron gates, on which "Exotic World" was inscribed, "You would have to honk the horn of your car three times," a signal to which Evans would respond. She would the teeter out down the long dusty driveway dressed in sequins and feathers, "like a cloud,"[9] and proceed to give you a tour around the museum.

Russell Shelnut lived near the ranch in the early 2000s. He would come by the goat farm once a week to check on the older women who resided on the property and occasionally take them for dinner. I asked Russell to describe Exotic World:

It's super hot, 100 plus degree heat in the summer. Dust everywhere. You had the dust devils blowing around. It was like the pictures that you might see of movies of some farm house way out in the middle of the desert.... If you're going along the road, you come to the farm house to the left with a pool [around which the Miss Exotic World competition was held]; next to that, on the right you have the museum. And all over the walls there were various souvenirs. She had a set of Sally Rand's fans from the Fan Dames and Sally had donated one of her G-strings and that was in a case. I think she had a sofa that belonged to Jayne Mansfield. But it's real flat and real dry, dusty, hot. It was very much a weird experience—like being in another planet or something when you walk into the place.[10]

Russell described the atmosphere and feel of the Exotic World when the reunion opened to the neo-burlesque community and the interactions between these young performance artists and Dixie:

They did this for Dixie, and I think that's just beautiful. She had the prime table [and] everyone came up to say hi to her and give her a hug. She's the custodian of burlesque. I'm so glad to know that this has been moved to Vegas where many, many more people can appreciate it, because, boy, that was an hour drive for me. And...I'm already out in the sticks. It was another hour to a more remote area.[11]

After Jenny Lee's death in 1990, Dixie Evans ran the museum until 2005 when the collection was moved to Las Vegas and renamed the Burlesque Hall of Fame. The present Burlesque Hall of Fame (BHoF) director, Dustin Wax, suggests that the need for the move stemmed from concern that visitorship was curtailed by the farm's remote location—it was just off Route 66. However, it may also have been the marginal nature of the content of the museum that dissuaded the general public and thus curtailed potential revenue. Others have different narratives surrounding the closing of Helendale, which include the heat damage to the property and even foul play on the part of a new generation of burlesque enthusiasts attempting to usurp power from Dixie. As Big Fannie Annie asserts:

It [the reunion] was actually very nice. They'd have little hamburgers and hot dogs and cold drinks and if you wanted your own beer you'd go get it. And we'd all sit around and look at each other—twenty, thirty of us there and it was wonderful.... The first year they had the contest there was probably 200 people from all over the world including press, cameras. It was something. And the older girls out there will tell you that was just something unbelievable. So, it grew from that, and a different generation took it over, and they've kind of changed it. Certain things happened which I won't go into because it's not good to talk dirty about people or say things about people. But whatever. It's changed. It depends on whose story you hear.[12]

Bambi Jones at home in Las Vegas, 2015

Tensions between the former Exotic Dancers League members (now called "legends") and the young generations at the present-day Burlesque Hall of Fame and a sense that their once "legend only" social club has been assumed and appropriated are recurring themes in many of the legends' interviews. However, none of the women who have shared such opinions in detail have wanted to be identified in this project. The interactions between the neo-burlesque generation and the legends, which are often positive for individuals involved but sometimes not, will be discussed later.

At present, a portion of the former Exotic World collection is now show-cased in two small rooms of a former health services building turned shared arts space, Emergency Arts situated in downtown Las Vegas, while the remaining artifacts are in storage. Downtown Las Vegas, "old Vegas," or "'50s Vegas" are terms given to the area to differentiate it from the Las Vegas strip in location, architecture, and sensibility. The area, which seems to be the ruins of the discarded Las Vegas of the 1950s, iconized by its old neon signage and aging casinos, is currently undergoing something of a rejuvenation. Young, often artistic and alternative, local Las Vegas residents have embraced and transformed these old buildings into coffee shops, bars, and arts spaces. This rejuvenation sits as a parallel story to Exotic World and the burlesque revival more generally. For it is here, in a former health services building turned (or hipsterized) communal art space, in the rejuvenated and historicized '50s Vegas, that Exotic World, now renamed the Burlesque Hall of Fame, lives.

Dustin Wax was hired in 2011 to oversee the curation, storage, and maintenance of the collection. As Wax explains, allowing anyone who came through the farm in the desert to try on sixty-year-old costumes with feathers and sequins is not the best way to maintain the artifacts. Further, as "time is the first enemy of everything"[13]—"feathers decay . . . you stick them in a box and they smell really bad," and "cockroaches love synthetic materials"[14]—the process of restoration has been a challenging task.

My relationship to the Burlesque Hall of Fame archive as well as other archives used in this project has been similarly complex. For one thing, due to a lack of space in the Emergency Arts Building, the majority of the BHoF archive currently inhabits a storage locker, and as a result, accessing the materials and having space to engage with them is difficult. Su Kim Chang, a librarian in the Special Collections at the University of Nevada, Las Vegas (UNLV), oversees what researchers in the field endearingly term "the showgirl collection." Chang has been working to build a connection with the Hall of Fame in order to help care for the collection and offer a research space to those viewing the materials. However, to date, little progress has been made.

As with the spaces in which these two collections are held—a university library, an arts space, and a storage locker—the attitudes toward the collections and the artifacts themselves are rather different. The UNLV's collection contains hundreds of archival documents and photos on showgirls in Las Vegas largely from two donations; one donation comes from Dorothy Mack, the widow of famed burlesque agent and manager, Jess Mack, and the other is from the Minsky family, a famed (if not the most famous) burlesque-producing family in New York and later in Vegas. When looking through this collection, one gets the sense that contents of desk drawers and filing cabinets—dog-eared contracts; coffee-stained scripts of vaudevillian comics; yellowing promotional photos of young, hopeful strippers; and a Christmas card from Tempest Storm—were emptied straight into boxes, and it is in this same condition that you find the materials.

The Burlesque Hall of Fame's collection, by contrast, has a much more diverse set of benefactors who have all donated just an item or two from their collective storage rooms and scrapbooks. In this way it is both less and more complete. A pair of rhinestone-encrusted high heels, Gypsy Rose Lee's traveling trunk, a framed golden G-string, programs, posters, printed ephemera, and a box of sixty-year-old pasties fill out the collection.[15] Engagement with these artifacts has presented a number of issues for me as a researcher. For one, I want to note the inherent seduction of these objects—Tempest Storm's framed, golden G-String, for example—and ask how one makes use of such an object and further critically engages with it. It was also crucial to treat the materials with respect, something that they were not necessarily accorded in the past.

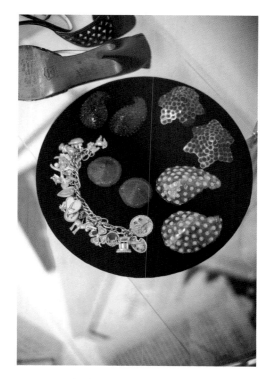

Pasties on display at the Burlesque Hall of Fame, 2015

As these objects are the remnants of erotic entertainment, they are probably things that were deemed "smutty" or not worth keeping.

However, erotic performance or not, performance archives are surrounded by a history of supposed inferiority in contrast to other art forms, and further problems involving how one actually archives a performance have been discussed at length throughout academic scholarship. Jacques Derrida suggests that performance does not remain and, as a result, it is always in a place of "loss."[16] Peggy Phelan has similarly discussed the impermanence of performance and its subsequent inability to become an archival "object," making it the defiant, political bad boy of the artistic mediums.[17] However, in direct contrast to these theories, Rebecca Schneider focuses on the residue, or "remains," that performance leaves behind. In this way, she does not pull performance out of the archive but rather expands the parameters of the archive to include performance.[18] That is, the archive can be shaped—and in fact is shaped—by individuals and their relationship to remains created by the performance. This concept is very much at play within the treatment of both the artifacts and the stories present in this project at the Burlesque Hall of Fame and, in particular, the homes of the legends.

Artifacts in the homes of the legends eschew conservative forms of categorization proposed by Schneider. Rather, in these homes, the objects are displayed and sorted in a way that has been determined by the legend rather than an external archivist figure. Further, as the dancer has always been present when introducing me to her performance artifacts, these items always exist in relationship to that dancer, her stories, and her use of the artifact. By example, a fifty-year-old costume might live in a closet next to a cooking apron; an old feather boa might be used to decorate a dressing table; costume jewelry might share a drawer with diabetes medication; and former promotional posters might be framed beside pictures of grandchildren and family members. In this way, these performative artifacts exist in direct conversation with their owners—the performers—and their present-day bodies and reality. The items are less fragments of the past than they are objects of the present as they remain in use in the home and hands of the performer. Further, these objects are also presented and described by that dancer through personal memory or practiced telling (as often these anecdotes have been told many times). This interaction between the performer and her own artifacts arguably sits in contrast with traditional archives, which position objects as historical and catalogue them for the benefit of the visitor to the archive. In contrast, rather than being catalogued as history for visitor observation, the objects in these homes are still very much living.

Diana Taylor rejects the polarity between embodied performance and the archive. Rather, Taylor suggests the term "acts of transfer," which implies that all transmitted knowledge is mediated and transferred in multiple ways. There are "many ways in which the archive and the repertoire work to constitute and transmit social knowledge,"[19] which can act in relationship with the sociopolitical, philosophical, and historical implications of the performance. Taylor thus calls for a joining between the transmission of the performance and the transmission of archive.

Utilizing Taylor's theory, where both the archive and the (in this case) still living history sit in conversation with each other, the UNLV and the Burlesque Hall of Fame (BHoF) archives become a reference point, which then allows me to enter into the oral history or ethnographic study. For me, these archives became a jumping off point. Often, when I was meeting with a dancer or being entertained in her home, my mentioning a piece she had donated to the BHoF led her to show me a "more important" costume piece with which she could not bear to part, or resulted in our spending hours flipping through a scrapbook. Thus, for this project, the collection became a reference for each dancer and a way of noting her previous fame or status (and clearly these women must have been famous if their costume pieces were in a museum). From this place of acknowledgment, it often seemed easier to move more naturally through the conversation. That is, the artifacts allowed me to note the dancer's previous fame and status within the BHoF collection and this was often greatly appreciated.

Aside from these two collections (the showgirl collection at the UNLV and the artifacts from the BHoF), the other archival resource for this project was the Gypsy Rose Lee papers housed in the Performing Arts Library in the New York Public Library. Gypsy Rose Lee and Sally Rand are the only dancers who are heavily featured in this project who were not part of the BHoF community. They are included because they are prominent dancers within the history of burlesque and also because they were regularly invoked in the interviews in this project. Both Gypsy Rose Lee and Sally Rand worked with women interviewed in this project. They become secondary players in relation to the dancer speaking, but they play an important role as in all cases they represent a different period in burlesque. More specifically, they represent the golden age of burlesque that allowed dancers greater fame and distance from patrons, which in turn, often created greater options and opportunity than those allotted to the women involved in this project.

Dusty Summers' Scrapbook on display at the Burlesque Bazaar, 2015

Just as the women interviewed in this project had fewer opportunities than the famed burlesque queens of two decades earlier, the BHoF archive struggles with its visibility and funding opportunities. Securing government funding for a sex-based performance history is always a challenge, especially in the surprisingly conservative state of Nevada. Thus, the majority of the museum's budget is derived from the annual reunion—lovingly called the "Weekender."

The Hangover Pool Party at the Burlesque Hall of Fame Weekender, 2015

The Burlesque Hall of Fame Weekender

THE WEEKENDER HAS MADE ITS home in the Orleans, an off-strip hotel where during the week, conference room rates begin at $35 a night, and which is, as I have now been informed by a few cab drivers, "the place the locals go." Having greatly expanded from its goat farm days, the Miss Exotic World pageant now draws neo-burlesque performers from around the world to compete for a variety of titles. These include Best Burlesque Troupe, Best Burlesque Group, Most Comedic, the King of Boylesque, and the most coveted award, Miss Exotic World.

The resurgence members have also helped to shape the reunion into the large-scale burlesque convention. At the Hangover Pool Party and Fashion Show, neo-burlesquers sport many creative variations on retro-inspired bathing wear. Similarly, at the Barecats Burlesque Bowling, teams compete adorned with a variety of sexually explicit party-themed accessories. Other events such as Stitch n' Bitch, a burlesque-themed sewing class, and Naked Ladies Reading (fairly self-explanatory) have also helped flesh out the four days of this event.

The Burlesque Bazaar is open daily in one of the hotel's large conference rooms. Vendors line the four walls selling a range of erotica goods such as nipple tassels, vintage clothing, and a variety of fetish accessories. Walking through this vending room are the young, counterculture burlesquers, stopping at vending tables to chat, buy goods, and express their admiration. Neo-burlesque performer Kitten LaRue and her wife, drag king Lou Henry Hover, stop beside a table of rhinestone pasties to pose for a selfie. Leslie Anne Hooker, a descendant of General Joseph Hooker, who allegedly first brought groups of woman over to America to pleasure servicemen, stops to talk and proudly explains the origins of her notable surname.

Lining the entire exterior of the room, facing the latex and bondage gear, is a procession of folding tables. These are the "legend" vending tables, at which the former Exotic Dancers League (EDL) ladies display their yellowing scrapbooks and piles of forty-year-old publicity photos available for autograph and sale. The autograph sessions present an interesting dynamic. These former strippers may not have been famous during their time performing; in fact, as

Opposite page: The Hangover Pool Party at the Burlesque Hall of Fame Weekender, 2015

Kitten LaRue and Lou Henry Hoover pose for a selfie at the Burlesque Hall of Fame, 2015

Jo "Boobs" Weldon, headmistress of the New York School of Burlesque, noted, "They aren't really celebrities, they weren't really famous. Tempest [Tempest Storm—interviewed later in the book] was really famous but that is so rare and a lot of women that are coming to the Burlesque Hall of Fame weren't famous like that."[20] However, whether it is by way of their title, "legend," the structuring of the Bazaar's "legend autograph sessions," or BHoF's general star treatment of the women, these former, possibly "not famous," strippers get to be remembered here at the Burlesque Hall of Fame, accurately or not, as burlesque stars.

The weekend is also a time when legends are able to reconnect and reminisce with each other. In this way, the BHoF Weekender has also provided a space where I was able to engage with and observe the legends in a group setting. This meant that when recalling events, the legends could fill in for each other, or disagree with each other, or argue over facts and dates—all of which often made for much richer and more nuanced stories. The group atmosphere also allowed me to observe the relationships between the legends. These interactions revealed disapproval of dancers who were possibly more explicit, danced in a later period and subsequently were required to show more, or dancers who had crossed over into other forms of sexual entertainment, such as pornography (these themes will be discussed in relationship to Kitten Natividad's interview). Additionally, the group interactions revealed hierarchical relationships between legends based on the degree of former fame and disputes over the mandate of the Hall of Fame as the organization tries to balance its former political role and its present place as a social club.

Although these social spaces, both those that are structured into the weekend program and those that are not, have been an important resource for this project, for most who attend the Weekender the main focus is on the evening entertainment. The large-scale evening shows at the BHoF Weekender span the four days of the reunion. The Movers, Shakers and Innovators Showcase opens the event on the Thursday evening of the weekend. The Friday Annual Titans of Tease: Legends Showcase is the heart of the reunion, where the legends performer their original routines. Saturday evening is the Miss Exotic World pageant, which draws neo-burlesque performers from around the world to compete for a variety of titles such as Best Burlesque Troupe, Best Burlesque Group, Most Classic, Most Comedic, the King of Boylesque, and, the most coveted award, the Queen of Burlesque. Finally, Sunday night is the Icons & All Stars Showcase, which features pageant winners from previous years.

Leslie Anne Hooker in Las Vegas, 2013

Waxie Moon at the
Burlesque Hall of Fame,
2015

At each of these events it is customary for the audience to dress in extravagant fashion. Formal attire, such as long sequined gowns, is interspersed with exaggerated representations of sexuality and self. Waxie Moon, a tall, bald-headed, male-bodied individual, with a mustache and muttonchops covered in sparkles, wears stiletto heels and a low-backed floor-length gown. Lola Pistola, a large-bodied woman, chooses to fashion a gown out of artificial flowers to give the welcoming appearance of mother earth. A variety of members from the trans and queer communities in their finest fill out the audience, and a general sentiment of body positivity and personal expression reverberates throughout the crowd.

The intergenerational interaction between neo-burlesquers and legends has proved to be an additional resource for this work and, subsequently, has become a large theme throughout the project. At the Weekender, each legend is assigned a younger person, often an individual from the neo-burlesque community, who acts as the legend's "escort." This companion generally oversees the legend's timetable and picks up the legend from her hotel room to escort her down to her respective events. The escort might also help the former dancer in selling her goods at the burlesque bazaar and in dressing for evening events—generally remaining on call. This escort-legend relationship often sets up a mutually beneficial exchange between the two. The legend receives more attention and care than she likely receives at any other time of the year. For the escorts, as they are often newer members to the community, they are given a sense of importance and inclusion as well as an opportunity to learn from the legend with whom they are paired.

Neo-burlesquers the Schlep Sisters take a selfie at the Burlesque Hall of Fame, 2015

Other points of connection between the two groups during the weekend are the Legends' Panel, where neo-burlesque performers are able to ask the legends questions about burlesque of the past, and Burlesque Finishing School, where the younger community learn about burlesque dance of the mid-twentieth century. Here legends often teach skills such as negligee removal, stocking peels, chair dancing, and other staples of the movement vocabulary of traditional striptease. Attending and sometimes assisting in these classes, observing the panel, and having continued engagement with and examination of interactions between the legends and their escorts has shaped much of my thinking around neo-burlesque's identity formation as a community, the community members' interpretation of burlesque history, and their perception and framing of the legends as a whole.

Burlesque Revived

EVOLVING SEPARATELY FROM THE EXOTIC Dancers League in Helendale, California, was the burlesque revival or neo-burlesque movement. Though these two old and new groups would eventually converge in many ways, their origins emerge out of vastly different communities in different corners of the country.

Generally, "neo-burlesque" is a term used to describe the subculture movement that originated in the New York performance art community in the 1990s. These performances, involving elements of performance art, circus, and striptease, would eventually be seen as the beginning of the burlesque revival. Lynn Sally, however, who both writes about and performs neo-burlesque, has suggested that initially performers did not use the term "burlesque" to define the work.[21] Michelle Baldwin similarly notes that the World Famous *BoB* was performing numbers such as an act set to 1950s music dressed in a Marilyn Monroe wig, in a gay bar in the East Village, when it was suggested that what she was doing was actually burlesque.[22] Utilizing the review format and burlesque iconography, neo-burlesque performers began creating shows that operated within a recognizable cabaret or variety act structure but then inverted some of the staples of the performance form as a means of questioning gender norms, stating political views, or including marginalized body types. Neo-burlesque communities began forming across the United States, Canada, and the United Kingdom. Tease-O-Rama, a convention where neo-burlesque performers from a variety of cities unite and share their work, first took place in New Orleans in 2001.

The birth of the neo-burlesque movement also notably coincides with Mayor Rudolph Giuliani's campaign to limit, and even close, strip clubs across the Manhattan area. In 1995, the New York City Council and Planning Commission approved a zoning code that would push sexually oriented businesses to the outskirts of the city. Although the clampdown was not solely directed at strip clubs, the impetus for such actions is often attributed, in large part, to the five-year boom[23] period when the number of strip clubs almost doubled in major American cities. Thus, although other forms of

Opposite page: Lola Frost and Rita Starr compete in the Titans of Tease Showcase, 2014

Burgundy Brixx competes for the Miss Exotic World, Queen of Burlesque title in the Tournament of Tease, 2014

sexual enterprise (X-rated book stores, pornography and video shops)[24] were also implicated, it can be argued that at the heart of Giuliani's anti-pornography campaign was the strip club.

Neo-burlesque performances emerged during this period as a city-approved mode of stripping. That is, they represented historical "re-creations" of stripping, in contrast to contemporary "real" stripping. This is not to say, however, that neo-burlesque performances were necessarily tame or gentrified. Quite the opposite; most of these founding performances were rather transgressive and arguably pushed forward both possibilities for erotic entertainment and elements of the performance art of the 1990s in New York City. They raised questions about naked bodies in performance and proposed ideas that bodies could simultaneously be hypersexualized, beautiful, and arousing while also being ugly, unappealing, and grotesque. In 2006, actor Matt Fraser was asked to host Burlesque on the Beach on Coney Island, which he describes as a venue "where neo-burlesque started." After seeing acts from foundational neo-burlesquers, such as Bunny Love and Bambi the Mermaid, Julie Atlas Muz, the reigning Miss Exotic World and Miss Coney Island, performed. In Fraser's words:

> Then I saw Julie do her act, and it's a famous act called "the severed hand," where a severed hand puts her into a spell, strips off all her clothes, [engages in simulated sex with her] and kills her. And I had never seen a striptease artist or a glamorous woman allow herself to be so ugly on stage. She was screaming. It was like watching a horror film on stage. And I was so intrigued by this artist entity that would be both simultaneously glamorous and ugly, sexy and frightening, and all in one weird mix.[25]

This description of Muz's "the hand" is a good example of neo-burlesque and its ability (when it is done well) to utilize the traditional striptease format and then push up against those parameters, questioning our relationship to the erotic body and the accepted presentation of women's bodies. In this act performed to "I Put a Spell on You" by Screamin' Jay Hawkins, Muz pretends her right hand is both disembodied and possessed, as it seduces, and then assaults and kills her. The performance references a golden age burlesque trope, where dancers would wear a puppet (traditionally the Devil or Dracula) on one hand, which would touch and caress the innocent dancer. However, Muz inverts this golden age structure, as the performance becomes sexually quite explicit and ultimately violent. The performance raises questions about ownership of women's bodies, as Hawkins's voice howls, "I don't care if you don't want me because I'm yours. I put a spell you because you are mine." Additionally, "un-attached," dehumanized sex, and perhaps even issues of emotional or physical abuse seem to be themes in this performance. However, humor is also present in this act for, "the hand" is ultimately Muz's hand, over which she of course has control. Thus, the performance also seemed linked to liberation, a relinquishing of power and giving in to one's own physical desires.

As a result of this foundational work, I have heard Julie Atlas Muz referred to as the "queen of neo-burlesque," as her performances have continuously pushed forward artistic standards for the community, particularly in its early period. The resurgence community now encompasses a wide variety of performers and enthusiasts, some of whom claim to be classic performers who attempt to "authentically" re-create burlesque as it was in the 1940s and 1950s. Others might arguably be more closely allied to contemporary performance art but still subscribe to the burlesque/variety format and utilize striptease as a construct for subverting, questioning, or reinscribing gender norms.[26] The Burlesque Hall of Fame awards prizes at the aforementioned annual pageant for "Most Classic" or "Most Innovative," which highlights the dichotomy in the neo-burlesque community between political, ironic, and comedic performance versus performers aiming to adhere to a traditional aesthetic.

Julie Atlas Muz and Peekaboo Point perform at the Burlesque Hall of Fame, 2015

However, this is not to suggest that most resurgence performers do not fuse both these forms. Julie Atlas Muz's "severed hand" sits in contrast to a much more classic routine she performed, which won her the Miss Exotic World title in 2006. In this piece, which she also performed in the 2010 film by French director Mathieu Amalric, *On Tour*, she gracefully dances to the classic ballad "Moon River" while floating a large balloon around the stage. Muz then struggles her way inside the balloon, vocalizing her discomfort in doing so. Once inside the balloon, she looks as if she were a stunning human snow globe; her silky limbs seem to float in space until she pops the balloon to reveal her naked body. A vastly different performance to this much more subtle "Moon River" piece is one I first encountered at the Slipper Room[27] in New York. Dressed in a nuclear radiation protection suit under black light, Muz strips off her costume to reveal glow-in-the-dark pasties, lipstick, wig, and nails. She then picks up what looks to be a glowing nuclear pellet. She swallows the pellet and undulates her body to give the illusion that the radiation is moving through her body. Finally, a glow stick slides out of her vagina and she throws it into the audience.

These three performances from Julie Atlas Muz's corpus of work are good representations of the breadth of neo-burlesque as performance art. They all offer new takes on the performance of striptease and fuse traditional elements of erotic entertainment with nontraditional props, movements, and themes. Further, these performances are both reverent and irreverent toward the naked body and sex. They are, of course, centering on these two entities and thus the body and sex often become the focus of these performances. However, in neo-burlesque there is often an underlying thread that seems to disrupt traditional formality, social stigma, and shame around the body and sex, and that pokes fun at conventional engagement with these topics.

Tournament of Tease at the Burlesque Hall of Fame, 2014

In Michelle L'amour's "Butthoven's 5th," the reigning Miss Exotic World 2005 walks on stage dressed as an orchestra conductor in black morning suit jacket with tails. She sits on a piano bench with her back to the audience, and in doing so flips her jacket tails to reveal her naked bottom with a bowtie at the bottom of her spine. She then flexes her glute muscles in time to the music to give the effect that her "Butt" is conducting the "Butthoven" orchestra. This piece, which has become something of an Internet sensation, does not seem to make an overt statement, political or otherwise. It does, however, mock traditional striptease and further presents a woman claiming control of her body while also being irreverent toward many of the confines and much of the subsequent seriousness placed around sexuality.

More recently, as the burlesque resurgence has grown and become much more established, both through the formulation and structuring of festivals and competitions across the world and also through its increasing entrance into mainstream awareness, the resurgence as a subcultural space for avant-garde performance has been somewhat overtaken by a wave of much more classical re-creation work. These performances are often characterized by lavish costuming with a focus on adhering to the aesthetic and the movement vocabulary of mid-twentieth-century burlesque.

A similar aesthetic is often present at the Tournament of Tease, also known as the Miss Exotic World Pageant. At the grassroots level, neo-burlesque communities have been praised as body positive,

Kitten LaRue and Lou Henry Hoover compete in the Tournament of Tease at the Burlesque Hall of Fame, 2014

feminist, and queer safe spaces. However, when I was given the honor of judging the pageant in 2014, I found that at its highest level the process of competition normalizes, regulates, and is profoundly incongruous with these philosophical underpinnings of the neo-burlesque community. That is, as I experienced it (or perhaps, as I "judged" it), when re-creations of these historic performances—once mainstream ideals of sex and beauty—are performed with great accuracy at a highly competitive level, it is likely that the same narrow views of beauty, body type, and sexual orientation of mainstream exotic dance (both past and present) are simply being perpetuated. In this pageant space, the "multitude of physiques occupy[ing] the neo-burlesque stage"[28] that dance scholar Sherril Dodds has suggested are present in the neo-burlesque community are greatly diminished—as are the displays of "imperfections,"

Drag King Lou Henry Hoover competing for the King of Boylesque title at the Tournament of Tease, 2015

such as "sagging breasts and wobbly bellies," which are celebrated over "the idealized and unattainable bodies of consumer capitalism."[29] Additionally, the queering and challenges to heteronormative views on sexuality, which often permeate smaller productions and festivals, also seem to be omitted. In fact, 2015 was the first year that drag king Lou Henry Hoover was allowed to compete in the "King of Boylesque" category.

Though this development of Lou—the small-bodied dancer who appeared on the BHoF stage in a sailor's uniform and painted on moustache (see page 54)—was regarded positively by many drag, queer, and trans performers in the community, some remained discouraged. They explained to me that much stricter rules remained attached to the much sought after "Miss Exotic World" category and that it would be a long time before a drag queen would be included on that much coveted competitor list.

However, the internal politics of the Miss Exotic World Pageant aside, generally the unifying factor of the burlesque resurgence is a sense of an alternative community. The resurgence community has redefined burlesque as a space for exploring and performing a variety of forms of sexuality and an alternative lifestyle choice. At a grassroots level, it has also tended to have a strong

Miss Exotic World 2004,
Dirty Martini, at the
Burlesque Hall of Fame,
2013

Neo-burlesque performer at the Burlesque Hall of Fame, 2013

relationship to the positive body image movement that has argued for a broader spectrum of beauty represented in the commercial media over the past twenty years. From this perspective, in communities across the Western world, the neo-burlesque movement has created spaces where a variety of body types, identities, orientations, and lifestyle choices have been accepted, embraced, and celebrated.

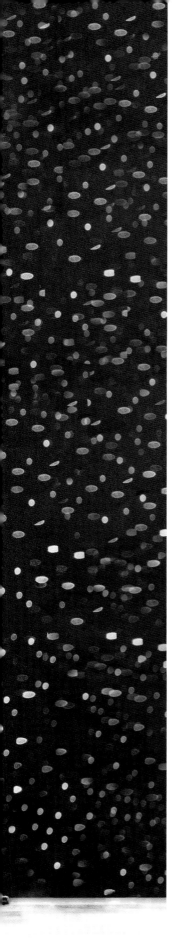

Feminism, Class, and the Category of Whiteness

IN THE BURLESQUE RESURGENCE, THE term "burlesque" often connotes self-awareness, empowerment, and personal agency. Thus, though many of the former dancers or legends involved in this project think very little of or even state that they have oppositional relationships to the term "feminism," many newcomers to the burlesque resurgence see the community as a safe space where many of the goals of modern feminism, including the right to sexual agency, sexual health, and personal exploration, may be enjoyed.[30] Some scholars have even utilized the resurgence in a boas-over-Birkenstocks debate as a testament to the progress from what has been interpreted as the rigid, humorless, and sexless second wave feminism of the '60s and '70s.[31]

From this perspective, the neo-burlesque community has often aligned burlesque history with sex positive feminism.[32] Growing out of the feminist sex wars of the 1980s, sex positive feminism took issue with a singular matriarchal voice assuming that all women should be unified by degradation and power imbalance, further advocating sexual agency and free choice. This movement in turn influenced ongoing debates and discussions among feminist and gender studies scholars in the area of sex work and included the development of much more diverse work being conducted on exotic dance.[33] It is from this ideological standpoint that former burlesque dancers—who may have even been seen to be (and also might see themselves as) at odds with the women's movement at the time in which they were dancing—have been reinstated as feminist icons. These legends (at times unknowingly) embodied topics, lifestyles, and discussions that have been rejected by sex work exclusionary radical feminist (SWERF) discourse. By embracing these legends and listening to their views and voices, the burlesque revival community often attempts to rewrite both their own and the legends' feminist history. Thus, for the neo-burlesque community, these old strippers often represent the mothers of an expanded or an alternative women's movement.

However, some of these legends often don't relate to or may even take issue with the term "feminist." Marinka, whose interview appears later, has described being hounded by college groups of second wave feminists in the 1960s.

Opposite page: Burlesque Noir competes in the Tournament of Tease, 2014

The Ruby Revue give their title-winning performance in the Tournament of Tease at the Burlesque Hall of Fame, 2014

In one account, she recalls arriving at a theater in Cedar Rapids, Iowa, and being met by the shouting of what she describes as "feminist college" students protesting her performance. Below, Marinka discusses the women's liberation movement and the advent of the birth control pill, which she perceived increased the availability of sex and ultimately lessened her power:

The main thing was they wanted to be equal and they started to think about equality. So they didn't need men to come and see women dance for fantasy because any girl who was on the pill would go out with their boyfriend and have sex. It was very negative. The birth control pill, the women's lib...I think killed show business in general because show business is not what it used to be; there is no more show business...because I think a woman is most liberated when you have the adoration of a man. I think this puts you on a pedestal and gives you the upper hand. I can't stand those men who feel they don't have to act like a man and open the door for you or give you this kind of gentleman thing to a lady. So it was negative, yes. Women lost a lot with liberation. They won a lot but we lost a lot.[34]

Juxtaposing "they" (the winners) that Marinka refers to versus "we" (the losers) represents a class divide between the educated, presumably second wave, college students protesting and the exotic dancers working to make a living. Many women dancing during this period who have been interviewed in this project seem to perceive their bodies, and their ability to sell those bodies, as their most valued commodity. Their "beautiful bodies," from a mainstream, heteronormative perspective, distinguished them and may have given them greater options than other women in the communities from which they came. Tempest Storm grew up in an impoverished community in rural Georgia during the Depression. She often cites her large breasts as her personal resource, which enabled her to leave an abusive environment. Stories such as this are common, if not the norm, within the group of legends who began dancing in the 1950s. For many of these women, feminism thus presented a threat to their source of income and way of life.

Marinka articulates feminism as a threat in that she perceived that gender equality neutralized her sexuality and ability to commodify it. That is, she didn't want to be equal; she wanted to be "on a pedestal." The adoration Marinka perceived formed her own personal agency, or as she describes it, "the upper hand" that gave her status within the striptease industry and ultimately financial independence.

The Ruby Revue give their title-winning performance in the Tournament of Tease at the Burlesque Hall of Fame, 2014

Ginger Valentine competes for the Miss Exotic World, Queen of Burlesque title in the Tournament of Tease at the Burlesque Hall of Fame, 2014

This sentiment and positive terms such as "pedestal" have been observed in contemporary strip clubs in which dancers use positive and empowered terminology about their bodies and performance as a means of constructing a powerful identity.[35] Though the project reported in this book is one of the first of its kind to be constructed around the legends, a similar phenomenon seems to be at play in their interviews. Almost all the women who participated in this project construct positive, empowered, and fiscally independent identities and use terms such as "on a pedestal" and "glamour." Statements involving the adoration of men are integral to many of the legends' stories. As Marinka states above, "a woman is most liberated when you have the adoration of a man." For Marinka, the term "adoration" becomes synonymous with control and safety in contrast to exploitation and vulnerability. It is from this standpoint that many of the legends reject gender equality for fear that it would (or some believe it did) lessen this power.

However, this complete rejection of the term "feminism" is not consistent among all the legends interviewed here. When I asked San Francisco–based dancer Holiday O'Hara about her relationship to the term "feminism," she explained, "There were a couple of women who were like, 'you know, you're dancing for men.'" She mimicked them in a rather patronizing voice. In response

Holiday explained, "No, I'm dancing for me and I'm making money and having a good time. Period. The end." Holiday then stopped herself and further clarified:

> I really do care about what people think, of course I do, but I don't suffer fools gladly. . . . I was a hippie. 1968. "Question everything. Question authority." I was a biker chick. "Screw you." This was a fat, too tall, ugly girl, who all of a sudden was getting paid for what she looked like, and her grace, and her ability to entertain and keep you interested. You think I was going to let anybody tell me, stop?[36]

Holiday's relationship to feminism is much less absolute. Where Marinka has a decidedly negative feeling toward the woman's movement, Holiday, through her questioning of "everything," seems to look at the movement as simply yet another form of authority, an institution that in turn must be railed against. Additionally, she notes that in contrast to Marinka's experience, she was involved in sexual-positive politics, a new development in this period. Throughout this project, there has often been a correlation between the legend's age, the period in which she was dancing, and the perceived threat of feminism. Holiday is fourteen years younger than Marinka and as a result entered the burlesque industry at a different period of the women's movement. As a result, time and

The Ruby Revue give their title-winning performance in the Tournament of Tease at the Burlesque Hall of Fame, 2014

Perle Noire competes for the Miss Exotic World, Queen of Burlesque title in the Tournament of Tease, 2015

context seem to play a substantial role in these dancers' interactions with the women's movement.

However, regardless of time period or the ways in which the legends perceive and articulate their relationship with feminism, these personal associations between legends and feminism often differ from the depiction of the legends put forward by many members of the resurgence. As a result, there remains a common dichotomy between legends, some who felt feminism ultimately led to the demise of their careers and personal power, and the largely sex-positive feminist burlesque resurgence community who often like to uphold the legends as feminist icons.

My own interactions and interpretations of the legends within this project have presented similar problems. When entering this community some five years ago, I, like many members of the resurgence, had expected to use a sex-positive feminist lens, which is in line with much of the work surrounding burlesque history. However, in meeting the legends, I became immediately aware of the potential problems with such projections on these dancers and their history.

Labeling the legends with the term "feminist" is often overly simplistic, not only because many legends do not define themselves as such but also because the use of the term can relate to the historic class divides that have (in the case of tensions between second wave feminist groups and exotic dancers of the 1960s) and often still do (in the case of some neo-burlesquers' relationship to the legends) exist. Sherril Dodds has noted that the neo-burlesque community is often a site of class privilege in that performers, by way of financial and intellectual capital, are able to produce such performances.[37] Further, she suggests that a defining element of the neo-burlesque community is that their performance practice is rarely driven by commercial pressures, which permits performers to exercise the freedom to defy normative, and often limited, representations of beauty. This de-emphasis on commerce allows for greater freedom because as performances have less concern with commercially viable sex, they are more focused on sexual exploration and safe space. The neo-burlesque community includes and celebrates difference, including diverse physiques, sexual orientations, and identifications, which are often embraced and celebrated in direct defiance of the narrowly defined beauty ideals espoused by consumer outlets.[38]

A few legends, such as Isis Star, very much ally themselves with the principles of the neo-burlesque movement. Isis states that when she began dancing in the 1960s, "burlesque was effectively dead, and it was just striptease. The movie *Gypsy* was very instrumental in me wanting to become a stripper, so I always stripped from the burlesque [revival] perspective."[39] Later, when neo-burlesque emerged in the 1990s, she returned from retirement to involve herself in the neo-community. Isis's take on what she calls a "new age" perspective on burlesque, can be found in her interview.

By contrast, English-born dancer Gabriella Maze suggests that unlike some of the tattooing and piercing, which often defines the neo-burlesque community, "We were not allowed any of those privileges." Gabriella explained the pressure to look a certain way "or you didn't get work. It was a tough life. It was not an easy life. But they tend to make it seem like everything was glamorous. But it's not always glamorous. Sometimes you've got to fight to get your paycheck."[40] Similarly, Judith Stein's interview expresses concern about the issue of class privilege within the resurgence, which she feels dissociates neo-burlesque from its historic roots:

> I relate more to the working stripping kids [contemporary exotic dancers] than I do to the [neo-]burlesquers. The burlesquers are hobbyists. I adore them and they're great but they're hobbyists. What can I say? If they're denying the stripper roots, that means they're denying us—the legends— and all of us that came before them.[41]

Drawing from Beverley Skeggs,[42] Sherril Dodds further suggests that in contrast to the working class, the middle and upper classes have the privilege to enact alternate class identities and characteristics, a condition that is habitually present in the neo-burlesque community. This is analogous to the Salome craze (or Salomania)[43] more than 100 years earlier, in which—inspired by Oscar Wilde's play *Salome*—middle-class women en masse purchased Salome costumes to perform sensuous veiled dances in their homes, utilizing the disconnect of "ethnic" difference.[44] Women re-creating Salome dances were allotted a safe space to explore sexual agency under the pretense of simply "dressing up" in "Oriental" attire[45] as opposed to showcasing their own white sexuality, which would have felt far more personal or "real" and thus inappropriate. Similarly, the resurgence, through simplifying this history, has often been able to "dress up," utilizing the pretense of cultural historicism and art to enable this new safe space. They are not strippers or sex workers but empowered burlesque artists.

The category of "whiteness" is an additional thread throughout this project. In her book *Choreographing Copyright: Race, Gender, and Intellectual Property Rights in*

American Dance,[46] Anthea Kraut situates the origins of whiteness studies from within a discussion of class. Here, Kraut draws from W. E. B. Du Bois's 1935 book, *Black Reconstruction in America 1860–1880*,[47] which found that white workers were more likely to identify with other whites outside of their class than with former black slaves, with whom they worked side by side. However, whiteness as a categorization did not really emerge until the late 1980s, with a more formal study of whiteness truly taking hold of scholarly attention in the early 1990s.[48]

Analyzing the category of whiteness from a performance studies perspective, Eva Cherniavsky suggests that a problem with defining whiteness from the perspective of white privilege creates a comparison between privilege and "colorless/unmarking."[49] Cherniavsky argues that categorizing whiteness as unmarked and race as a differentiating mark is limiting and that this conceptualization of the unmarked versus the marked body supposes that outside of physical bodies, all lives are also lived identically across racial lines. Also engaging with this concept of marked versus unmarked bodies, from the perspective of dance studies, Susan Manning, in her book *Modern Dance, Negro Dance: Race in Motion*,[50] positions the unmarked whiteness in dance as the "social and artistic privilege," reading this as "the legitimate norm against which bodies of color take their meanings."[51] Manning's reading of "unmarked" whiteness in dance is important to heed within the context of this project. While in-depth engagement with issues of race is beyond the scope of this project, the traditions of this once rather white and (in earlier temporal periods) segregated dance form are—if not overtly—systemically present throughout.

In Joann Kealiinohomomoku's groundbreaking 1969 paper, "An Anthropologist Looks at Ballet as a Form of Ethnic Dance,"[52] Kealiinohomomoku points to hierarchies in dance that enforce and replicate histories of racism and colonialism. Although this project engages with a dance form that arguably sits on the opposite end of the hierarchal spectrum of American dance, burlesque (the low, working-class, entertainment) was additionally inscribed with race-based binaries both in terms of remuneration and prejudice among dancers themselves. As African American legend Toni Elling describes:

> Yes, it was very, very hard because there were so many places that we couldn't play because of our blackness. And we didn't receive the same pay as others, no matter what. But if we wanted to work, we had to accept what was offered.

> Among the girls [in the dressing room], there was something that got my goat too. I found out they were looking to see if I had a tail, a T-A-I-L. They thought black people had tails. And one of the girls finally told me. And I thought, how ignorant could you be?[53]

Historic racial prejudice, inequitable treatment, and pay disparities between black and white performers permeate Toni's account of her career. Further experiences can be found in Toni's interview. Additionally, racially segregated clubs are present in this project, such as San Francisco's Chinese club, Forbidden City, outlined in the late Ivy Tam's interview. Similar racial inequities in the exotic industries can still be observed.[54] The historical racial tension in burlesque is currently a major point of discussion in the neo-burlesque community. Troubled by the void of material documenting the role of African American women in burlesque, neo-burlesque performer Pearl Noir (see photo, page 56) has begun forming a video archive where neo-burlesque dancers reenact traditional routines. In addition, the Burlesque Hall of Fame showcased the exhibition, "Not-So-Hidden Histories: Performers of Color in Burlesque" in 2013.[55] In 2016, Poison Ivory, became the first African American neo-burlesque performer to be crowned the Queen of Burlesque, Miss Exotic World. However, many within the community have questioned why, in a movement built on acceptance and difference, this progress has taken so very long.

That is, even within the context of the (supposedly inclusive) neo-burlesque community, where—one would hope—such racial discrimination between dancers in dressing rooms is no longer present, the covert category of whiteness is still present. A notable element of the neo-burlesque movement is not simply that participants in this primarily recreation community have the necessary means to attend and perform at burlesque festivals for leisure, but that much of this (often educated and middle-class) community is also white. Thus, though neo-burlesque performances often have very different mandates from those of the burlesque of the mid-twentieth century (many times questioning societal norms surrounding representations of bodies, sex, and gender), the community at the Burlesque Hall of Fame has a racial makeup remarkably similar to that which it nostalgically emulates.

As a result, in engaging with this community, I am aware that it is easy to take for granted what Margret L. Anderson has described as the "invisible character of whiteness," a construction that "supports the hegemony of white power and class structure."[56] Both the social class, which often distinguishes the neo-burlesque community from the legends and, even more so, the racial makeup of the Burlesque Hall of Fame event, which—at times eerily—aligns itself with a discriminatory burlesque of the past, are invisible characters in this project, which permeate the oral histories throughout.

Aging Burlesque Bodies

I N 1969, JUDITH BUTLER SUGGESTED that ageism is "systematic stereotyping" and "discrimination," and Bernard Starr proposed in 1985 that it carries an even greater stigma in relation to sexuality. The majority of literature examining later life sexuality and presentations of the body is rooted in the context of nursing homes,[57] predominantly invisible within popular discourses of the elderly and yet one of the only sites in Western society in which others are directly confronted with late-life sexual expression. Largely neglected in the existing literature are discussions regarding performances of the body outside of these insulated institutions. From this perspective, this project positions the Burlesque Hall of Fame annual reunion showcase as a unique space where issues of both later-life sexual identity and the public presentation of aging bodies can be distilled and analyzed.

As recent events suggest—for example, the findings of the employment tribunal against the BBC for firing aging female presenter Miriam O'Reilly, or the current uproar surrounding Madonna's latest album and her sexual display inappropriate for a woman in her fifties—the publicly aging female body is often deemed to be, by most societal standards, decidedly un-erotic and even inappropriate or distasteful when framed as such. In her essay, "The Fear of Flesh That Moves," Joanna Frueh refers to the aging body and the state of decay, which is epitomized by contemporary culture's abhorrence toward aging, loose skin.[58] That is, rather than tight and youthful skin, old skin sits in a constant state of excess. Along these lines, Kathleen Wood has theorized that the invisibility of a mature woman's body actually results in hypervisibility.[59] With this project I seek to draw from the legends' community their perceptions of their aging bodies and their performances of late-life sexuality in order to confront issues of social abhorrence toward aging women in performance.

The interviews in this project also explore the process of aging out of exotic dance. Sabastiono Timpanaro[60] proposes the concept of physical limits, calling these physical limitations and a subsequent inability to work "natural limits." In this instance, however, when experiencing the shift between theaters and

Opposite page: Gina Bon Bon performs in the Titans of Tease Showcase at the Burlesque Hall of Fame, 2013

lap dancing clubs, the members of the Exotic Dancers Leagu
project did not have to stop dancing because of physical strain
lost their ability to attract patrons. That is, their natural limits
tional but of an aesthetic nature. Club dancing often de
younger dancer than staged striptease, which is a much mo
The close proximity of dancers to patrons may have highligh
Sociologist Carol Rambo Ronai suggests that in the context
non-theatrical striptease, even a very "young" woman can
sense, old becomes a descriptive term for dancers who are r
appealing to patrons, a concept that is discussed alongside M
In both Marinka's and Suzette's interviews, "mother" becom
age in exotic dancers. That is, "older than my mother" or "as
seems to be a breaking point in careers and a way of distingu
an appropriate working age from those who are decidedly '
ther describes the emotional impact of growing old in the inc
it took on her identity and sense of self. Subsequently, she br
methods of self-preservation, which include drug and alcoh
ciation, and contempt for clients.[62]

As the theatrical frame of burlesque shifted over the twen
the burlesque theater became obsolete, many members of
moved past "natural limits" of their ability to attract custome
past the potential for financial gain. A thread throughout tl
is then formally discussed in relationship to Marinka's expe
tion of precariousness and retirement: Does a sex worker ev
especially those who continue to perform? At the Burlesc

Weekender, the EDL members are not dancing for money but they are indeed dancing, often the same numbers for which they were paid some decades earlier. The reunion showcase thus somehow resembles a limbo that postpones precariousness and (perhaps eternally) the looming retirement.

In this way, the project additionally examines the performance as a labor of love. Performance scholar Nicholas Ridout suggests that the performer realizes something that "looks and feels like the true realm of freedom—not the 'free time' of capitalist leisure—but knowing, very often, that in that very attempt, they risk subsuming their labors of love entirely to the demands of the sphere of necessity in which they must make their living,"[63] Ridout's definition of amateurism exemplifies the Burlesque Hall of Fame as being—in its most idealized form—a noncommercially driven, communal, safe space.

However, though Ridout's term "amateur" notes the sense of freedom and love present in this community, the word falls short within the context of this project, as it undermines both the commercial status these dancers once had as well as issues of survival, described in many interviews throughout the book. To return to my question above—Can a sex worker ever retire?—for many members of the EDL this relates to issues of identity. That is, the relationship to striptease, and the need to continue to perform it, can be a tension-filled space. For many of the legends, exotic dance was primarily a means of survival, which implies that their other options were limited. From this perspective of need and

Titans of Tease Showcase at the Burlesque Hall of Fame, 2014

Val Valentine performs in the Titans of Tease Showcase at the Burlesque Hall of Fame, 2015

Gina Bon Bon at the
Burlesque Hall of
Fame, 2013

limited choice, it is hard to conceive that dancing striptease today can ever be completely unencumbered and recreational for this group.

Thus, in employing the term "legend," a word used by the both the neo-burlesque community and the legends themselves, I am referencing these dancers' past professional careers, complex histories, and current role, performing in the context of this primarily hobbyist safe space in the Titans of Tease Showcase.

BURLESQUE—DEAD, ALIVE, AND IMAGINED

What Is Burlesque? Striptease Synopsized

IN THE FALL OF 1868, Lydia Thompson, a British music hall dancer turned famed burlesque pioneer, arrived in New York with her troupe of "British Blondes," launching the tradition of American burlesque as well as a multi-million-dollar industry across the United States and Europe. The performances of the British Blondes comprised combinations of dancing and singing as well as parodies of plays, often involving women playing male characters and wearing (scandalously) form-fitting tights.[1] Theater historian John Kenrick notes, "On top of having the tights, these women looked at the men in the audience, were audacious to them, were sexually enticing, said very suggestive things."[2] However, these shows did not involve the act of striptease, which now has become synonymous with burlesque, until sometime later.

Though there are many differing stories involving the first daring chorus girl to actually remove an article of clothing, historians often link the beginnings of social acceptance and understanding of striptease to the introduction of belly dancing into American culture.[3] This "exotic" form of "Oriental" dancing was made popular in Western culture in both Oscar Wilde's *Salome* (1891) and Little Egypt's belly dance or "cooch" dance at the Chicago World Fair two years later.[4] Burlesque performers utilizing names such as Little Cairo or Little Alexandria[5] mimicked cooch dance performers and began removing portions of their costumes as an allusion to Salome's "Dance of the Seven Veils."[6]

With World War I, the "exotic" became a less favorable mode of performing sexuality and a homegrown, safer, whiter form of eroticism was introduced to the mainstream. The term "cheesecake" entered American slang in 1915 when journalist George Miller suggested the all American images of curvaceous women known as pin-ups were better than cheesecake, a concept further championed by Florenz Ziegfeld. The *Ziegfeld Follies* capitalized on the ideal of the pretty, approachable, and quintessentially American chorus girl and further solidified the burlesque variety format by introducing famed comedians such as W. C. Fields, Bob Hope, Fanny Brice, and Charlie Chaplin to their shows. The entrepreneurial Minsky family is often credited with establishing burlesque as a multimillion dollar industry in New York. These shows moved into historic Broadway theaters and were characterized by large sets, elaborate costumes, and famed dancers such as Gypsy Rose Lee. This period, which peaked in the 1930s and is lovingly labeled the golden age, is likely the most recognizable period of burlesque history.[7]

Concerned by the boom and accessibility of the working-class or lowbrow entertainment, mayor of New York Fiorello LaGuardia waged a "moral war"[8] on burlesque in 1937; this culminated in a refusal to grant licenses to any theater that used the term "burlesque" or the name "Minsky" on a marquee and subsequently pushed burlesque out of the city. Robert C. Allen's authoritative burlesque history, *A Horrible Prettiness*, credits the death of burlesque to LaGuardia's concern with the moral landscape of New York City and the systematic removal of burlesque from Broadway. Although Allen argues that LaGuardia caused the end of burlesque's golden age,[9] in fact, burlesque just left Manhattan; as Bambi Jones observes in her interview, "we all moved to New Jersey."

Further, the burlesque variety act format and striptease continued as traveling shows and at fairs and in theaters and nightclubs well into the 1960s and 1970s. In the mid-1950s, Harold Minsky, who features in many of the interviews in this book, moved his father's and uncle's burlesque shows to Las Vegas, pioneering the Las Vegas showgirl construct. While these shows continued to feature both comics and exotic dancers, the emphasis increasingly shifted to striptease.

Bambi Jones's scrapbook, 2015

The 1960s then also marked substantial shifts in the industry, influenced by the new accessibility of nudity made available by the sexual revolution, the introduction of pornography into the mainstream,[10] and a variety of more modern erotic entertainments such as go-go dancers. Theater historian Kristen Pullen has suggested that the first pastie-less or topless go-go dance in the United States was performed in June of 1964 at San Francisco's

Performer in the
Tournament of Tease at
the Burlesque Hall of
Fame, 2014

Lou Lou D'vil in the
El Cortez Hotel, downtown
Las Vegas, 2015

Condor Club,[11] when the eighteen-year-old cocktail waitress Carol Doda danced atop a hydraulic grand piano that was slowly lowered to stage level to gradually reveal her bare breasts. Doda and topless go-go were an instant success.[12] San Francisco became the front runner for nude entertainment, merging elements of traditional burlesque and topless go-go. The city is also the location of the Mitchell brothers' O'Farrell Theater, a former x-rated movie theater that pioneered a type of more personal striptease performances known as *lap dancing* in 1980.[13] *Pole dancing* later emerged and is often credited to entrepreneur Michael J. Peters who introduced a concept of continuous and rotating girls performing at any point when a patron might enter the club, as opposed to previous assigned show times.[14] Both lap dancing and pole dancing are often credited as the source of the strip club boom, between 1987 and 1992, when strip clubs roughly doubled in cities across America.[15]

Missy Lisa competes in the Tournament of Tease at the Burlesque Hall of Fame, 2014

Downtown Las Vegas,
2015

RUBY SLIPPER
2007

Burlesque after Dark

RUNNING PARALLEL TO OR AT times in conjunction with the strip club boom is the development of the resurgence community and subsequently the increased scholarship on both historic burlesque and the resurgence. In contrast to the continuous chronology I've outlined above, most scholarship often categorizes burlesque into three historical periods or "booms."[16] The first boom, sparked by British musical hall dancer Lydia Thompson, refers to the parodies of plays that flourished in the late nineteenth century.[17] The second boom reached its peak in the 1930s when burlesque moved into historic Broadway theaters.[18] Many versions of burlesque history then paint a dark age when burlesque died, at some point in the middle of the twentieth century, only to be succeeded by the rebirth or resurgence.[19]

In some cases, the death narrative has allowed scholars exploring the resurgence to avoid association with some of the socially problematic debates that sit at the heart of scholarship involving contemporary strip clubs. This scholarship often focuses on issues of exploitation versus emancipation.[20] One side of this debate situates stripping as an encapsulation of ongoing systemic misogyny, suggesting that public displays of sensuality lead to further violence against women.[21] The other end of this spectrum situates dancers in a position of power. Some scholars see the exotic dance industry as "anti-establishment, a feminist act, and a strike against patriarchy."[22] To this end, Dahlia Schweitzer goes so far as to say that "with the men the suckers and women pocketing the cash, the striptease becomes a reversal of society's conventional male/female roles...one of the few outlets in which women exercise unchallenged command over their bodies."[23]

Conversely, Suzette Fontaine's interview paints a bleak portrait of this industry. She speaks openly of the limited options for a "poor Hispanic woman," recalling the pressure of club owners, which forced her to overstep her personal boundaries for purposes of survival. By contrast to Suzette's experience, Gabriella Maze found personal agency and independence in the industry. In her interview she speaks of empowerment when she suggests that it is unfair for outsiders to label striptease as degrading when "it's the only job that you're comfortable in because it's the only job that people accept you. That is very, very empowering."

From a historical perspective, scholarship has focused on a number of topics. Robert C. Allen charts the origins of American burlesque from the British music hall in the mid-nineteenth century into the twentieth-century American burlesque show; twentieth-century burlesque, post–World War II burlesque in western Canada, and censorship of burlesque in Boston have similarly been explored; additionally, individual dancers such as Josephine Baker, Mata Hari, Lydia Thompson, topless go-go dancer Carol Doda, Oscar Wilde's Salome, and Gypsy Rose Lee[24] have been discussed. However, the diversity of scope and focus aside, the death narrative is observed throughout most of this literature and is acknowledged with near unanimity. That having been said, the point at which this death occurred and the factors that contributed to the decline are debatable.

Bernard Sobel suggests that burlesque thrived for about ten to twenty years after prohibition but eventually met its death due to financial difficulties arising from the increasing demands of the stage hands' union and an inability to compete with motion picture prices.[25] Rachel Shteir, in her chapter entitled "Who Killed Striptease?," states that one of the last burlesque houses closed in Kansas City in 1969 and points to three changing cultural forces: feminism, the sexual revolution, and pornography. Shteir explains that of the remaining "decrepit grind theaters"[26] across the United States through the 1960s, none were able to survive on dancers and comics alone. Thus, theaters were forced to add 16-millimeter adult films and peep shows to their lineups to encourage patronage. Second, the freedom of "free love" made nude bodies more available and accessible than ever before.[27] Finally, the birth of the women's movement, which saw the burlesque dancer as a symbol of female objectification and repression, is regarded as an immensely important factor in understanding the shifts in burlesque theater attendance. Others hypothesize that burlesque may have seemed a throwback to a previous decade representing sexual repression, sexual hypocrisy,[28] and misunderstanding of the human body as dissociated from nature. For others, burlesque may have been a tangible representation of either systemic or overt women's oppression.

In 1967, Irving Zeidman published his observations of the then present-day American burlesque show and its decline. Noting the changing structure and emphasis of the spectacles, Zeidman describes the decline of the comic and other variety act entertainers and suggests that the sole focus of burlesque had moved to striptease:

Since there is no influx of new male performers in burlesque, the old faces, and they are really old, are now reappearing, one after another, in harrowing procession. The comics look as ancient as their jokes. Age has withered and custom has stalled their infinite vulgarities. . . .

The girls are mainly new . . . the most recent crop of busty favorites diligently advertising the exact dimensions of their billowy breasts, which they are not [averse] to displaying in slow or rapid motion, up, down and sideways.

. . . Finally, burlesque without comedians, straight men, singers, chorus, or scenery—just strippers—has managed to survive in all girl nightclubs as burlesque after dark.[29]

Robert C. Allen situates the death much earlier and argues that burlesque began to decline as early as the 1930s. Allen explains that New York Mayor Fiorello LaGuardia's "personal war" against burlesque, culminating in a refusal to grant licenses to a theater that used the term "burlesque" in any way, drove the spectacles off Broadway, "out of middle class consciousness,"[30] and out of New York City. Although burlesque did continue in cities outside of New York and eventually moved to the traveling show format, Allen suggests that the core of the industry had been eradicated. He states, "When burlesque stopped there, it left the body of the burlesque industry brain-dead. It was only a matter of a few years before burlesque passed from the scene entirely except as a misleading signifier for nightclub strip shows."[31]

Ben Urish also utilizes the nightclub as a signifier of a fundamental change in burlesque. He situates what he terms the "Nightclub Era" in the years between World War II and the mainstream emergence of youth culture (1945–1966). In these years, he suggests, burlesque was no longer suitable as a viable theatrical form. He argues that the nightclub environment put the emphasis on striptease performers, whose acts became longer and more elaborate with this change in space. Mainly, he credits the advent of television, which eventually led to smaller venues, as an impetus for the end of the nightclub era:

"By the early 1960s, only resort cities and specialized clubs featured striptease on a grand scale.... By the mid to late 1960s, many strippers found themselves performing in bars to rock and roll from a jukebox, where they had once performed on stage to their own carefully selected orchestrations."[32]

These scholars note factors contributing to shifts in the performance form that took place in the mid-twentieth century, including the movement out of large theaters, the rise of pornography, and the birth of the women's movement, all of which had differing influences on the industry. Arguably, the most notable shift in the way striptease was performed was the institution of the more intimate format of lap dancing, where dancers were asked to step off the stage to interact and dance with, or on, patrons, thus further eroding boundaries between performer and audience. In contrast to the scholarship outlined above, the interviews in this project suggest that burlesque did not sit in an isolated capsule but rather that all these shifts, lap dancing included, are a part of burlesque history. That is to say, the "misleading signifier" as proposed by Allen, performed to the "rock and roll from a jukebox" suggested by Urish, all intersect with and are indeed a part of the burlesque narrative.

In her book *Undressed for Success: Beauty Contestants as Merchants of Morality* (2005), Brenda Foley quotes burlesque dancer Susan Mills, who performed at Boston's Pilgrim Theater in 1974: "When the show opened the girls were really very nice, like in real burlesque and by the time the show closed they were using coke bottles between the legs."[33] Foley then utilizes the trading of comics for coke bottles as a metaphor for the evolution of striptease from the large-scale Broadway productions of the 1930s to contemporary lap dancing, concluding with Mills's sentiment, "That was the progression of strippers."[34] Although I have yet to conduct an interview that involves a coke bottle, many of the women involved in this project, who danced during the supposed "death" of burlesque, speak of similar transitions, dancing both in burlesque theaters and early strip clubs, often moving between the two performance venues. While Foley does not focus on the evolution of burlesque but rather briefly notes or even laments shifts in the industry within a broader context, my hypothesis that burlesque's history is much more complex than the predominant narrative concurs with Foley's interview, which notes the changing focus of the burlesque show format.

Additionally, I would like to add that the term "burlesque after dark" proposed by Zeidman may also be overly simplistic in that it demeans itself in relation to a past burlesque that is somehow more "authentic" or "real," the "after" implying a difference from what happened before. Mills's statement, "like in real burlesque," implies that she herself never actually danced in "real" burlesque but rather danced something like it.[35] This concept, that there was once a "real" burlesque, is something that many dancers in this project reflect on and try to get back to by way of re-creation, or what they deem to be moral performances, to link back to a simpler or purer time. This theme will be further discussed in this project. For it is often the search and desire for "real" and "living" burlesque, or rather, the imagined, socially uncomplicated burlesque that unites the legends and the resurgence community.

Neo-burlesquer performs in the Tournament of Tease Showcase at the Burlesque Hall of Fame, 2014

Teasing Out Terms: Space, Face, and Function

FACE: BURLESQUE, NOT STRIPPING

AT THE BURLESQUE HALL OF Fame weekend in 2012, Jo "Boobs" Weldon, a strip club dancer turned famed member of the resurgence community, took to the Orleans' stage: "When people ask me 'what's the difference between burlesque and stripping?' I say, a stripper would never ask what's the difference between burlesque and stripping."

This distinction between burlesque dancers and strippers has traditionally been complex and contested issue in the resurgence community. For many members of the revival, the term "burlesque" often connotes self-awareness and personal agency rather than stripping, which might be thought of as exploitative, demeaning sex work. British pop culture commentator Caitlin Moran states that unlike stripping, neo-burlesque shows are feminist activities insofar as the power rests with the individual women performing.[36] Moran concludes: "Most importantly, burlesque clubs feel like a place for girls. Strip clubs—despite the occasional presence of a Spice Girl, ten years ago—do not.... [W]atching good burlesque in action you can see female sexuality: A performance constructed with the value system of a woman...instead of an uncomfortable, half hidden erection and silence."[37] This sentiment is echoed in much of the literature surrounding the neo-burlesque movement.[38] Similarly, as Debora Ferriday theorizes in her article, "Showing the Girl: The New Burlesque,"[39] striptease clubs are examples of hypernormativity—that is, an often narrow, heteronormative view of sexuality and sexual attractiveness, as opposed to the modern burlesquer who questions or subverts female nakedness for predominantly female audiences rather than male spectators. Further, David Owen asserts that "(neo)burlesque is not stripping" as a burlesque show is "more about the tease and the art of the reveal rather than about simple exposure."[40] Joanna Mansbridge concurs with this sentiment and suggests that in contrast to strip clubs, burlesque shows offer an "opportunity to gather and a stage on which to develop ideas, create personas, and make fun of our cultural fixations around sex."[41]

Though in many cases the distinctions between contemporary strip clubs and neo-burlesque are correct, such structured binaries between the two forms are often overly rigid. It is important to note that like historical burlesque

Miss Exotic World, Queen of Burlesque, 2010, Roxi D'light performs in the Icons and All Stars Showcase at the Burlesque Hall of Fame, 2015

performers from whom neo-burlesque performers receive inspiration, the connections to contemporary strip clubs or other forms of erotic entertainments are possible, as the boundaries of neo-burlesque can at times also be rather fluid. Roxi D'light, who in 2010 was crowned the Burlesque Hall of Fame's Miss Exotic World, works in strip clubs in her home town of Windsor, Ontario, between neo-burlesque festivals. Similarly, some of the foundational members of the neo-burlesque community also came from mainstream exotic dance of the 1990s. Jo "Boobs" Weldon comments on the distinctions between strip clubs and the early days of the neo-burlesque scene:

Jo "Boobs" Weldon at the Burlesque Hall of Fame, 2015

The transition isn't that clear for me. I was a feature dancer in strip joints in the early '90s and I didn't like traveling alone from strip joint to strip joint. At least when I travel from festival to festival I know a lot of people. . . . The [distinctions] are not that clear—it's not like, "I shall stop stripping and become a burlesque dancer." That never ever, ever happened. For most people that were doing burlesque and started doing it twelve years ago, that didn't happen because doing burlesque for a living didn't exist. The circuit where I am now didn't exist then and I don't know if it will exist three years from now.[42]

The burlesque festival circuit that Weldon mentions is small and very few dancers are able to make a living from it. Thus, while some neo-burlesque dancers may dance in strip clubs as a source of revenue, for many involved in the neo-burlesque community, striptease is recreational. In this way, neo-burlesque is about choice rather than financial need, which often becomes a unifying element of the community.

Though the socioeconomic class of the individuals involved in the resurgence can vary, the lack of emphasis on financial gain is often a common factor of the resurgence. This de-emphasis on commerce allows for greater freedom, as performances have less concern with commercially viable sex and as a result are more focused around sexual exploration and safe space. Sherill Dodds suggests that the neo-burlesque community includes and celebrates difference and further that "a multitude of physiques occupy the neo-burlesque stage. While the overt display of 'imperfections,' such as sagging breasts and wobbly bellies, is embraced and applauded, the idealized and unattainable bodies of consumer capitalism are a rarity."[43] Further, it is also argued that neo-burlesque presentations of bodies, which often sit outside of mainstream norms of sexual attractiveness, can be seen as a political statement. When speaking about the plus-sized dance troupe, the Fat Bottom Review, Baldwin suggests that the troupe has the power to "change perceptions about full-figured women everywhere."[44]

Stephanie Blake, Miss Exotic World 1997 and 1998, performs at the Burlesque Hall of Fame, 2015

From the perspective of this anti-commercial, safe space, discussions of exploitation in contemporary commercial sexual entertainment and other hazards of such industries are often not relevant or helpful.[45] These structured (and at times inaccurate) barriers around what burlesque "is" help historic burlesque to be remembered and subsequently neo-burlesque to be re-created free of socially problematic factors and interaction with other forms of sexual entertainment such as nude go-go outlined in Kitten Natividad's interview or peep shows described in Gabriella Maze's interview or prostitution outlined in Suzette Fontaine's interview.

Mansbridge also refers to the neo-burlesque community as a "generation of young urbanites."[46] This statement is also rather narrow. It is true that the members of the neo-burlesque community are almost always younger than the legends. However, as the foundational members of the resurgence who began the community in the 1990s move into their late forties and fifties, such age distinctions between "young" legends (also known as "baby legends") and seasoned neo-burlesquers has become less concrete. As Penny Starr Jr., who has been attending the Burlesque Hall of Fame reunion since 1999, states, "It's interesting how some people just fight it like, I'm not a legend, no, and I'm like, you're closer to them, more than a twenty year old." Further, Penny Starr Jr. suggests that over her fifteen years in the neo-burlesque community, more and more "nubies" have entered the community, and legends, as they are not a renewing resource, have decreased. She theorizes that this new ratio has created more prejudice toward contemporary "strippers":

> It's same sex sexism, you saying you're better than that woman. And, I find the people who protest most are the people who have never actually been to a strip club or talked to a stripper. I'm like, no . . . they're us, we're all sisters under the pasties. We get that backlash from the belly dance community, which again, I'm like, we're wearing the same costumes, would you feel down on a naked Merce Cunningham dancer? Would you call them a whore?

So, no, it's one of the things I'm a big proponent on is, no, no, you don't get to say those things, because essentially that's what you're doing, you're slut-shaming someone, when you, yourself, are sensitive to being slut-shamed, like, how does that work?[47]

The reference Penny Starr Jr. makes to the distinctions between nudity in "artistic" dance versus exotic dance will be discussed in relationship to Kitten Natividad's interview. Starr's comment regarding lack of contact with contemporary strip club strippers, however, is of great relevance to the current discussion. It is possible that with this saturation of new neo-burlesquers in ratio to legends, the proximity of recreational, nonsex industry, neo-burlesquers to "strippers" has decreased. That is, with fewer legends remaining a part of the community, contact with commercial striptease is diminished and as a result, it is possible that there might be less understanding toward women who work in the contemporary sex industry. One constant theme throughout all my interviews is that for the legends, such distinctions between burlesque dancer and stripper are only relevant today in articulating the burlesque resurgence as a separate movement from contemporary stripping. That is "stripper" versus "burlesque dancer" is a very recent distinguisher. The legends involved in this project tend to use the terms interchangeably during their time in the industry. Below, Tiffany Carter, who began performing burlesque in the mid-1960s, does not describe herself as a burlesque dancer but as a stripper who happened to perform in burlesque shows:

In my day I was a stripper. To me, burlesque is a group of different performances; you had comedy, magic, fire, maybe some belly dancing, etc., etc., and strippers are a part of burlesque. I did do some duo, group, and acts with dancers so that's the part of the burlesque I have done, but for the most part I was a stripper.[48]

Judith Stein reciprocates this sentiment:

They're [neo-burlesquers] not strippers? If you were taking your clothes off in front of people, to music and getting paid in some way or another, either being paid money or in recognition or applause, you are a stripper, honey. There's no such thing as a burlesque dancer. It was a burlesque show that had strippers. A burlesque show was comedians, dog acts, jugglers—and they brought in at the very end, they brought in a woman who took her clothes off, who was called a stripper. . . . It's this neo-burlesquy bullshit.[49]

In addition to the distinguishing of terms ("stripper" and "burlesque dancer"), the space in which burlesque was performed is also often a means of creating polarity between the strip club and the burlesque theater. These two spaces as distinct entities represent an epistemological dichotomy: burlesque as art form and stripping as sex work. As contemporary burlesque celebrity Dita Von Teese stated in a recent interview with Fox News,

Performer in the Tournament of Tease at the Burlesque Hall of Fame, 2014

Obviously there's a difference between what you might see if you walk into your average strip club in 2013; the modern burlesque scene is a tribute to the striptease of the past.... Right now, a lot of the best performers are not just creating replicas of burlesque [theater] shows that were popular in the '30s and '40s. We're retaining the spirit of what a burlesque show would have been.[50]

In some of the neo-burlesque narrative, the strip club, in contrast to the theatrical burlesque shows, symbolizes the great difference between "striptease of the past"[51] or "what the burlesque show would have been"[52] and modern exotic dance. However, from the perspectives of the legends interviewed in this project, such distinctions between the two performance venues were far less concrete.

SPACE: THEATER, NOT CLUB

Both the burlesque theater and the American supper club are generally believed to have reached the height of their popularity in the early to mid-twentieth century, and both initially employed striptease dancers, comics, singers, and musicians. From a 1960s' perspective, Marinka, a headliner who began her career in the early 1960s, outlined three main types of clubs. She lists them in ascending order from what she deemed to be low- to high-level club. Her observation appears consistent with views of other dancers from the period:

Mixing Clubs
The show was all girls [strippers] and they had a lot, a lot of girls [strippers] and they had one emcee. Usually the emcee was a very big heavy woman who did singing or risqué jokes in between each act. The girls had to mix... some girls loved the mixing clubs—believe it or not—because they had the opportunity to meet men and some of them married the clients.... That was one type of club.

Supper Clubs
There were the supper clubs, and in the supper clubs there was always a singer, a comedian, and exotic dancers. And usually in those clubs you had to work very nice, very mild, have a good wardrobe, usually we did a negligee... something very mild because it was a supper club. People were eating. And often there was both men and women.

Hotel Clubs
The nightclub of the hotels, you had to have a name, they wanted only the features. And the reason for that was because you shared the bill with pretty well-known people... and it was very rare you would see a man [by] himself [In the audience]. He would have a lady on his arm.[53]

In large part, the hierarchical status by which Marinka rates the clubs is allocated based on gender demographics in audiences. Similar to Moran and Ferreday, who differentiate the burlesque revival as a place for women rather than the strip club which is perceived as a place for men, Marinka looks at the Hotel Club, which she rates the highest in status, as also a show for women. Women (particularly white, middle-class women) as the moral compass of an entertainment form and performance space is a recurring theme in interviews with dancers. This discussion is expanded on in relationship to Tempest Storm's interview.

Additionally, mingling or patron interaction is concentrated at the low level, by Marinka's account, which is also in line with frequently recorded concerns of women in modern strip clubs.[54] Bic Carrol, one of the only dancing boys in the legends community, clarifies that "no matter what they say," all dancers in mid-twentieth-century burlesque participated in mixing and received commissions on drinks sold during these interactions, which was known as "B drinking":

> *Bambi Jones and Judith Stein (other legends), we'll talk honestly about the B drinking. But some would go, "Well, we were such big stars, we didn't have to do it." Well, I worked with Sally Rand[55] and she did it. I don't care who you were, you had to do it, no matter what they say. Because, it was all about selling drinks, and if you didn't sell any drinks . . . you could be packed, but if the cash register wasn't ringing, what good did it do? You were dispensable.*

It is relevant that Bic suggests that even in the nicest clubs with the biggest stars, interacting with patrons, or "B drinking," was essential, and without it, one was dispensable. Such interactions with patrons blur lines between performance and emotional labor and further complicate the dichotomy often present between sex work and entertainment in twentieth-century burlesque.

To clarify, Bic defines B drinking as the following:

> *Hustling drinks at night—because the law said you couldn't work in the club and be on the floor unless you were employed. So I had to figure out a way that these girls were employed. They would start out on the chorus line, and a couple of weeks later, I would teach them enough to be a stripper. . . . Anyway, [you'd be on the floor mingling], and [with your drink] you got a plastic stirrer, and each stirrer was a different color, and you saved them, and at the end of the night, you turned them in. So, the value of each drink was a different color stirrer. Say you had a 7-7, that would be a one-color stirrer. And, then if you had a gin gimlet, it was another color stirrer. And, if it was champagne, they just knew . . . because everybody went for champagne, it was worth the most—even though usually it was made in the back room out of vinegar and 7-Up, so you didn't want to drink it. If the customer demanded he actually see you drink it, you would take the shot and you*

would spit it back under the ice at the top of the glass. Now, some places would put a drop of olive oil on top of the ice, then they'd put the shot of liquor, so that the liquor floated on top of the olive oil, if they wanted to smell the drink. Then, you just moved the ice with your tongue, and you sipped the Coke underneath it.[56]

In this scenario Bic asserts that he was hired to teach girls working "on the club the floor"—that is, how to solicit patrons to buy drinks—and move these women from the "B" list to onstage talent. Starting as a chorus girl and subsequently becoming a stripper was a common trajectory for many of the women interviewed in this project. Bic's comment suggests that as the women were not allowed to solicit drinks without formalized employment at the club, he was hired to teach them to dance and enable them to make the transition to chorus girl, and later, solo stripper.

What is notable about Bic's statement is that these women were working first, and performing as a secondary necessity. Further, as noted in his previous comment, even the most famous of dancers were "expendable." Such a claim is an interpretation and will be disputed by Tempest Storm in her interview, but as soon as patron interaction becomes a factor, the lines between dancer, bar maid, and as they pretend to drink their "date's" purchased liquor, sex worker, become further distorted. Thus, though supper clubs ranged in level of respectability, as outlined by Marinka, according to Bic, regardless of the establishment, there was always patron interaction, which required dancers to leave the boundaries of the stage and enter a real audience with potentially real expectations.

However, in analyzing the politics of the club floor, I do not wish to suggest a polarity, which positions burlesque theaters as good and clubs as dangerous. In contrast to my discussion above, and further, in contrast to many of the conceptions within the neo-burlesque community, which often view the low-brow clubs in contrast to the artistic and theatrical burlesque, former dancers interviewed in this study do not always make such a distinction. If they do, it is often the inverse perception. In the 1950s and early 1960s, clubs often attracted a much more sophisticated clientele than the theaters and provided dinner-friendly, co-gender entertainment space. Thus, many dancers from this period will position most clubs in a higher status position than theaters. This is in contrast to the clubs of the 1980s, which began introducing lap dance, a much more intimate dance format that, by most dancer accounts, had a very different sensibility than anything found in their predecessor the supper club.

A challenge to the purist, discontinuous, death narrative, which often positions theatrical burlesque as separated from other forms of erotic entertainment and burlesque theaters as entirely separated from stripping and the strip club, is the claim that all the former dancers involved in this project danced in both the burlesque theaters and nightclubs and further, they moved back and forth between the two. April March, named the First Lady

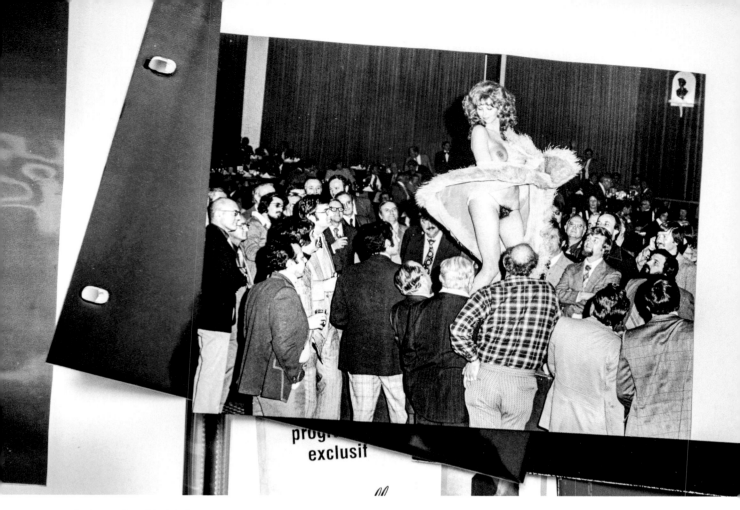

An image from Marinka's scrapbook, 2013

of Burlesque for her resemblance to Jacqueline Kennedy, danced from 1952 until 1978 and performed at theaters, supper clubs, nightclubs, and eventually clubs that would look similar to the modern strip club. Below she describes some of the establishments in which she performed at the end of her career:

> I was dancing in theaters. But the theaters were ending…and I would open up clubs or theaters for Stan Shankar, who I went to work for in Miami in 1960. The last place I worked was the Silver Slipper nightclub in Washington, DC. But I also worked at a theater called the Plaza Theater.[57]

April performed similar striptease routines for the entirety of her career, regardless of performance venue, moving freely between theaters and clubs with similar costumes, music, and choreography. Her statement suggests that the end of burlesque and the beginning of the strip club are hardly distinct moments in time and, rather, enforce the continuousness of the dance form amid changing physical spaces.

Preferences between dancing in theaters versus clubs vary throughout the interviews in this project. April March's choice to perform in theaters was based on safety concerns, a sentiment that will be outlined in April's interview. By contrast, some dancers in this project describe the theaters as lewd working-class establishments, exposing dancers to harassment—different from supper clubs that offered much more favorable working hours in a sophisticated and niche environment. These sentiments are outlined in my interview with Ivy Tam, who owned Forbidden City, an upscale Chinese supper club in San Francisco. Another performer, Tiffany Carter, also danced in both theaters and clubs during the same period and preferred the clubs to the theaters;

> I danced in clubs and theaters. I preferred the clubs much more, the hours were always the same in the evening; at theaters you would work pretty much all day, starting at noon, and shows spread out all during the day until midnight. Also, I liked the atmosphere at the clubs more; some theaters were really raunchy, and guys would jack off—yes you heard it right—jack off in the front rows widely exposed and no one stopped them; that was horrible.[58]

Tiffany was dancing in theaters during, if not after, a time much of the resurgence community and scholarship term the "death period" of the late 1960s and early 1970s. This period indeed saw burlesque theaters struggle financially and subsequently implement a number of cost-saving devices such as screening pornography, which may have accounted for the irreverent behavior of the audience members toward live performers. Nevertheless, Tiffany's experience is still somewhat contradictory to the many popular tellings of burlesque. To opt for the club over the theater is in active opposition to the revival's construction of burlesque history, which depicts the theater as a place where women are respected, glamorized, and empowered in contrast to the strip clubs. Instead, Tiffany depicts the theater as a lewd establishment, exposing its dancers to harassment, in contrast to the club that offered much more favorable working conditions.

FUNCTION: ART, NOT SEX WORK

Similar to the neo-burlesque community's common rejection of the word "stripper" and the construct of the club, the legends often distinguished their performances as separate from modern adaptations within exotic dance, such as pole dancing. As Alexandra the Great 48 (named for her bra size) states, "In our day, you couldn't just find a pole and slip on it."[59] Lap dancing is also a frequently noted differentiator (though some women, particularly the younger legends who danced in a later period, engaged in lap

dancing). Marinka had the following to say about the contact involved in lap dancing:

> We never allowed men to touch us, we always conducted ourselves like ladies, we tried to get the respect. Plus we always demanded money—and money for our work, not money for being touched by a man which in those gentleman clubs, that's what they do. I'm nobody to criticize anyone but that, to me, is just prostitution.[60]

In this way, through enforcing such discriminators, former dancers are also at times actively involved in the retelling from their vantage point of having danced in an earlier period. That is, rather than simply noting evolutions or changes between stripping then and now, they often actively dissociate themselves and employ terms like "prostitution" in order to push modern exotic dance and legends who danced in a later period further from themselves, their careers, and their experiences. In addition, emphasizing lap dancing's proximity to sex work—"being touched by a man for money"—also enforces the distinction that modern exotic dance is closer to sex work than mid-twentieth-century burlesque. In this way, Alexandra and Marinka position their performances closer to art than modern striptease, which they posit as a sexual commodity. Additionally, such tellings and their subsequent shaping and interpretation as well as portions that are extracted from the stories are often encouraged and rewarded by many members of the neo-burlesque community as they enforce their believed narrative.

April March, "The First Lady of Burlesque," recounted an incident she experienced at Chicago's 606 Club in 1956:

> I met a gangster. I don't remember his name because I think he took over Al Capone's mob. . . . But anyway, when it was time for me to leave, my contract expiring, they said I wasn't leaving. And I said, yes, I am. And they said, no, I wasn't. . . . [S]ome of the other girls, they told me that I had better listen because over in Cicero, girls that didn't do what they were told and tried to leave had acid thrown in their faces, stuff like that. . . . The way I got out of there was the young cop helped me. He told me to, every night, take a little bit of wardrobe, take something with me, but the last night, to leave an old costume, to leave something there, so they didn't know I was leaving permanently. So, I went and picked up my dog and the rest of my luggage and he (the cop) gave me a little box of NoDoz pills and a thermos of black coffee. He said, drive and don't stop until you get to Oklahoma City. So, that's what I did. That was my exit out of Chicago. . . . I used to think Chicago . . . that was all comic book stuff, but it really wasn't. That's what went on back in those days. I never returned to Chicago to work again. In fact, I've never been back to Chicago, except to the airport.[61]

I have heard Miss March recount this story twice, once to me personally (from which the above transcription was recorded) and once within the context of a burlesque convention, where she stood and told the story to an audience of neo-burlesque enthusiasts. This second and public telling was very different from my first time hearing the story. In this second instance, I noted the admiration in the audience, through giggles and verbal expressions of excitement, as April casually mentioned Al Capone, the planting of an old showgirl costume in a dressing room, and the Mafia presence in 1950s burlesque. From my interpretation of the situation, these primarily female members of a neo-burlesque community seemed almost to overlook the inherent brutality and abuse in the story. Many members of this (what I assume to be) liberal, feminist audience appeared to allow nostalgia to blur the circumstances expressed in the narrative. That is to say, they appeared unconcerned by the threat of an acid attack.

To state that burlesque was a safe place for performers (particularly female performers) in the 1940s or 1950s is contestable. Below, Bic outlines an experience when he first started working in 1953, which further highlights Mafia violence toward female dancers:

The first place I ever worked, I saw a girl get shot onstage. Her boyfriend was a punk mafia guy, and he thought she was cheating. And he walked in, right in the middle of the show, he shot her. They closed the curtain. Redd Foxx [the emcee] came out and told some jokes. They opened the curtain, and nobody ever saw the body again, and the police weren't called. And I was seventeen; I went, okay, got this picture. But see, everybody, we worked for the mob. You have to understand that. [The clubs] were all gangster operated, even in Europe. And you just learned that you do your job, you keep your mouth shut, and you get paid. It was that simple.[62]

It is the omissions in burlesque history, which often enable resurgence members to position burlesque history as a liberated and artistic performance form, without the potential complexities these women may have historically faced, such as shaming, or ownership, or abuse. Similarly, historian Jorn Russen theorizes that historical characters can, at times, be seen only in terms of temporal difference to the present and that this is often an oversimplification.[63] Temporal difference, viewed from the vantage point of the present, often allows for disposal of facts, which gives a much more surface version of a person or situation.

However, it is possible that even within Russen's theory there is a generalization and oversimplification. Temporal distance and inaccessibility of the event allow for omissions. These omissions are, in turn, used in quite complex ways for the participants involved in the telling of the history. As this relates to the burlesque resurgence, there is a vested interest in omissions as they help to reinforce an interpretation of burlesque that is important to this community. This interpretation is that burlesque is, and preferably always was, a safe, cultured, and feminist space.

I asked director of the Burlesque Hall of Fame, Dustin Wax, about historical omissions within the resurgence and the necessity of historical accuracy. He replied:

> *People go into it [burlesque] today with the idea of—you know, they filter the glamour out for themselves. There's never the idea of "I'm going to go into this so I can do this shameful horrible thing, and constantly be subject to physical intimidation and manhandling." It's a personal choice that people have made in sort of reviving this art form....[I]t's like Dixie [Evans] and all of the others would talk about; when they were done with their set they had to go sit in the audience and try to get people to buy drinks. And that's a practice that doesn't exist anymore....It exists in strip bars, but it's not part of [neo-]burlesque. They [the resurgence] transformed burlesque into primarily a theatrical art rather than a sort of strictly erotic entertainment in the back room of a seedy bar.*[64]

The transformation of burlesque from an erotic entertainment to a theatrical art form has relied on the interpretation of the stories told and additionally the temporal distance of these stories to the present. That is, the passage of time has provided a selective and nostalgic lens through which to view burlesque. The women are no longer dancing, the men are no longer gazing, we are not confronted with living reality. For example, for most people familiar with the resurgence of burlesque, the image of a burlesque dancer with a feather boa accompanied by a mobster feels very different from the image of a contemporary exotic dancer with Lucite heels accompanied by a strip club owner. For many within the revival community, the former image can be observed and glamorized through a historic veneer. The latter is present and accessible and therefore exposes issues one might find morally problematic and distasteful, or over which one may exercise judgment.

Further, I would like to make note of Wax's use of the term "glamour," and "filtered" glamour at that. Glamour is a word that is employed liberally within both the legend and neo-burlesque communities and as a result it is ever present throughout this project. Carol Dyhouse has suggested that "glamour" implies "a form of sophisticated feminine allure" and has a history that is interwoven with "changing constructions of femininity, costuming, popular culture, fashion, and celebrity."[65] When the term first came into common parlance during the nineteenth century, it was akin to sorcery or magic charm. However, in the 1930s–1950s the term "glamour" became strongly associated with Hollywood's golden age,[66] a period in American cinema that ran parallel to its less refined relation, burlesque and the burlesque golden age. Perhaps in an attempt to draw legitimacy from Hollywood, burlesque performers did—and from the interviews in this project, it is clear they still do—use the term "glamour" to elevate their work. In the same way that Dustin Wax employs the term to reference the most positive elements of the industry when stating the neo-burlesque community "filters" the glamorous aspects out of this history, for the

Judith Stein performs in the Titans of Tease Showcase at the Burlesque Hall of Fame, 2014

legends, glamour is one of two, if not the, penultimate descriptive terms. Along with referring to "class" or being "classy," being glamorous connoted a shift in the social order. To be glamorous is to rise above the unsavory elements of the industry and to elevate oneself closer to the "class" of a Hollywood movie star.

However, in mainstream media of the 1960s, likely due to the rise of the women's movement (or second wave feminism), glamour became a "dirty word."[67] Similar to theatrical burlesque itself, the term in this period became associated with the objectification of women and contrived sexuality in contrast to "natural" beauty and free love. Thus, "glamour" fell out of mainstream fashion for about two decades until the birth of "glam rock," championed by musicians such as David Bowie in the 1970s. For the legends in this project, however, the term is enduring, as they lovingly evoke the presumed "class" of burlesque's golden age.

Nigel Thrift has theorized that glamour is reliant on three cultural pillars. The first pillar is the effect of "standing in the world without troubles or with the troubles you want."[68] The second pillar is the employment of, or the engagement with, an alternate version of self, which can act as an imaginary norm. Finally, Thrift suggests that glamour's third cultural pillar is a calculation but one that must seem effortless. "Glamour is selling. It is manipulation. It is seduction. It is a certain form of deception. But it is something more too. It is meticulous selection and control."[69] From this perspective, when Wax describes the process of filtering the glamour out of some of the trying circumstances or events involved in burlesque history, he is actively referencing a wish to stand in the world "without troubles." Further, he is speaking to this "certain form of deception" where an imaginary norm is constructed through a process of "selling," "manipulation," and "seduction."

However, perhaps it is missing the point to focus on the omissions, inaccuracies, and even "deception" in the revival's predominant narration of burlesque history, and to instead introduce a more complex telling that connects the mid-twentieth-century burlesque to the strip clubs of today. Almost a year after her speech at the Burlesque Hall of Fame, I sat down with Jo Weldon and asked her about her statement regarding "striptease" versus "burlesque":

> *My comment about strippers never get asked that? In the entire time*
> *I worked in strip joints nobody ever asked me the difference between strip*
> *joints and burlesque, and I worked in strip joints from 1980 to 1998; nobody*
> *ever asked me that question ever. I don't know if strippers now get asked*
> *that but I doubt it, I seriously doubt it.... The vast majority of people who ask*
> *that question know the answer and they are just trying to be buck wads.*
>
> *There is a huge difference; it doesn't have to be a class structure difference*
> *or a difference in levels of feminism; there's just a huge difference except*
> *when there is no difference at all.*[70]

Here, Weldon is referring to the current burlesque resurgence in comparison to contemporary stripping rather than to my previous statements, which compare mid-twentieth-century burlesque of the 1950s to contemporary stripping. Nevertheless, I wonder if perhaps I am the "buck wad" for pointing out the inaccuracies within the resurgence's telling. For it is possible that the omissions and the revised history are in fact one of the defining features of the revival and perhaps burlesque in general.

Russen argues that history is not a simple summary of facts. A history must possess a certain quality, "a connection of past and present."[71] That is, history is created by people in the present by their making sense of the past. Therefore, history should be understood as a "construction," even as an "invention." From this perspective, imagined narrative constructed around the dance form and the ways in which it has been consumed and perceived from the mid-twentieth century until the present are essential to both the understanding of this community and also the current telling of burlesque history.

The burlesque revivalists, in both their actual dance performances and their choice of lifestyle, dress, and demeanor at such conventions, are not necessarily concerned with factual or historical accuracy but with a believed "glamour" or "spirit."[72] That is, this believed spirit of burlesque stands for an ideology the community wishes to represent that is usually of a liberated, sexually healthy/free/aware, feminist, inclusive, and artistic nature. This spirit then fills in or smooths over any omitted portions of the history. The body and sex positive tenets of the neo-burlesque movement are often very inclusive and welcoming, and they further build what is often seen as a safe space for members of this community.

However, in constructing this safe space, neo-burlesquers often, as Joanna Mansbridge nostalgically remarks, "revive a memory of a different world" that is "steeped in glamour, glitter and nostalgia." With a history that has been "embraced by a sexually savvy generation that in search of authenticity is interested in all things retro and vintage, burlesque offers, perhaps, a more enchanted image of the past, one less vexed than the more politicized history of feminism."[73] This definition of neo-burlesque clearly exemplifies an all too common, romanticized version of burlesque. An attempt to gentrify and remove vexation or to depoliticize the story into a more palatable "retro," "vintage," and "sexually savvy" narrative can at time trivialize the experiences of the women who lived that history. Despite this, the omissions constantly threaten to expose themselves and reveal a burlesque history that is complicated, unfiltered, and potentially lacking—or of a different—"class."

Good Old Daze

The revival is in many ways based around learning from, historicizing, and honoring the "living legends,"[74] dancers from the 1950s and 1960s, when burlesque was "living." However, many of the legends involved in the movement perceive themselves to be the last of the burlesque dancers from the dwindling days of burlesque, often describing a desire to re-create the burlesque of the good old days, when the performance form was in its heyday. Below, Dusty Summers, a very active member at the Burlesque Hall of Fame, reflects on Leslie Zemeckis's documentary, *Behind the Burly Q*:

> *Just finished "Behind the Burly Q" by Leslie Zemeckis and while I thoroughly enjoyed it, I thought she put the death of burlesque a few years early. I didn't start in burlesque until 1965 and while it didn't have the glamour of the burlesque's heyday, I did get to work in some theaters with comics like Monkey Kirkland, Bob Mitchell, Charlie Vespia, and Art Watts. I was even in the chorus line of a burlesque show in Phoenix where they tried to revive "olde tyme burlesque" in about 1968. I appeared in "Olde Tyme Burlesque" in Las Vegas on and off in various casinos from the early '70s until about 1980.... By the time I opened my own club in 1983, all that was left of burlesque were the features who still had the beautiful wardrobe but not the glamorous settings and stages of days gone by.*[75]

Summers's statement lends much to this discussion. First, her career charts a clear evolution from burlesque into the contemporary strip club format. As the strip clubs of the 1980s would have looked quite similar to contemporary clubs, Summers outlines a linear transition from theatrical burlesque, complete with famed comics, into a modern understanding of exotic dance. Additionally, Summers positions the death of burlesque around her own career, a topic that will be discussed further in the next section. However, what is perhaps the aspect of this statement most relevant to this discussion as a whole is that Dusty Summers, who teaches classes for the Burlesque Hall of Fame on the "living" burlesque of her day, also "revived old time burlesque." Summers's burlesque "revival" in 1968 not only puts into question what exactly the current revival, again predominantly based around dancers and dances of the late 1950s and 1960s, is actually reviving, but also what and when "old time burlesque," or what Summers describes as the "heyday," actually was.

By contemporary accounts from the period, burlesque was perceived to be dying in the 1950s.[76] On January 4, 1956, *Variety* magazine published an article entitled "Burlesque...Its Rise and Demise."[77] This article opens by stating, "I am the last of the burlesque producers and show owners on the western wheel" and looks back on a former burlesque that was a "Cradle of Comedians, Once a Family Amusement" rather than a "Burlesque [which has] Succumbed to Smut and Strippers."[78] Similarly, dancers from this period speak of basing their dances on this idealized former burlesque.

Many dancers interviewed for this project look longingly at the prior generation. As April March notes in her interview later in the project "back in the '50s they were beautiful,...they behaved beautifully; they were nice women earning a living taking their clothes off." Further, women who danced during the 1950s and 1960s often note that they looked to the burlesque of twenty years prior as the heyday of the performance form. As Marinka explains, "I learned from the women from the '30s and the '40s so I stuck to what

I learned;...all the way I tried to keep it nice."[79] Even so, Bambi Jones, who began dancing in 1949, states in her interview that when she went for her first burlesque audition, burlesque was on its way out: "I went to the theater, and by then, it was a dump, the theater in 1949....[B]urlesque was on its way down, and then it moved into the nightclubs."[80]

Further, an article published in 1931 also in *Variety*, entitled "The Killer of Burlesque," speaks of burlesque's current, 1930s demise, and looks back to the cleaner burlesque of two decades earlier:

> Shortly before 1910 the Western Burlesque Wheel gave dirty shows. Not as dirty as stock burlesque of the present, but dirty enough for those times, with the chief dirt the cooch, as always. Only then one coocher was featured per show. Now the entire chorus cooch to show how simple it is after all, even for the stage unexperienced.
>
> The Western Wheel like all dirty shows saw their audiences fade to stags and from that to zero...burlesque as a title for an entertainment is washed up forever. It's the name of dirt...dirt shows narrow the audience. There is no new business.[81]

Further still, a patron recalling a burlesque performance in 1915 recorded the story in an article published in the *Cavalcade of Burlesque*, entitled "The Good Old Daze." It begins:

> It was back in 1915...and it [was] one of those little mid-west towns, when Friday night at the Opera House was a big affair. In fact, the opera house has seen better days, and the interior with its gay red plush bespoke of the gay nineties.[82]

The *Cavalcade of Burlesque*, an industry magazine, had a vested interest in promoting burlesque in a positive light and thus all articles from the publication tend to reflect this optimistic view. Nevertheless, the account by this burlesque patron from 1915 acknowledges that the theater the burlesque show was reduced to was one that had "seen better days." The statement implies that like the burlesque of the 1950s, which nostalgically remembered the burlesque of the 1930s, and further the account of burlesque of 1931, which would meet its demise due to its decline in standards since 1910, this representation of a 1915 burlesque show was performed in a once great theater of the 1890s. Thus, burlesque, presumably similar to all erotic entertainments that necessarily push boundaries to excite their patrons, was always "dirtier" than its earlier incarnations. That is, it was likely always dying and only really "lived" in its vintage form (a term that, in general public use, is awarded after twenty years). The strip club then is but another "too dirty" modern entertainment, and the resurgence nostalgically longs for the clean, glamorized, empowered, real, and "lived" burlesque.

Walking the Line: Boundaries and Limits of Safe Space

Though the concept of the death of burlesque may not exist as a concrete period of time, for many dancers it seems to exist as the end of a personal safe space. Almost every dancer I've interviewed positioned the demise of burlesque in relation to her own career or decision to leave the industry, which also often coincided with an incident or event where the boundaries or lines surrounding her own comfort level were overstepped or threatened. I have never interviewed a dancer who did not have a "line" for herself. These lines might exist around questions of morality, health and safety, class, or what dancers deem to be classy or classless; what is perceived to be "real" sex versus performed; and issues of admiration versus exploitation.

April March stated she would "never spread [her]...legs open"[83] without a G-string and further, when she began perceiving pressure to do so, she felt the burlesque business was over and subsequently left. By contrast, Tiffany Carter, former Miss Nude Universe, claimed, "I never got down on the floor, that was dirty;...once I did and I got crabs."[84] Such lines operate as a safe space in which dancers might map out and then preserve their own comfort zones.

For March, spreading her legs without a G-string felt both immoral and not "classy." Maintaining such a boundary enabled her to construct a space that elevated or maintained her own class status and allowed her to perform in a manner that she deemed to be ethical. In this instance, two predominant themes in this project collide, the shifting space and framing of striptease and the perceptions of class(iness), and these often position striptease performance as art rather than sex work. The need to be perceived as having (a level of) class was, for April, the main parameter dictating the construction of her personal safe space. In fact, for many dancers interviewed in this project, the need to be seen (both by themselves and by others) as a performer rather than a sex worker seems to fuel many of their decisions around the construction of personal boundaries. It is arguable, though less overt, that Tiffany Carter's lines are also constructed around class although from a different perspective. In our discussion, Tiffany emphasized floor work, which she described as "dirty" both figuratively and literally. Floor work—a term for sexual movements and at times simulated sex while dancers would lie, roll, or grind on the floor of the stage—came into fashion at the end of Tiffany's career. The pressure to get down on the "filthy," "sticky" floor of the stage pushed up against her limit. Tiffany further suggests that this advancement, the pressure of floor dancing, marked a relative endpoint in burlesque history.

Some—though by no means all—of the dancers interviewed in this project saw the advent of lap dancing as fundamentally at odds with the ability to maintain personal boundaries as well as a formal and permanent crossover into the role of a sex worker. Holiday O'Hara, a former stripper turned emcee of a striptease theater in San Francisco, describes the first night lap dancing premiered at the theater where she worked:

> In 1983, I quit, and the reason I quit was because they changed the format, and I said, no one's going to touch my girls for a dollar. A dollar?! You gotta be kidding me? I mean if we're going to be getting into touching people, maybe $1,000, but a dollar?!!!... The management said we can't compete with the Michelle Brothers [San Francisco club often credited as the pioneers of lap dancing]; we need girls to crawl down off the stage and do lap dancing. There was no opening and closing act. There was just girl, after girl, after girl. And me saying "and now we have so and so"—I didn't even come out on stage, I didn't even wear a gown. I just opened the curtain, fiddled with the light a bit, but nobody cared. I'd say "here's so and so," and she'd dance for a heartbeat and then she'd crawl off the stage showing her pussy, getting money. And then when she was doing that, the rest of the girls who were in the audience, they were clothed, they were in lingerie—panties and a bra—and they were basically dry humping people. Dry humping people for a dollar.[85]

Similar to the statements above, Holiday O'Hara clearly explains the boundaries that construct her concept of safe space and is able to articulate the moment at which these lines were crossed. In addition, she notes a moment when physical space and the framing of striptease shift in a profound way.[86] In this new scenario, Holiday no longer wears a gown or walks on stage to announce or frame the performers. The technical elements, such as lighting, seem insignificant. Finally, the dancers leave the stage and climb on to the laps of patrons, where they continue their performance. This transition, where dancers move from theatrical framing and staged performance into lap dancing is indeed a fundamental shift, not only in the framing of the dance form but also in the way the dancers, as performers, were framed and subsequently viewed. Holiday's statements both describe the death of the dance form from within her own personal experience and clearly map out the porous nature of burlesque history. Burlesque and its dancers moved between different performance spaces and entertainment mediums. Thus, burlesque history is a messy one that, unlike the traditional tellings, transforms, and evolves as it vacillates between art, dance, sex work, and, more often than not, many shades in between.

Working Girls and the Wonderful Bubble

At the Titans of Tease Legends' Showcase, after Tammi True took her bow in a red G-string, fishnets, and red sparkly pasties, Imogen Kelly, a former stripper turned sex worker advocate, turned performance artist, turned 2012 Miss Exotic World, emerged from the wings. In a pink, sequined gown, she found her spot, raised her glitter-encrusted microphone, and spoke:

> It is my absolute honor to be here to do the Legends Walk of Fame. Or to even be a part of this night, which is so important to me. Because without these legends, I don't know what would have become of me....I'd worked in these really violent strip clubs. I was a stripper. The ladies behind me are strippers. We were working girls, you know, we worked, and I just say that only to remind you that we are creatures of privilege in burlesque. This is such a wonderful bubble where you don't have to deal with so many of the elements that working strippers do. I mean we've taken this thing, we've sneakily taken this thing, from the world of misogyny, and men, and the male gaze and we've made it beautiful.[87]

Kelly then introduced the Legends Walk of Fame and read the names and biographies of each former dancer. As the legends paraded, shimmied, and were escorted or wheeled across the stage, depending on their level of mobility, I reflected on the uncharacteristically silent audience. Kelly's words were—and still are—probably the most honest articulation of the revival community I'd encountered. However, I was unsure and still am about how the audience, both revivalists and legends alike, generally perceived it.

If, as Russen theorizes, history is an "invention"[88] constructed by, for, and in relation to the present, and this construction is then taken as truth, it is potentially disruptive for the creators, believers, and perpetuators of this history to be depicted this way on the Burlesque Hall of Fame stage. Kelly's speech ties burlesque and the legends back to the continuum of modern exotic dance and exposes the potential gaps in this narrative.

However, through the concept of the "wonderful bubble" proposed by Kelly, free "from the world of misogyny, and men, and the male gaze,"[89] it is arguable that the neo-burlesque movement has given life to a burlesque that likely never actually "lived." The movement's de-emphasis on commerce allows for greater freedom. As performances have less concern with commercially viable sex, they are more focused around positive body image, sexual exploration, and expression.

Val Valentine performs in the Titans of Tease Showcase at the Burlesque Hall of Fame, 2015

In this way, the Burlesque Hall of Fame Weekender offers a new, idealized version of burlesque, which, in turn, has created a safe space where older exotic dancers and their aging bodies are celebrated.

However, this relatively fictionalized version of burlesque history has the potential to inadvertently stigmatize women in erotic entertainment, both past and present. The common narrative surrounding burlesque is that it died in the mid-twentieth century and is thus an isolated event from other forms of erotic dance or entertainment. The interviews in this project suggest this history is much more nuanced and further that it is disrupted by, and intersects with, many other forms of entertainment—lap dancing, nude go-go, pornography—spaces and timelines. This is a project that lives in those disruptions. It lives in the nightclubs, in the traveling shows, in the peepshows and porn theaters. Further, the women interviewed made careers off their bodies. They have been seen, but they have not always been heard. With the following interviews, I hope to offer you, the reader, the opportunity to—arguably for the first time—hear about careers and experiences of the women who transitioned through and continued dancing past the so-called demise of the twentieth-century burlesque.

Legends perform in the Titans of Tease Showcase at the Burlesque Hall of Fame, 2014

*Bambi Jones at her home
in Las Vegas, 2015*

BAMBI JONES

I N THE LOBBY OF A nondescript retirement home on the outskirts of Las Vegas, Matilda (photographer) and I were greeted by a booming and effusive "Hello!!!" Dressed all in white—complete with matching leggings, thigh-high go-go boots, and marabou—and with her thin arms outstretched above her head to highlight her enthusiasm, this was Bambi Jones. The nearly ninety-year-old showed us to her apartment within the complex—a small but loved space that was also home to a life-size stuffed tiger, large plastic bags filled with theatrical props, and a sizable collection of rhinestone-studded baseball caps. Atop the television set was a denim cap with "USA" written across the front in rhinestones, which Bambi suggested I wear for the duration of our interview. I did.

Bambi and I sat in two Lazy Boy armchairs positioned side by side and, by way of a few astrological questions, she quickly ascertained that we shared the same birthday. We were bonded by April 29th, and frank conversation commenced quickly. Bambi explained that for a large portion of her later life, she "was in the burlesque closet." She was very secretive about her past exotic career at the request of her daughter's husband, daytime TV host Montel Williams, who feared the potential shame of being associated with Bambi.

However, after her daughter's divorce, Bambi was able to "come out," apparently prouder than ever, and has been lecturing about burlesque history to retirement communities in the Las Vegas area ever since. Below Bambi shares her own personal history. She outlines New York Mayor Fiorello LaGuardia's closure of burlesque theaters on Broadway and the subsequent exodus of burlesquers out of Manhattan and into—in her case—New Jersey.

I was working in a beautiful club in Buffalo. A group of maybe twenty people would come into the club late at night and order the best champagne, the best steaks, and the best of everything. Special attention was paid to them. I asked who those people were. I was told they were the burlesque people.

From Bambi Jones's
collection, 2015

I said, "Well, what is burlesque people? I don't understand." They said,
"Well, they're at the theater downtown."

I went to the theater. The first stripper that I saw was Rose La Rose. I said,
"Oh, my God." She did a beautiful number, but at the end, she posed and
she was naked. I was in shock. I went back to work that night and to the girls
I said, "Would you believe she was naked?" Nobody blinked. I said, "Did
you hear me? The lady was naked on stage." One of the girls turned around
and she said, "How much do you make a week?" I said, "$49. $7/night."
"How many shows do you do?" "Three shows/night, four production
numbers a show." "And you get $49/week?" "Right." "What would you say
if we told you that Rose La Rose gets anywhere from $5,000/week and up?"
It took the wind out of me and I looked at them and I said, "But the bitch
doesn't even dance." All she did was walk around, parade. It was all walking
and she had her big production of bedroom scenes. You had the bedroom
there, the clothes. She walked around and did everyday activities, except at
the end when she took everything off. Then I found out she was notorious

for that, but she was the top one in the burlesque world. I started, "Well, I'm going to start looking into Burlesque."

We used to get a paper that had all the information of all the shows. I saw in there an ad that said "Be a booster for Milton Shuster." This was an agent in Chicago. I called and said, "I'm on my way." I packed my big trunk. I got on a Greyhound bus and I went to Chicago. I stayed at the YMCA, which was $2/night, which was close to the theater. I went to the theater, and by then it was a dump. The theater in 1949 is when most of the places…anyhow, burlesque was on its way down. It moved into the nightclubs.

Yes. It was on a downhill spiral. What was sad was most of the entertainers like Rose La Rose had a warehouse of props [with nowhere to go]…. The theaters were closing, the burlesque theaters, especially in New York where La Guardia kicked burlesque out…. Minsky and the word burlesque were not allowed on a marquee because [La Guardia] ran on a bill to clean up New York, and burlesque was the first thing that he went after to close. Everybody went to New Jersey, but the ladies that worked with the animals, with snakes, with birds, with doves, with monkeys a lot of them just quit, because they had nowhere to go.

Bambi, like many of the dancers discussed in this project, situates the end of burlesque within the context of her own career. That is, though the burlesque performers interviewed here continued to dance professionally well into the 1990s, from Bambi's perspective, her idealized version of twentieth-century burlesque was on already on a "downward spiral" in 1949. As noted in the first section of this book, burlesque has often been thought to be "dying"—that is, the present often looks back at erotic entertainment of the past, when it was cleaner and classier. It is here, at the beginning of this supposed death period, that this project lives. It exists in this space created by Bambi's statement, "they had nowhere to go." This book seeks to inhabit this supposed "nowhere" and give voice to the women who continued to live and perform "now-here."

I called and said, "I'm on my way. I packed my big trunk. I got on a Greyhound bus and I went….

Ellion Ness performs in the Titans of Tease Showcase at the Burlesque Hall of Fame, 2015

ELLION NESS

ELLION MET MATILDA AND ME in a small suite of the Orleans Hotel, which the Burlesque Hall of Fame had kindly allowed us to transform into a portrait studio for the duration of the weekend. In a floor-length red-beaded gown, Ellion held the arm of her escort, Eddie Van Glam, self-proclaimed "Seattle's Number One Super Star Boylesquer." Eddie carefully helped Ellion across the brown speckled hotel carpet on to the white paper backdrop to have her portrait taken. Politely explaining that he would be competing for King of Boylesque title later that evening—with a routine performed to a recording by the Village People, involving the statement "Macho Glam" inscribed across a red sparkly speedo—Eddie excused himself. At this Ellion leaned forward, puckered her lips and planted an adoring kiss on the young, neo-burlesquer's mouth; though Ellion's mobility was limited, her spirits clearly were not.

When I asked her age, Ellion responded: "I've said I was twenty-two since I was fourteen and I don't want to change it now," and she gingerly adjusted the straps of her dress as Matilda began to test her lighting. I helped Ellion place her feather boa around her shoulders and she smiled and reflected:

> *People have this idea of you as you get older—and you do get older. You've been there and that's it. But today, to see the way that the legends are revered and respected, it's so rewarding to me. . . . And then they have the Legends' Night where the legends perform. It's just beyond. If someone would have told me thirty years ago that this would be happening, I would laugh in their face. I just would not ever conceive of, believe of it, that this could happen.*

The interviews in this project cover both time periods depicted in Ellion's statement, the history of mid-twentieth-century burlesque and the annual reunion at the Burlesque Hall of Fame, where these dancers perform, decades later, with now aging bodies and in a different frame and context. I asked Ellion about the differences between the current Burlesque Hall of Fame Reunion and the period when she danced, the 1950s. Below she shares her account of her first days in the industry working for one of the most acclaimed burlesque

Legends Night . . . If someone would have told me thirty years ago that this would be happening, I would laugh in their face.

Ellion Ness performs in the Titans of Tease Showcase at the Burlesque Hall of Fame, 2014

producers of the early to mid-twentieth century, Harold Minsky, and of catching the wardrobe of big stars as it was stripped off and thrown into the wings:

There was the showgirl line and there was the dancer's line. I started in the showgirl line. I wanted to be in the dancer's line although [that dancing] was a lot harder than [what] the showgirls [did], but I wanted to learn it.... I got to learn with the dancers, and it was a new show every Friday, so that meant rehearsing from Tuesday in between shows and Wednesday and Thursday after the show. We would be there until maybe 1:00 or 2:00 in the morning and then the new show would start on Friday and there would be new acts. That's kind of how I learned the burlesque field.

I'll tell you a funny story. They told me one time, I think I was there a couple of months or something, and they said I had to get the key to the curtain. They said I had to get the key to the curtain. I said, where is it? They said the comic had it. So, I went to the comic and he said, "I don't have it, I think Grace has it." So, I went to Grace. Grace sent me to the musicians. The

*musicians sent me to the straight man. They said, "Oh, Ruthie has it."
Ruth was Minsky's secretary. I had to go out front to the office and get the
key. So, I go out and Ruthie says, "Is something wrong"? I said, "Oh, I was
looking for the key to the curtain." As I was saying that, Minsky came out
of his office, and he said, "What brings you out here?" I said I need the key
to the curtain so we can open the curtain. He just looked at me with all this
power and he just kind of smirked and he said, "You go back and get ready
for the show. The curtain will open." I thought, "Oh, okay." There was
no doubt in my mind that the curtain
was going to open. So, when I went
backstage the stage manager said,
"Did you get the key to the curtain?"
I said, "No, I guess Mr. Minsky has
it because he said the curtain will
open."*

*That was my school. That's where
I learned the art of being on stage,
stage presence, working with great
talent. I worked with Tempest Storm
at Minsky's when I was in the chorus.
And the chorus girls took turns
catching wardrobe for all the acts.
It would be like six or eight
burlesque dance acts. We took turns
and my turn came up, and I was
catching wardrobe to Tempest,
I caught her wardrobe. And when
Dixie Evans was there it was my turn
to catch the feature's wardrobe, and
I caught her wardrobe. I was just
thrilled when I came to the
Burlesque Hall of Fame and they
were both there.*

Ellion, looked over her shoulder, and
smiled at Matilda's camera lens before
breaking into laughter. She then continued telling her story. Below, Ellion
clearly maps out transitions in burlesque such as the termination of live
musicians and subsequently the coex-
istence and interaction with topless go-go. She further explicates her own
personal demise in burlesque due to the pressures of alcoholism and the
subsequent career she found beyond the footlights.

*Ellion Ness at the
Burlesque Hall of Fame,
2014*

Ellion Ness performs in the Titans of Tease Showcase at the Burlesque Hall of Fame, 2014

I love the theater. I love working in the theater. The nightclubs, they were fun to work, too. I got to meet more people, more of the audience, because I was right there with the audience. In the theater, there's separation. I like both of them, but I guess I would have to say I preferred the theaters. Maybe because I started in a theater. I would be on a road show and I would travel with a group of people, the comics—not the musicians who were in the theater, but the comics and some of the girls, the burlesque dancers. We'd all take the same train after the last show on a Thursday night and then we'd go to the next city, say, from Philadelphia to Pittsburgh. We'd be on the train together, and it would just be one big party, a lot of laughs and a lot of fun. I think that had a lot to do with it.

The one I think that was most depressive [about the end of the burlesque theaters] was when they started taking out live musicians and they started using tapes, reel-to-reel tapes. It takes something away. There's something about live musicians that just is more moving than to dance to a tape or a recording. I think another big change was when they broke forward into topless dancing. They still had burlesque going, but it wasn't the big thing.

But when the topless came into the nightclubs, and I believe it was Carol Doda who started that at the Condor, it went on from there. The Chichi was still going. That was burlesque, and they had a lot of burlesque dancing going on. For a while, they were both going. It isn't like topless came in and burlesque went out. It was a transition.

The truth would be I'd had a drinking problem. I became allergic to alcohol, and every time I would drink I would get into a rash of trouble. So, I stopped drinking. It took a while. It wasn't overnight. And then at that time I had to drop dancing. When I sobered up in 1980, I went back to school….I was hesitant, but…I got a resume and I sent that in and then I was hired…for ten years as an alcohol and drug counselor. It was rewarding. It was very rewarding. I loved working with the police, I loved working with the clients, and most of the staff.

For some [striptease dancers] alcohol was a problem. I was one that had a problem. When you're working in nightclubs, not theater so much but nightclubs, you're in the atmosphere, the environment of drinking, and we used to kind of join in. Then, if it gets out of hand it's out of hand. It doesn't happen for everybody. Everybody doesn't have the gene or DNA or whatever it is that that happens. In a way, I'm very grateful because I got into a life that absolutely changed my life. If I was still on that, I never would be doing Burlesque Hall of Fame. I love my Alcoholics Anonymous family, and I love my burlesque family and my family family. It's just amazing. Life just keeps getting better.

*April March
performs in the
Titans of Tease
Showcase at the
Burlesque Hall of
Fame, 2015*

APRIL MARCH

APRIL MARCH AND I STEPPED out of the hot Las Vegas sun and into the icy air-conditioned foyer of the Lied Library, University of Nevada, Las Vegas (UNLV). April has long blond hair, magical eyes, and a dislike of the term stripper. As a result, when speaking about her profession she employs the term "ecdysiast," which the *Oxford English Dictionary* defines as "the process of shedding old skin (in reptiles)." As a woman who has been married eight times—"same as Liz Taylor," she reminds me—the concept of shedding old skin seems to be a theme in both April's professional and personal life.

On this occasion, she was interested in looking at the UNLV collection, with the aim of finding some past promotional imagery housed in the university's showgirl collection. At the special collections desk we met Su Kim Chung, the librarian who oversees the collection. Su Kim had added a leopard print scarf to her traditional archivist attire, which I believe was in celebration of April's visit, and had pulled out a few boxes that might contain some images of April.

And so, with white gloves, I sat with the archivist and the ecdysiast as we looked through piles of vintage nudie pictures, searching for treasures. April grew up with her grandparents in Oklahoma and thus found her way into burlesque in Oklahoma City. As we opened files and worked through the paper trail of burly-q history, April reflected on the following:

> I lied about my age and went to a place called the Derby Club in Oklahoma City, where they had striptease dancers. I'd never seen a striptease dance in my life. Well, I applied for a job as cigarette and flower girl, which I got. And I used to watch these beautiful women, back in the '50s; they were beautiful. I mean there was nothing vulgar, they dressed beautifully, they behaved beautifully; they were nice women earning a living taking their clothes off. Now, I told myself, geez, they're beautiful but I could never do that. I'd never take my clothes off.
>
> So, anyway, one night I set my tray down, I went to the little girl's room, and I came out and I bumped into this gentleman. He says, "Have you ever

He said, "Here's my card. . . . I can put you into burlesque . . . the rest is up to you . . . you may become a movie star."

thought about getting into show business?" Of course I was young, trying to act older: "Oh yes, I want to be a movie star." I said. He said, "I'm Barney Weinstein. I own the Theater Lounge in Texas, and my brother, Abe, owns the Colony Club." And he said, "Here's my card. If you ever decide to get into show business, I can put you into burlesque, and the rest of your career is up to you . . . who knows, you may become a movie star some day."

. . . I got on a bus and I took my roller skating outfit with me. So, off I went to Dallas, and I took a cab out to the Theater Lounge. And Barney, he was really surprised to see me because he didn't think that I would ever come: "You know, we've got to get you a stage name." He said, "We can't use Velma Fern Worden. It just wouldn't fit on a marquee." So he thought about it and one afternoon I was rehearsing, and he came to me, "I've got it, I've got it. April March." And I said, "No, March comes before April." He said, "Not in your case." So I stuck with April March. And you know, I started feeling more like April than Velma.

Most people changed their name half a dozen times. They'll be something out of the sea, or they'll be this, or they'll be that. They'll be Bambi Jones, and they'll be Neptune Anne. Well, you can't do that if you became the feature. I was a big draw . . . like Tempest was a big draw, Blaze Starr was a big draw, I was a big draw.

April March at the
Burlesque Hall of
Fame, 2015

Unsuccessful in our search, Su Kim opened another box, and we pulled out three new folders of pictures, programs, and posters. April was nicknamed the First Lady of Burlesque in 1961 due to her resemblance to Jacqueline Kennedy. However, according to April, her involvement in stately affairs extended past her stage name. On one occasion, after catching the eye of a Saudi Arabian prince, she accepted an invitation to dine with him. By her account, the American government found out about the impending meeting and asked her to deliver a sealed letter. Though April did not know its contents, she explained "something must have been in that letter because later the prince was assassinated."

April shifted in her blue silk top seeming to tire of our fruitless hunt. I then showed her a pile of contracts signed by theatrical burlesque producer Harold

April March performs in the Titans of Tease Showcase at the Burlesque Hall of Fame, 2015

Minsky, for whom she performed, and she smiled in recognition. Though we didn't find an image of April that day, this Minsky reminder allowed April to reflect on her decision to enter theatrical burlesque. Later, when we walked outside into the sun again, she recounted yet another encounter with murder, an incident she experienced in Miami. In this account April described her decision shed her skin once more and leave nightclubs for the more labor-intensive theater circuit. She noted that there was much less patron interaction in the theaters, which made them a safer workplace environment:

> I started working in the theaters in the '60s.... In theaters, you didn't come in contact with your audience.... I went into theaters after the shooting, the killing at the Place Pigalle nightclub in Miami Beach. That scared me enough to get the heck out of nightclubs.

> [We were in the Place Pigalle.] I was sitting having coffee under the spotlight in a white cocktail dress. [I was with an] old girlfriend, by the name of Sharon Sutton, that I had known back in Oklahoma City when I was a cigarette girl and she was a stripper. She had become an alcoholic and

I hadn't seen her for years. So, I got her a job on the show at the Place Pigalle in Miami Beach. She was drinking [I was in the club having my coffee] and heard the singer from Canada had been shot and killed, and the doorman was shot in both legs. And Sharon came [in during the action and saw the gunman] and she said, "Oh, that gun isn't loaded." About that time, I remember screaming because I heard gunfire. And Sharon had come in front of me, and I thought I was shot. It wasn't me, it was her; she took the bullet instead of me. She stepped in front of me. Anyway, she wound up in the hospital, lost her leg.

I went to see Sharon every day in the hospital. And I took her home after they took her leg off. She didn't know what she was going to do. Anyway, I took care of her as best I could. Then, I had to work, because I had a daughter to support. My daughter was eight, nine, eight, something like that. Anyway, I decided to go in the theater circuit. I said, oh, no customers, no drinking, nice theaters, do a lot of shows. It's better than the nightclubs.

It was more work in the theaters, seven days a week, four [shows] during the week, five on Saturday. And you do all those shows, and you still travel on that seventh day. You travel from Buffalo to Seattle, and had to be there for 10:00 rehearsal. The show was 11:00 something…

[but] I had a little bit of notoriety, and I had a big name in Miami Beach, because I worked the clubs. The press was very nice to me, but I'm nice to the press. Whenever they'd do a story or anything, or TV does anything, I always send them a thank-you note. And they remember that. They always remember. Most of the girls don't send thank-you notes.

*April March at the
Burlesque Hall of
Fame, 2015*

I'm going to be a class act,
I'm not going to be a flash in the pan,
I'm going to become a big star and

KEEP IT CLASSY.

~Tempest Storm

*Tempest Storm at Red Rock Canyon,
Nevada, 2013*

TEMPEST STORM

A T VIVA LAS VEGAS, a vintage car show held annually in the parking lot of the Orleans Hotel two months before the Burlesque Hall of Fame reunion, Tempest Storm sat at a wooden folding table selling photos from days gone by. Her sales booth was surrounded by a sea of 1950s-attired attendees, mid-century hot rods, and retro-enthusiast vendors peddling memorabilia and nostalgia. Tempest Storm, who dated Elvis Presley, was offered contracts by MGM, and had a high-profile relationship with John F. Kennedy,[1] is generally considered one of the most famous burlesque dancers of all time.[2]

Born Annie Blanch Banks, Storm's ambition and perfect "bust," also named the "best props in Hollywood"[3] by Dean Martin and Jerry Lewis, enabled her to escape abuse imposed upon her in her hometown of Eastman, Georgia, and, in her words, "become a star." At the age of twenty, with two marriages behind her, Banks moved to Hollywood and began working as a chorus girl. She adopted the name Tempest Storm in 1950 and changed it legally in 1957, shortly after her breasts or "money makers" were insured by Lloyd's of London for $1 million dollars.

Standing on the hot asphalt of the Orleans' parking lot, I helped Tempest's manager, Harvey Robins, organize the piles of sixty-year-old promotional photographs depicting Tempest at different points of her career. Harvey explained:

> For me, if a person, at some point in life is a star, I always feel that they will always be a star. A person can make a hit record in 1957 and then by the time fifty years go by, that record is a memory; some people might know the song but the artist is relegated to the background. To me, they're always a star. If you earn that quality and you earn that title, then you continue to possess it.[4]

Harvey also noted that of the masses of merchandise sold online, which utilize images and the name Tempest Storm—posters, surfboards, t-shirts, lingerie— Tempest receives none of the proceeds. Consequently, Harvey has worked to find revenue sources for the burlesque queen.

Tempest Storm and manager Harvey Robins at Tempest's signing table at the Burlesque Hall of Fame.

A sign tacked to Tempest's table reading "Black and White Photos: 20 dollars, Color: 25 dollars; Have Your Photo Taken with Tempest: 20 dollars" began to peel from its placement in the Nevada heat. As I added an extra wad of sticky tack to the back of the Bristol board, in an effort to keep the sign in place, a gaggle of burlesque aficionados began to form in front of Tempest's booth. Finnish neo-burlesque artist LouLou D'vil handed Tempest $20 and excitedly gave her iPhone to her strong man, sideshow carnival performer boyfriend, the Baron, so he could take a picture of the two women. LouLou stood for the photo, angling her body to reveal a tattoo of Tempest, which covered most of her upper arm. As I watched Tempest and the image of Tempest on LouLou's right arm pose for the picture, I wondered what it was that made a farm girl from Georgia, turned icon of American erotica, relatable to this young Scandinavian some sixty-five-years later.

An image often used to gentrify burlesque history is the figure of the burlesque queen or famed burlesque dancer. Fame glamorizes and further removes its subject from unsavory or salacious connotations, enhancing mainstream consumption. Thus, the famous burlesque queen is often employed in the neo-burlesque telling of historic burlesque as a means of purifying this history.

Although there were some famous burlesque dancers in mid-twentieth-century burlesque—dancers who, like Tempest Storm, were able to move out of marginal erotic entertainment and into mainstream consciousness—this was not the norm. Additionally, the mid-twentieth century marked the end of theatrical burlesque. With this shift in theatrical format, the small potential for stardom in burlesque decreased even further until such possibilities virtually disappeared. By noting the uniqueness of Tempest Storm's story, I'd like to propose a further complicating factor to the traditional telling of burlesque by questioning the famed burlesque queen narrative.

Construction of a Burlesque Queen and the Illusion of Availability

Roland Barthes has theorized that at a high level, the striptease dancer creates layers or barriers, "a whole series of coverings placed upon the body of the woman in proportion as she pretends to strip it bare."[5] These barriers are varied, not the least of which is the actual stage itself, as it physically distances the dancer. Costuming, exoticism, props, and the spectacle all distract from genuine nakedness, enabling dancers to hold themselves above the inherent eroticism and move into mainstream acceptability.

Barthes's analysis of striptease took place in the same period that Tempest Storm was performing, and we can assume that he would have observed performances similar to hers in similar spaces and through similar frames. Thus, his theories contribute additional context to the case study. Below, Tempest describes her show in Las Vegas that was performed at the Dunes Hotel, which would later become the Bellagio:

> Well, I did a production. I had a set. I had a chaise longue and a cocktail bar and French doors and…two guys…one guy would have a tuxedo. He escorted me onstage. And he did a dance. And we sat up at the bar, the prop of the bar, like we were having a drink with each other. And then we would put our glasses down. And he would act like he was leaving. And then, I would walk up behind him and put my leg around him and do certain movements. And then, I would leave him and I'd go over to the chaise. All of this was pink. And I was doing certain movements on the chaise longue.…And then, another guy comes through the doorway. And he has just a hat and very tight pants and a tie or a scarf around the neck and no shirt. And he's doing movements toward me. And then, I go into my number. It was very interesting.…you had to entertain couples…because, especially the women, they loved to see the costumes. They would come and ask me about my costume. And they always said it was very, very sexy and classy. I had a lot of women fans.

Here Tempest describes the many layers—the soft, pink color of the set and furniture and the framing of her performance by two male dancers, the lush costuming—that sat between her audience and the exoticism of the striptease. Joseph Roach's "it" effect suggests that distance is crucial for celebrity status. He describes the "tease" of greater intimacy, which paradoxically distances and renders the celebrity unavailable.[6] Pairing Roach's theory with the work of Roland Barthes on the layers helps in explaining the process of distancing and framing and the barriers that theatrical burlesque dancers skilfully construct in order to limit the availability of their visibly available bodies.

Tempest's emphasis on entertainment for couples, particularly the women in the audience, indicates the general acceptability of her performance. Female patronage, particularly white, middle-class patronage, has long been regarded as a barometer[7] of decency and good taste in lowbrow entertainments such as burlesque. With their acceptance, middle-class women create a moral safe space, signaling that an entertainment has entered the mainstream.[8] Therefore, when Tempest notes that she "had a lot of women fans" and "they always said [her performance] was very, very sexy and classy," she is situating her act in the middle-class mainstream.

By this same token, the drop in female patronage—which Tempest places in the 1960s, suggesting that it coincided with G-string removal—becomes problematic:

In the early days, we had a lot of couples. The husbands would bring their wives. When they started taking everything off, then you lost the women. . . . When I played London, the owner came after the show because I wore two G-strings. And I took the one off. And the other was like a flesh color. And the owner, after the show, he said, "Everything is fine. You're very classy and sexy. But could you take that last G-string off? You're entirely in the dark." And I said, "We don't do that sort of thing in America." And [then], when I got back [to America], that's the first thing I saw. They were taking everything off.

Tempest's statement raises questions about the interplay between theatrics and striptease in performances: Is it the nude body or the display and framing of the nude body that is truly at stake in this discussion? Tempest felt that regardless of the nudity, she had an ability to gentrify her bottomless performance by using "a lot of those feathers, back and forth, and tied it around me. It was a 'did she or didn't she?'" Tempest's use of feathers then sits as another barrier or "layer"[9] between the audience and her physical availability.

Throughout her long career, Tempest was able to enforce her own personal boundaries from within the context of the "slum," a feat that would eventually enable her to leave the slum and move into a burlesque queen status:

Well, about burlesque, when I started I always wanted to be a class act so that was in my mind; I didn't want to do anything that, you know, would be called risqué or nasty—"Oh she's a nasty performer"—or take off too much. That was my motto when I started: I'm going to be a class act, I'm not going to be a flash in the pan, I'm going to become a big star and keep it classy.

Here, Tempest demonstrates her understanding that there are some ways she might perform striptease that were acceptable and marketable to the mainstream middle class and some that were not. By noting that she did not want to be a "nasty performer," Tempest suggests awareness that she had choices that allowed her and her performance to exist outside and separate from the slum. In addition, Tempest alludes to a connection between being "classy" and becoming "a big star," or having mainstream appeal. That is, she needed to "keep it classy" or operate within the confines of a social class that was higher than her own.

It is clear that Tempest Storm had, and still has, a strong understanding of the illusion of availability, layers, and the need for theatrical framing, which she uses to offset the intimacy involved in her performances. When speaking of her performances, Tempest always emphasizes the spectacle—the props, the costumes; these are the layers that limit her availability and ultimately construct her burlesque queen status.

However, questions of theatrics, class, and G-string removal aside, the shift in burlesque audiences in the late 1950s and into the 1960s signaled another change. Concurrent with the pressure of increased nudity, pop culture and mainstream media's response to and treatment of striptease altered, as can be observed in numerous pop culture publications from the period.[10] On January 4, 1956, *Variety* magazine published an article entitled "Burlesque—Its Rise and Demise."[11] The article, which I drew from earlier, looks back on a former burlesque that was "once a family amusement" rather than a "burlesque [that had] succumbed to smut and strippers."[12] This sentiment is similarly summarized in Tempest's statement below, which contrasts mainstream media's perception of contemporary striptease versus 1950s striptease:

> *And now, they look down on it. They [mainstream media at the time that she began her career] had respect for it because, like I told you, all the stars, they would bring their wives on Saturday night. Of course, they called that "slumming."...They're going to see the "burley-q"...but the news media now looks down on it. They think burlesque dancers are hookers. They look down on them now.*

The mainstream perception of burlesque as a space where stars could be seen with their wives and which subsequently allowed the burlesque dancers themselves to move into mainstream consciousness gradually changed. That is, the frame through which burlesque was viewed altered both physically and culturally. Culturally, there was indeed a shift in the couple-friendly nature of the entertainment as can been seen in the declining female patronage,[13] and thus, the social acceptability of the performance form.[14] Physically, there was a shift in the framing and the actual staging of the performance form. Quite literally, the physical removal of the stage and the introduction of the much more intimate strip club format introduced in the latter half of the twentieth century, would have made the strategic framing of the naked body and distancing of public intimacy problematic.

Until her retirement in 1980,[15] the same year that lap dancing was introduced, Tempest continued to perform on stage and did not venture into the audience. As she explained, "that was always in my contract," suggesting that stepping off the stage was the limit to her public intimacy but indeed "by the end," she lamented, "there was no more illusion." The pink chaise longue, the dancing boys, the bar, and the French doors were the layers that sat between this burlesque queen and her audience. Without this "whole series of coverings"[16] and spectacle, the space and possible framing of the celebrity burlesque queen became vastly different.

Layers and Lamé: Performing the Personal

The first time Tempest met Gypsy Rose Lee, she wore a gold lamé dress to be interviewed on the San Francisco-based television talk show, *Gypsy*. Speaking before the show, Gypsy shook Tempest's hand, looked the young burlesque queen up and down, and said, "I have the same dress." The parallels between these two performers extend far past metallic lamé. Both women had strained relationships with family and experienced difficult childhoods. In each one's peak period, both were arguably the most famous burlesque dancers and ultimately household names for striptease. And both were renowned for their very public romantic relationships.

Lee's first marriage in 1937 was arranged in large part by her studio, 20th Century Fox. The studio had suggested that it would be helpful in cleaning up the famed stripper's image if she were to marry a "nice, ordinary man, a civilian, just to make her more like everyone else."[17] Arnold "Bob" Mizzy, a dental supply manufacturer, was just such man. In the two years that followed marrying someone like "everyone else," Gypsy was contracted for five feature films with 20th Century Fox.

Tempest Storm's suitors, among whom were Louis Armstrong, Nat King Cole, and the infamous mobster Mickey Cohen,[18] were also of concern for her potential studio, MGM. The most serious of these relationships, and the one that would have the gravest implications for her career, was Tempest's marriage to jazz singer Herb Jefferies. MGM studios forbade the relationship between the interracial couple and, as a reaction to Tempest's choice to go ahead with the marriage, MGM dropped all future contracts with her.[19]

Forty-five years later, when I asked Tempest about the implications of her interracial marriage, she recounted the warnings during her engagement:

> A reporter up here, Ralph Pearl, who wrote about me a lot, he called me one night. And he said, "After your show, meet me in the coffee shop. I want to talk to you." I said, "Oh, my god, what the hell did I do now?" He said, "You have got the world in the palm of your hand, at your beck and call. Why are you marrying this guy?" ... But I didn't listen to anybody. ...

In 2009, Tempest met Harvey Robins on a cruise and asked him to manage her. Harvey jokes, "I had never managed anyone before. I have enough trouble managing myself. But it's Tempest Storm. So in this case, I said yes." Thinking about Tempest's principled choice and her statement, "I didn't listen to anybody," I asked Harvey about Tempest's relationship with Jeffries:

> She truly never saw color even though she grew up in the outskirts in Georgia. She didn't have any prejudice. In fact, the people who were black treated her with dignity and respect and a lot of white people she came into contact with, including her family, treated her terribly. Herb Jeffries was not a black/white issue to her. He was just a good-looking guy that she fell for. She always fell pretty easily for good-looking guys as you know.[20]

Thus, Tempest did not comply with MGM's requests as Gypsy had done with 20th Century Fox a few decades before. She did not sufficiently "cleanse" her lived reality and subsequently her image. It is arguably for these principled reasons that Tempest was not granted the opportunity to cross over into "white," middle-class mainstream entertainment as Gypsy had before her. Tempest's story is one based on a belief system. She married for love, not convenience. Her story also suggests that the construction of a burlesque queen was not simply made from one's performance on stage but also her performance off stage—her personal life. And that was a step too far for Tempest.

The Sexiest Stripper of All Time

A few days after the Viva Las Vegas convention, I sat on the floor of Tempest's apartment refilling her photo stock, surrounded by piles of leftover photos, scrapbooks, and magazines. One of the most recent publications was a 1995 magazine, *Leg Show*, in which a sixty-seven-year-old Tempest was featured. The cover of the edition proclaimed "Tempest Storm: The Sexiest Stripper of All Time."

I opened *Leg Show* magazine and read the article in which Tempest reflected on her time on stage at the Dunes hotel, her grand performances, and the star-studded audience who came to adore her. I flipped the page and was presented with a very young Dita Von Teese, who at this point was using the stage name "Diva." Here Diva, the stunning young dancer and fetish model, was photographed before her marriage to Marilyn Manson, her work as a spokesperson for MAC cosmetics, or her contract with Cointreau. Here, in an August edition of *Leg Show*, Diva, who with her current 2,000,000 Twitter followers is arguably today's most famous or "sexiest stripper," was photographed sitting on a toilet, legs open and shaving herself. I was stuck by the rebellious, raw, counterculture image, which stands in sharp contrast to her current polished and carefully constructed persona.

Tempest Storm and Dita Von Teese at the Burlesque Hall of Fame, 2014

What is remarkable about this seemingly insignificant, mid-'90s X-rated magazine is that these two articles, placed side by side, exhibit both after and before the construction of these women's exotic celebrity-dom. Here, both women were pictured; one reflecting upon the "layers" of her time, one yet to find and shape her own personal layers to frame sex stardom.

Tempest will likely always remain, as reported in that 1995 copy of *Leg Show* magazine, one of the "sexiest strippers of all time"; as Harvey says, a star "will always be a star." In fact, LouLou, the young Finnish dancer with Tempest tattooed on her arm, who later that year would go on to win the Burlesque Hall of Fame's 2013 title as Miss Exotic World, Reigning Queen of Burlesque, is a very active performer. Therefore, by way of LouLou's right arm, Tempest is still dancing today.

While burlesque dancers of theatrical burlesque had the option of layers and framings not available to contemporary strippers, there still remained a constant pressure to implement these layers and play them right. Though the current telling of burlesque states otherwise, there was always the possibility that dancers, by the loss of a layer or two, public or personal, could slip further from the status of entertainer and into the realm of the "slum." In mid-twentieth-century burlesque, the dancer who was able to skilfully bump up against middle-class boundaries was the one who ultimately gained mainstream burlesque queen status. And it is rare to find a better example of such skill than the one and only Tempest Storm.

Toni Elling at the
Burlesque Hall of
Fame, 2015

TONI ELLING

I N A SPECTACULARLY BEJEWELED PINK ball gown, World Famous *BoB* introduced Toni Elling's performance at the Titans of Tease Showcase. *BoB* began by explaining that when Toni's mother, out of concern for her daughter's chosen profession, spoke to their pastor, he supported Toni's choice stating, "Let Toni be great. Let her be a star!" Bob comically speculated, "I have a feeling that pastor was making sure he had some singles [dollar bills] in his pocket" and then finished by announcing, "She is here for you tonight. She is a huge, huge star known as the Duke's Delight. Please welcome to the stage, Toni Elling!!!"

In a long purple gown, purple bob wig, and purple boa, the eighty-seven-year-old, named for her relationship to Duke Ellington, shuffled onto the stage. With a cheeky glint in her eye she waved at us with the tail end of her boa. She slowly drifted across the stage while searching for the zipper at the side of her dress. Having found it, Toni then meticulously unzipped the garment, revealing her thin legs. She then removed the dress entirely to exhibit a white bodysuit, which had strips of chiffon floating off the back.

Toni played with the chiffon and slowly wandered around the stage, with a great sense of emotional—if not physical—freedom. The crowd seem exceptionally, even for this audience, touched by Toni's lightness of being. Perle Noir, star of the neo-burlesque scene and advocate for African American burlesque history, sobbed almost uncontrollably. Finally, though the music had stopped, the audience's applause and vocal sounds of support continued. At this, Toni pulled down the top half of her body suit and flashed her naked breasts. Perle sobbed harder.

Toni Elling performs in the Titans of Tease Showcase at the Burlesque Hall of Fame, 2015

Later, I sat with Toni in a coffee shop in the front foyer of the Orleans casino. Somehow, amid the constant clang of slot machines and streams of nearly naked neo-burlesquers moving past us, it seemed very peaceful at our table.

Toni Elling assisted by Tigger in the Titans of Tease Showcase at the Burlesque Hall of Fame, 2013

Toni had a soft smile and twinkling eyes; her aged hand held mine as we spoke. If Tempest's career had been affected by her marriage to an African American, I wondered what it was like for Toni, as a black dancer in the early 1960s. "Honey," she sighed, and then began:

> *I was working for the Michigan Bell Telephone Company . . . in Detroit and I worked there for nine and a half years, without promotion. Although I was always being patted on the back and told I was one of the best operators ever, I couldn't get promoted. And a friend of mine became a stripper and encouraged me to get into it too because she said you'll never get anywhere at the phone company. I had wanted to buy a house for my sister, my brother, my mother and father, and [help them] to pay the bills. But, as Rita Revere said—that's the stripper who encouraged me—it would never happen with me working at the telephone company. So, I should get into this and I could make more money and accomplish my dream.*

> *I started in 1960 at the age of thirty-two, which at that time was the age for most strippers to consider getting out of it, and I was just getting in. And*

yes, it was very, very hard because there were so many places that we couldn't play because of our blackness. And we didn't receive the same pay as others, no matter what. But if we wanted to work, we had to accept what was offered.

For instance, I worked a lot of jobs for $125.00 a week, six nights of work, three shows, usually. And that was not what a young, white stripper was making. They were making hundreds of dollars. Oh, it was hard, very hard, but I persevered. And as I said, I made a reputation for myself, so the people who hired me were happy to get me. That's as far as it went. . . . The highest paid stripper at that time, or part of that time, anyway, was Joanie Carson. And she made $1,000.00 a week and she happened to come to New York when I was working in New York at a theater and she decided that I should be the feature. And she went to the owner and told him so. And she said, "I feel bad taking my check, knowing that she's not making the same money, and she's as good as I am." And he told her that he couldn't do it. She told him he should pay me more. And he told me that he couldn't do it because he'd be run out of town.

A neo-burlesquer, with black hair and a 1950s-style kerchief tied around her head, stopped at our table to give Toni a kiss on the cheek. Toni smiled and said "Thank you dear." "They are my burlesque family," Toni explained to me before continuing:

In Hollywood, I worked at the Club Largo, which was the best club in Hollywood at the time, the Largo and the Pink Pussycat. And there was a convention in town of Texans and when I came out to dance, someone yelled, "That's right, nigger, show them how to do it." I was so upset. . . .

Something that happened often, club owners thought that I should do some kind of savage act and take off my shoes and act like a savage. The owner of Club Largo, before I went on stage to do the audition, he asked me to tell him about my act. And when I finished, he asked, when do you take your shoes off? Well, I knew exactly what that meant and I was just really angry. And I told him, "When I go back to the dressing room." He looked at me, he didn't know what to say. "Well," he said, "what?" And I said, "I take my shoes off when I go back to the dressing room and rest between shows." He said, "You don't take your shoes off and dance?" I said, "Why should I?" And I never did.

Historic racial prejudice, inequitable treatment, and pay disparities between black and white performers permeate Toni's account of her career. Ongoing racial inequities in the exotic industries highlight the value in retelling and reinterpreting these stories. These racial tensions are currently a major point of discussion in the neo-burlesque community. For Toni, however, the Burlesque

> There were so many places that we couldn't play because of our blackness.... But if we wanted to work, we had to accept what was offered.

Toni Elling accepts the award for Legend of the Year, 2015

Hall of Fame represents an idealized version of burlesque—free from hardship, need, and racial prejudice. It is here that she, an African American stripper of the 1960s, has been reframed and reclaimed. Toni, a woman who was told that she was physically unable have a child of her own, now calls the neo-burlesque performers her "burlesque children," this community her "BHoF family," and this Weekender her "burlesque home."

Toni Elling and Lottie the Body at the Burlesque Hall of Fame, 2015

Toni Elling

Lottie th

Ivy Tam at the Burlesque Hall of Fame, 2015

IVY TAM

I N DECEMBER OF 2015, I sat in the kitchen of my West London flat, dialed a San Francisco phone number through my Skype account, and waited for the voice of Ivy Tam to vibrate through my laptop speakers. I had met Ivy earlier that year, along with the ninety-three-year-old Chinese American burlesque star Coby Yee and the Grant Avenue Follies. The Follies, made up of a group of middle-aged women of Chinese descent, was directed by Ivy and Coby; it performed chorus line routines like those done in the Chinese American nightclubs of the 1940s and 1950s. Upon meeting them, I was told that the Grant Avenue Follies was a recreational group that included a real estate agent, a retired banker, and a school principal who all loved the companionship offered by the group and the thrill of performing. Thus, under the guidance of Ivy, they had traveled to Vegas to perform with her at the Burlesque Hall of Fame's Titans of Tease Showcase.

As I spoke to Ivy, I heard great excitement and lightness in her voice, and though I could not see her, I knew she was smiling. She told me about Forbidden City, the upscale Chinese supper club that she had owned with her late husband. The San Francisco–based club, which opened in 1939, was immensely popular during World War II. Ivy's story is dissimilar to April March's account, as April described opting for work in theaters over clubs for safety reasons. Conversely, Ivy saw the theaters as lewd working-class establishments that exposed dancers to harassment, unlike supper clubs, which offered much more favorable working hours in a sophisticated and niche environment. Further, in sharp contrast to the experiences articulated in Toni Elling's narrative, Ivy saw racially segregated clubs as a safe space, where dancers could be protected within the context of a community…even if Chinese strippers were hard to come by:

It was very hard to get Chinese girls to be in the show because Chinese families are so traditional. So we would hire Japanese, Filipino, whatever. They looked Chinese—but it was tough filling our chorus line sometimes. One day, I'm sitting there and the lady who worked in our office came out and asked how the show was going. I said, "We're still short one girl in the

Coby Yee at the
Burlesque Hall of
Fame, 2015

line," and then she looked at me and said, "What are you doing sitting here? Have you ever danced before?" I said, "Well, when I was teenager and then we had a lot of house parties, you know, when you have parties, and then the parties have dancing." Then she said, "Why don't you go out and try?" So all the chorus girls got in a line and told me to follow them. After she took one look, she said, "You will do!" And that's how I started dancing at the club.

During the war, it was really a booming time for the nightclub because of all the service men. They always stopped in San Francisco. They would come in and talk about being sent overseas. Because they didn't know whether they were going to come home, money was not an issue—they spent money before they were shipped out. That's why the nightclub was always filled with people. Then after World War II, everyone came home and they all started building families. And the TV came out—very popular—and then everyone was taking care of family at night instead of going clubbing. Life was changing then, you know? Especially with the Chinese, the businessmen started bringing their families over here.

But after that, when business was going down, we sold the club to Coby Yee. Coby is a really cute, nice Chinese stripper who was one of our stars at Forbidden City. She would travel [but] she would always come home to San Francisco and always come back to Forbidden City. Later, when she owned the club we'd always . . . go and visit her there. . . . One thing with the club, we were like one big family. We were good. After the show, and then after the club ended, we were still friends. We get together. All of our families. We are one big family.

In some ways, through the Grant Avenue Follies, Ivy is continuing this tradition of community and female companionship. In talking to Coby and Ivy, it seemed when confronted with the inherent racial discrimination present in mid-twentieth-century burlesque, the women of Forbidden City embraced sisterhood. They created a safe space, a home. For, as Ivy states, "They'd [the dancers] always come back to Forbidden City." Further, as dancers went on to have children, these children were brought into this community environment, as noted in Ivy's statement: "All of our families. We are one big family." Coby Yee's daughter, Charmaine, was in attendance at the Weekender and cheered as her ninety-four-year-old mother performed; she remarked, "Oh yeah, we are still all together."

I wanted to speak further with Ivy about her relationships with other dancers at Forbidden City. I wanted to know what it was like to run the club. I wondered if having a woman involved in running the club helped to instill this concept that "we were all together." But I never did ask her those questions. As we finished our call, we wished each other a Merry Christmas and I said that I would call her in the New Year. But that would be the last time I spoke with her.

> One thing with the club, we were like one big family.

Ivy passed away in spring 2016. The memorial statement on the Grant Avenue Follies' Facebook page stated that her passing was due to a "brief illness." The Follies cited Ivy as one of their most "beloved sisters," their "mentor" and "inspiration," who had "final approval" on all of their costumes, insisting that they "look just right."

She was never without a smile. Everyone loved watching Ivy perform her fan dances. She was like an angel floating on stage. She is now an "angel" watching over us and dancing [to] "It's a Wonderful World." She will definitely be missed, but will never be forgotten.[1]

Big Fannie Annie during the Walk of Fame in the Titans of Tease Showcase at the Burlesque Hall of Fame, 2013

BIG FANNIE ANNIE

MATILDA AND I VISITED BIG Fannie Annie—a former carnival stripper who made a name for herself as an obese burlesque dancer—at her booth in the Burlesque Bazaar. Here, at a vending table, she sold her renowned, homemade, ten-foot-long "Star Boas." "Are you the little girls from London, England?" Annie bellowed, while peering with wide eyes through her large goldframe glasses in an effort to "get a good look" at us.

In the same way that race segregated dancers in mid-twentieth-century burlesque, body size also could marginalize stripteasers. That is, though the neo-burlesque movement often focuses on positive body image and body acceptance, Big Fannie Annie's narrative suggests that historically, burlesque has relegated dancers with larger bodies to what she describes as a "specialty act," or an "oddity":

> I started out in the carnival industry as a young child; . . . they had girly shows there. I started out when I was probably eleven or twelve. . . . I kind of grew up around there, and I got to meet all the greats because they also worked in carnivals, like Sally Rand. So when I was younger I got to see her and a lot of other greats that did girly shows, too. That's where I started.

> I was the very first obese girl to start stripping, and I stripped nude. When I started the '50s shows I weighed 450 [and] anywhere up to 650 pounds because it varied. It went up and down. They said, "She's not going to do too well because who wants to see her?" But it turned out to be very freakish, and actually I was one of the most popular and highest paid; . . . men would come from 1,500 miles around to see me because they were into that type of body shape, which was never on stage before. A lot of girls didn't like me because I was making all the money; I was getting a big paycheck every week, plus the men would bring me gifts. The other girls thought, "what the hell is wrong with me? I'm prettier than she is." But it wasn't about that. It was about that I was the first one. They lined up to see me. And, of course, I was in every single newspaper every week because I was an oddity, that was called a specialty act.

They lined up to see me. . . . I was in every single newspaper every week because I was an oddity, that was called a specialty act.

Big Fannie Annie during the Walk of Fame in the Titans of Tease Showcase at the Burlesque Hall of Fame, 2014

I was also a question on Hollywood Squares one time. I remember who answered the question, and I remember the question. The question was, Is it true there's a 450-pound dancer? The question was asked to George Gobel; his answer was, "And in the first two rows they pass out hard hats!" Then the guy said, "Yes, it's true. She's from Seattle, Washington, and her name is Big Fannie Annie".... The first two rows they had to pass hard hats to because she was so big. You know what I mean?

Annie organized her boas across her table, exchanging a neon pink boa and a kelly green one. As she shifted the spacing of her creations, I wondered how it felt to be famous for her body size. I asked her if this kind of joking bothered her. "Why would it?" Annie asked frankly.

I'm the one who was making the money. I look at it this way: they paid to see me. I didn't pay to see them. It never worried me because actually I had a very good act. Everyone was entertained. I was a little naughty. I did stand-up, X-rated comedy because I was too big to dance for a half an hour, so I would be able to sit down and tell jokes to rest in between.

Big Fannie Annie sells
her star boas at the
Burlesque Bazaar,
2015

Annie suggests that as the first, and likely one of few exotic dancers of her kind from this period, her success was predicated on what she terms a "freakish" voyeurism. This is in contrast to the other dancers interviewed in this project whose performances were not alternatives but rather were the main sexual entertainments. Thus, for the majority of dancers interviewed the pressure to conform to narrow, normative ideals of sexual attractiveness was significant.

As Annie was coming from a place of difference, I wondered what she thought about the present-day neo-burlesque community as a space of body acceptance and empowerment. I imagined that she would think of it as a progressive step forward, but she corrected me:

> I never dreamed in my entire life that I would dance for mostly lesbian women. My entire life was dancing for men, and my whole career, all my jokes and everything, was geared to men and making them feel embarrassed and embarrass[ing] them personally, and abuse them and treat them like rag dolls. Like they did women. And the women loved it. The guys would talk so big and then I would get them on stage and pull their pants down and say look at this small prick. But it was all in fun, and people paid money to get me to pick them to go up there because the lines got so long I said we have to take the highest bidder. Sometimes I could get $500.00 to take somebody up there and humiliate [him], but a lot of times [the guy's] friends would pay for it and [he] didn't know it. The difference is it's not as sexy. People [in neo-burlesque] today, it's a hobby. They don't make the kind of money that we made by working every single day, every single week. In other words, when we bought a costume in the 1970s it cost $2,000, but you got the hat, the parasol, the gown, all the underpieces, and the panels. But today, they can't hardly afford $200.00, you know what I mean? Different shit. . . .

> It's changed. I don't know if it's for the better or not. I go every year [to the Burlesque Hall of Fame], I've been in the walk [of fame] the last two years, but I've been thinking out loud to friends [that] I think I'm about done. It's very expensive to go. Even to be in the walk of fame or the walk of shame or whatever you want to call it, it's expensive. I've got to hire a makeup artist. I've got to hire a hairdresser. I can't see to put on makeup anymore. I'm so blind close-up I can't see anything, so I have to have somebody do it if I'm going to look halfway decent. And then I always have to make a new bra and I spend money on rhinestones. It costs me $300.00, $400.00, every time I do it. So I said to myself, I think next year I'm going to get my teeth fixed and

maybe my eyes done and I'll take a year off at least....But Legends for
Legends, they all bitch about it but it's just for legends.

"Well, why do you still go?" I asked her. Annie leaned forward, placed her sizable, French-manicured hand on the table and responded: "Because it's my one chance to see girls every year that I haven't seen in thirty years or forty years and run into people that...some you worked with and some you just admired. That's why."

Big Fannie Annie did attend the following year...and the year after that.

HOLIDAY O'HARA

TO THE TUNE OF THE 1972 hit by Stealers Wheel, "Stuck in the Middle with You," Holiday O'Hara enthusiastically rolled onto the stage wearing a white bustier, stuck in the middle between her two neo-burlesquer assistants. Seated on a wheeled walker, she seductively peeled off her skirt and threw it to one of her helpers. She then removed her bra, and using her arms for support on the metal frame, she managed to stand, and coyly shimmied her shoulders to shake her world-wise breasts. In response to this movement, the audience exploded with enjoyment. When she was once again seated, her assistants wheeled Holiday across the front of the stage so she could, with her hands in a prayer position, bow her head in gratitude to her adoring audience.

One year later, in her room at the Orleans Hotel, Holiday maneuvered her electric wheelchair around to face Matilda. While doing this, she let out a groan of discomfort and closed her eyes to steady herself. Holiday has severe arthritis that causes her chronic pain. She explained that to be away from her hospital bed in order to attend the reunion is incredibly taxing on her body. Describing her pain level as about 8 out of 10, she stated her belief that each and every year would be her last year to attend the event. When I asked why she would endure this level of pain to come, she explained that it was simply who she is. Holiday is a performer. As she explained,

> My life has been a very physical one. I lost my virginity to a boy's bicycle when I was 12. . . . I had no idea what was going on, but I had broken my hymen. My mother said to me, "Well, it won't hurt when you get married." Even at twelve, I knew, "Mom, things are going to happen before I get married."

As Holiday spoke, Matilda pushed aside the mermaid-themed headpiece and accessories atop the hotel's chest of drawers and grabbed a mug of water sitting there. She handed the mug to Holiday, who readjusted her back and then took a sip and a deep breath.

Like Big Fannie Annie, Holiday's relationship to the Weekender is complicated. In the previous interview, Annie mentioned that her poor vision made

applying makeup and preparing for the Weekender taxing. Holiday's difficulty is dealing with chronic physical limitations, which are aggravated by attending the event. In part their continued attendance, in spite of physical adversity, is due to their commitment to the community. However, there seems to be an additional and arguably stronger pull to the event, which is connected to identity. As Holiday mentioned, this is who she is, inferring that she is a performer. An identity—regardless of physical limits—that one cannot retire from but that continues on as a deeply rooted sense of self.

I asked Holiday about her attendance at the event and specifically about her identity as a legend. She corrected me:

> Oh, Tempest Storm is a legend. She's a legend. You know, Blaze Starr, there we go, legends. Not me. I'm not famous. I mean, if you want to say [that] all the girls, all of us who danced, back in the day—1940 to 1970, those thirty years—[that] we're all legends, fine, I have no problem with that. But if you want to talk about people who were headliners all the time, or most of the time, that's not me.

> Sure, every once in a while, any of us who were on the road [were] featured. I mean, I featured a few times, but mostly, I didn't have the breasts for it, to be honest. I was 5'9", I was slim. I lost weight shooting speed in 1968; I went from 180 to 120 in three months. My mother hadn't seen me, [and when] I showed up on her doorstep, she burst into tears. It was the first clue I had that something was wrong. Because 120 is way too skinny for me.... Small is fine now, in these days, but my breasts were small and not that particularly great. I mean, I went incredibly far for a woman who didn't have great breasts. They were small. I was a 36C or a 38B, depending on the bra. But [my breasts] also are shaped. I have National Geographic breasts. Does that clue you in right there? With downward facing nipples—when I was slim [they] looked like they had sand in the toe. You know the kind of breast I'm talking about, they're flat on top and then they have all the milk ducts and everything at the bottom, and the nipples are at the bottom of the breast; they're not up high and perky. I'm not putting down my breasts, I want that to be very clear; I'm really practical about what worked then. If we went bottomless, I didn't take my bra off as first thing, I took it off as the last thing. I took my G-string off before I took my bra off because I looked better. There are pictures of me out there—well, [pictures] I have, of me—with no G-string on and a bra on.... I just thought, well, what am I going to do to make more money? Because that was it; I wasn't looking to become a star, I was simply looking to increase my pay grade.

> I went to Seattle and an old carny guy, because there were a lot of old carny guys around back then, gave me an act. He said, change your name to Holiday Heart, shave your hairs in the shape of a heart, sing this parody of "Kiss Me Once," and come out of a valentine. He made me a giant prop,

> Nightclubs are not fun anymore.... There's something wrong with that, don't you think? Sex is supposed to be fun.

made out of plywood, it had three sides, so you couldn't see. I sat on a little boudoir chair and there was a giant heart cut out in the front piece of plywood. Where I sat, there was a short curtain rod with that red flocked shower curtain material that looks like a whorehouse immediately. I would pull the curtain and the curtains would open and there would be me. It looked like a giant valentine card, and I was "Holiday Heart, every man's valentine." I'd pull the thing, I'd come out, and I'd actually, with a microphone, sing the song, called "Kiss It Once." "Kiss it once and kiss it twice and kiss it once again, it's been a long, long time." On and on with that song. Then I'd go and point to somebody dressed in gray, if there was, or something close, and I'd say, "There's a man all dressed in gray, he likes to kiss it all the day." And I'd throw a candy kiss out from my bra. "There's a man dressed in brown, he likes to kiss it all over town." "There's a man all dressed in black, he likes to kiss it in the crack. Oh, kiss it once and kiss it twice." That was my act. That was my first feature act. I toured San Francisco and Seattle and L.A. with that. It was a big prop and it was a drag to bring around. At one point, you couldn't do this now, but I had seven pieces of luggage, including this enormous prop.

Very different now. Very, very different. The burlesque world now isn't. We have neo-burlesque, but the stripping is all lap dancing, there's very few places that actually have real entertainment stripping. It's pole dancing and lap dancing. Pole dancing is great; some of those women are amazing. Amazing. Pole dancing was coming in just as I was leaving, and I remember thinking at the time, oh, I'm so glad I'm getting out of this, because that's not me.

I took Holiday's mug and placed it back among the mermaid accessories she would wear for her performance the following day. Holiday reflectively continued her train of thought and spoke of her time at a club San Francisco. She explained that she had been in a relationship with the owner of the club and "he was the first really good human being I'd been with. My lovers had gotten better and better, but, you know, it was a rough life. I fell in love with the best, I think, that was in my circumstance at the time."

Thus, Holiday remained in San Francisco working as both a stage manager and emcee until her final days in burlesque. Below she explains her decision to leave the industry, which she had seen change drastically:

I didn't even wear a gown. I just opened the curtain, fiddled with the light a bit, but nobody cared. I'd say "here's so and so," and she'd dance for a heartbeat and then she'd crawl off the stage showing her pussy, getting money. And then when she was doing that, the rest of the girls who were in the audience, they were clothed, they were in lingerie—panties and a bra—and they were basically dry humping people. Dry humping people for a dollar.... In 1983 is when I quit.... I worked for one week and I said, nobody is going to touch my girls for a dollar. A dollar? You've got to be kidding me.

In this statement, as quoted earlier, Holiday describes the beginning of lap dancing. Here, the technical elements mentioned in Tempest Storm's interview, such as lighting, props, and costume seem insignificant. Instead, the dancers leave the stage and continue their performance on a rather different stage—the laps of patrons. This transition, where dancers move from theatrical framing and staged performance into lap dancing, is a fundamental shift, not only in the framing of the dance form but also in the way the dancers, as performers, were framed and subsequently viewed.

Erotic entertainment needs to constantly push boundaries of what is exciting and titillating. Holiday's story highlights such transitions and maps out the continuous nature of burlesque history. From this perspective, burlesque didn't die; it evolved with the changing format of striptease in a constant effort to quench the thirst of desire. I asked Holiday about her personal boundaries within the context of this ever-changing history. I was curious about her limits. Where was her line? She had the following to say:

> When you let people touch you, who has the power? Money has the power, actually. Man thinks he has the power, but it's the money. If man didn't have the money, he wouldn't get any action, so it's the money that has the power, and you have to decide, as a performer, if that's what you want to do. Are you willing to compromise?...Or maybe it isn't a compromise. The women who were working for them [lap dancing clubs], for some of them it wasn't a compromise; some...thought it is, and so there's a lot of drugs and alcohol use. Those women are hard. Nightclubs are not fun anymore. I talk to people who go into strip clubs, they're not fun anymore. There's something wrong with that, don't you think? Sex is supposed to be fun. It's not supposed to make you bitter and hard. I worked one week [in a lap dancing club] and I was done. I was done doing that. I was done.

Kitten Natividad
at the Burlesque
Hall of Fame,
2013

Kitten Natividad performs in the Titans of Tease Showcase at the Burlesque Hall of Fame, 2013

KITTEN NATIVIDAD

MATILDA AND I ENTERED KITTEN Natividad's room at the Orleans Hotel, and Kitten invited me to sit down on the bed. Matilda scanned the dark maroon room for extra light sources. "Do you mind if I open the curtains?" she asked and proceeded to struggle with the thick patterned drapes. As the sunlight hit Kitten's face, she briskly stated, "Let me just finish getting my makeup on," and sat down to apply a fuchsia-colored lipstick. I casually chatted with her as Matilda snapped a test photo. Enjoying the presence of the camera, the sixty-five-year-old, dressed in black satin fingerless gloves, fishnet stockings, a black waist cincher and a sheer lace bra, would speak, then stop and strike a pose, and continue her story from where she left off. In between the batting of her green sparkly eyelids and a series of lip pouts, Kitten casually explained the genesis of her entry into erotic entertainment. She began with nude go-go, moving sequentially into burlesque, cult classic "nudie cutie" films, lap dancing, and finally pornography:

> It was '69. And you started off going onstage stark naked and you danced for forty-five minutes. It was like aerobics because you were young and you could really dance...and in forty-five minutes you can pick up $100.00, so it wasn't really that you were doing it for the hourly wage because they would only book you for two hours and I would make over $200.00. Then you would get in a car and drive to another club and you would do two hours there. Then you would drive to another club.

Kitten threw her head between her legs and tousled her dark red hair. She stood up, grabbed her large breasts and pushed them up toward her collar bone as if they would stay there once released:

> I also did hard core and they almost make you feel like you sold your soul to the devil. And you know what, ask me if I give a fuck. I do what I do because I have to do it. I did it because in Canada the ones who were making the most money featuring were porn stars. So I said, "Oh is that all it takes to be

in a fuck film? Fine I will do a fuck film so I can get back up." You always had
to play the game too; I didn't have to but I did. So what?

Kitten's career touches on many key evolutions in erotic entertainment over the latter half of the twentieth century and proposes further complications that muddy the commonly understood burlesque narrative. Her story provides an excellent example of the transitions that took place over this quickly changing period and the porous nature of burlesque history as it fused and interacted with various forms of sex work. The interview also brings into question boundaries surrounding "real" versus "performed" sex in nude go-go and particularly pornography, and it considers the real implications for the women who "performed" in these entertainments.

Porn Staring: The Golden Age and Sex Re-Framed

Kitten pulled her chair across the patterned, plum-colored carpet and up to the wooden dressing table in order to examine her face in the mirror. This inspection revealed that the edge of a false eyelash had come loose; she pressed it back into place with the side of her pinkie finger. Kitten then continued discussing the circumstances of the industry when she began her career in erotic entertainment in nude go-go:

That was almost at the end of burlesque and guys were into the horn stage
where they didn't want to see girls take it off anymore; they wanted her to
just be out there naked. I found that very boring so I went to Hollywood
where they still had [some] burlesque and then I got into the costuming and
acts. I met Sparky Blaine, a manager, and he put me in the Miss Nude
Universe [contest]. I won that and he took me on the road as a burlesque
dancer. [I did] my traveling shows with the theater circuit, not nightclubs.
Later [I did] nightclubs, and [overall] it was a span of thirty years so I did it all.

The "end" of burlesque mentioned by Kitten generally refers to transitions between the burlesque house and the modern strip club. This period in burlesque history coincides with the golden age of pornography, which refers to feature-length hard-core (full penetration) narrative films, viewed in theaters for a roughly ten-year period between 1970 and 1980.[1] This decade sits as an entr'acte, as Eric Schaefer describes it, "between reels of essentially pilotless underground stag films" from the early twentieth century, to the advent of video[2] and the rapid de-popularization of the porn theater emerging in the mid- to late 1980s.[3] This period of pornography's golden age provides a moment in time when the framing of pornography was closer to, and often viewed alongside, theatrical burlesque. The two forms of entertainment at times shared both performers and theaters. This meant that theaters would switch back and forth between burlesque shows and pornographic film screenings—sometimes in the same evening.

When I asked Kitten what it was like to follow the screening of a pornographic film as a dancer, she laughed and explained, "You didn't think about it but you knew in your mind and that was kind of like, oh god, this is fucked."

Taking an "if you can't beat 'em, join 'em" attitude, Kitten began a career performing nudie cuties, a film genre that fused the traditions of cartoon-like comedy, pin-up photography, and soft core pornography.[4] These films include innuendo humor, simulated sex, and multiple naked women who comically find themselves in sexually implicit situations such as hitting a man in the face with their uncontrollable breasts or performing oral sex on a banana. Arguably the most famous director of this genre was Russ Meyer, whom Kitten references below:

> They were "nudie cuties," and if you ever became a Russ Meyer girl, honey, you were really known. That's what got me the universal [the title of Ms. Nude Universe], you know, with men. You see...I'm a man-eater, honey. I like to perform for men. I was the star of everything, the films. I did a lot of T&A, like Takin' It Off and Takin' It Off 2. I mean these films made millions, and I was in demand. It was fabulous. It was a fabulous life.

As discussed in Tempest Storm's interview, the burlesque queen ceased to exist after the birth of lap dancing due to a lack of theatrical layers that framed the dancer. However, the erotic star indeed continued, as the burlesque queen was succeeded by the porn star. In some instances, such as Kitten's, burlesque dancers moved into erotic film for this very reason.

For performers who chose not to cross over to film and remained in striptease, the constant presence and comparison to erotic film was difficult. Kitten noted that "a lot of girls were strippers that looked down on you when you went nude and when you finally took it off; 'I will never show my pussy,' they'd say. You gotta do what you gotta do and I don't feel bad for them or put them down that they wouldn't take it off, but they shouldn't judge us."[5]

Kitten suggested that many dancers "looked down" both on the films and the women in them. Perhaps they resented the increased competition or felt threatened by the pressure from the nudie cuties and other new forms of erotic film, as these could push the limits of their own boundaries (increased nudity, eroticism). Regardless of being shunned by peers and exhibiting increased nudity, Kitten expresses a sense of power (at least over men in calling herself a "man eater") and further claims that life was "fabulous" because she was the "star of everything, the films."

To return to Kitten's statement above, that she "like[s] to perform for men," this was a sentiment echoed throughout our discussions, signaling that although many of her peers (both then and now) did not believe what she was doing was "ok," her male audience did. Rather than developing a sense of sisterhood with her contemporaries, for Kitten, her audience was her support system.

It was these men who ultimately constructed her layers of celebrity,[6] celebrated her, and made her a star.

Freeing Love: Nude Go-Go, Porn, and Performing Sex

To examine the added implications that both pornography and nude go-go introduced into the burlesque narrative, let us return to a previous statement where Kitten contextualizes the beginning of her career in nude go-go:

> That was almost at the end of burlesque and guys were into the horn stage where they didn't want see girls take it off anymore; they wanted her to just be out there naked.

Here, Kitten situates the "end of burlesque" in relationship to the beginning of live nude entertainment. The introduction of nude go-go to erotic entertainment can be seen as the industry's answer to the free love moment. Free love and increased public nudity put pressure on the burlesque industry to modernize its adorned, structured approach to sexuality. Nude go-go provided what seemed to be a fresh, less theatrically framed version of sexual entertainment.

Five years after Carol Doda's groundbreaking bare-breasted go-go atop a hydraulic grand piano in 1964,[7] the Condor Club introduced bottomless or fully nude dancing. As a newsreel from the period suggests, in nude go-go, "girls are not considered performers and as such, not restricted by the laws of the burlesque stage." This description lends much to the understanding of the progression of striptease dance. The classification of bottomless dancers as free-loving hippy girls rather than performers allowed club owners to showcase fully nude moving, shaking, and gyrating women.[8] This nonperformer status not only made full nudity acceptable but also made it more "real." This was not performed eroticism portrayed by performers' bodies, but "real" eroticism with "real" naked bodies. In this changing erotic climate, burlesque was being framed in many ways by erotic film and additionally was operating in comparison and competition with this new erotic dance style, hip and "real" nude go-go.

When I asked Kitten to explain the burlesque she performed in the early 1970s in comparison to her go-go days, she said:

> It's basically they sit there and watch your show and in those days you had to hold their attention for forty-five minutes. So that's why you would take the gloves off, the stockings slowly, the negligee, all that. And at the end you did the twirling and all that [flowing movements with an often see-through negligee].

This sits in sharp contrast to nude go-go, which as its name suggests, required no temporal waiting period for live nudity. The presumption that audiences could and would be engaged by a forty-five-minute striptease implies a sense of stardom or special quality that is not afforded to go-go girls. In addition, the highly energized and often sporadic movements associated with go-go, as well as the spirit and impetus behind go-go, was rarely thought to be as sensual as burlesque. Rather, go-go focused on a free, party atmosphere likely fueled by the presence of pornography, which would have pushed consumer expectation for greater nudity and immediacy.

San Francisco not only introduced nude go-go to the nation but also was the location of the Mitchell brothers' O'Farrell Theater, which pioneered more personal striptease performances known as lap dancing in 1980. Lap dancing not only increased that amount of nudity but also necessarily increased its availability. Interacting with patrons, both on a personal and more physical level, has now become an expected and essential element of the striptease industry. Here in this space, a more intimate and often more complex relationship between dancer and audience is a standard element of striptease performance. The strip club floor, with its booths and laps, presents a constant tension, where the audience is in very close proximity to dancers' real, naked bodies, who must nonetheless maintain a negotiated distance.

When Kitten found nudie cuties had come to an end with the close of the decade, lap dancing was an established tradition. I asked Kitten to describe the origin of lap dancing as she perceived it and questioned what it was like, after enjoying the stardom granted by the nudie cuties, to leave the film frame and move into the laps of patrons:

> Pretty soon all the nightclubs were hiring that kind of entertainment.... They wanted just to get down and dirty and do the lap dances and all that. So, I moved on to movies...because you've got to get so close to the guys. Who the fuck wants to do that naked, almost do a dry fuck? And, then I started drinking to cope with it....I don't put anything down, and I've done it all, baby, porn, everything.

Here Kitten very frankly notes several elements—in this case, substance abuse—that some modern exotic dancers utilize to create emotional boundaries between the audience and the dancers' own personal intimacy. On one level, lap dancing proved unappealing to Kitten because it offered a very different pay structure; formerly she had been contracted as a headliner or a featured performer, and now she had to pay to enter the establishment and perform shift work. This pay structure, which converts the dancers into contract workers, seems to be at the root of the problem for Kitten. As she states:

> When I was in L.A. I went to work for a club and they were doing lap dancing. But when they started to tell you that you had to pay $200 to work...I didn't feel right that I had to pay to do that.

In addition to this sense of inequity with payment methods, Kitten also felt that performing lap dancing overstepped the boundaries of her own intimacy. By mentioning that "you've got to get so close to the guys," and further questioning, "Who the fuck wants to do that naked, almost do a dry fuck?" Kitten indicates the actual intimacy with patrons or the realness of the performance. It is possible that in the same way that the women dancing go-go were "not performers" one might question if the same form of justification is placed on lap dancers. The perception of performed sex versus "real" sex sits at the heart of many questions posed in this project involving the boundaries and framing of erotic entertainment.

From this perspective, let us look at the way pornography is indeed a performance. In contrast to the burlesque performer who employs layers and a series of coverings[9] to project the illusion of the dancer's own intimacy, the performer in pornography replaces this shrouded intimacy with visibility. Here sex is visible. Further, this "performed" sex is not so much about the physical pleasure between the individuals involved in the intimacy but is rather positioned for camera-savvy angles. Thus the emphasis is placed on the "showing" of sex to the multiple viewers. In making the intimacy accessible, visible, and consumable for many people, the real intimacy shared by the actual individuals engaging in the act is reduced.

In utilizing the word "real" I am aware of the potential problems inherent within the term. Thus, for the purposes of defining "real" sex in opposition to "unreal" or performed sex, I will draw from Erving Goffman's definitive work, *Frame Analysis: An Essay on the Organization of Experience*:

> We often use "real" simply as a contrasting term. When we decide that something is unreal, the reality it isn't need not itself be very real; indeed, it can just as well be a dramatization of events as events themselves—or a rehearsal of dramatization, or a painting of the rehearsal, or a reproduction of that painting.[10]

Goffman links what is unreal to a dramatization of an event. That which is real then sits in contrast to the unreal. Thus, real is a relative term operating in relationship with, in this case, its dramatized version.

The theory of framing posed by Goffman extrapolated to real sex versus a theatrical version of sex can help us understand Kitten's choice to enter the very revealing nudie cutie films rather than to remain in striptease. Nudie Cuties were but dramatizations of her sexuality and desires.

From this perspective, I wondered if Kitten chose filmed pornography over lap dancing because it felt more like a performance than the realness of lap dancing. I anticipated that she would think of it much like her decision, a decade earlier, to enter nudie cutie films rather than remain in the burlesque house, which she viewed as "dying" and no longer endowed with the frame and social context that had potential for stardom. I hypothesized that hard core would offer her a similar frame of distance, an additional layer no longer available in the current strip club format. Instead, Kitten had a rather frank and somewhat sobering response:

> When I did porn it was in the '90s. It was because I wanted to get big money and you weren't getting it. Burlesque was not happening any more, just the lap dancing. So, I said, I'll just do porn. I'm not married. And, who knows, and probably nobody will ever see it. I did it. I was on drugs and everything. I can't take it back, so I did it.... I just did it for money. I didn't do it for fame or glory. I just wanted enough money to pay all the bills. It was scary. Let me tell you it was scary doing porn because already AIDS was in. I did go and get checked to see, and then everybody had to have a certificate, but I still didn't trust the guys. It was a scary thing.

Taking into account the threat of the AIDS epidemic, where this supposed sexual entertainment or "performance" could have such "real" implications, I tried to understand Kitten's decision. I asked about her choice of pornography over lap dancing. I wondered if pornography somehow felt safer than dealing with new patrons night after night. "No!!" she aggressively responded, annoyed with me. "I told you why. MONEY. I was a WHORE. Come on. Just accept that I was a WHORE. I did it for the money."

In the face of the AIDS epidemic, questions emerge as to whether sexual entertainment is ever fully removed from realness. For Kitten, the reality of pornography exists not solely as a social stigma, isolating her from her community, but it also affects her real body. Pornographic film, in its pursuit of the realness, seeks to affect the bodies of its performers in a variety of ways. It has been suggested that all porn seeks to persuade viewers that what they are watching is "not performed but the real thing."[11] Although in utilizing Goffman's definition, porn can be considered a theatrical version of the real event, it is hard to deny Kitten's real substance abuse to stifle her real fear of contracting a life-threatening virus. The reality of pornography thus exists as a space where real bodies, real people, have relatively real sex in the production of the work, for which the product (the screening, the VHS tape, the web material) is the supposed theatrical event.

All That Glitter and Shit

Kitten carefully unzipped the garment bag, which lay on the hotel bed beside me. She lovingly looked at the multiple costumes she had brought to the Burlesque Hall of Fame Weekender. She laid a hunter green corset and matching thong out on her bed and asked Matilda if she thought it would look better in the photos than the black set she was wearing. After quick contemplation, Kitten decided she would stick with the black as she had worn the green the night before in the Titans of Tease Showcase.

Kitten has been coming to the reunion since its days at the goat farm in Helendale and loves being able to spend time with old friends. That being said, the reunions have involved some difficult relations with other dancers who did not approve of Kitten's career in pornographic film, as by her very presence at the reunion she represents burlesque's malleable and movable history. Kitten, in her Burlesque Bazaar booth selling her DVD copies of her erotic films, sits in confrontation to a legend beside her selling 1950s cheesecake photography and has chosen to showcase burlesque history, and her place within it, very differently. As a result, interactions between Kitten and some legends have, at times, been strained:

> So, they would always tell me, "You're not a burlesque queen; you're nothing but a porn star. You sold yourself to the devil!!" I said, "It's a free country. I can do whatever the fuck I want with my body." [What they did] was catty. I would have, I think, definitely three girls that were really fucking with me all the time, so I told them off. That's just not me. I kept saying, "This is disgusting." And one of the girls that was doing that, finally they just threw her out of the Burlesque Hall of Fame. . . . She was the one that gave me such grief, like she would embarrass me in front of maybe five other legends [saying] "This is the one that sold her soul to the devil." And, you know, things like that. It was horrible. She was always putting me down to make themselves look better, I guess. I literally fucked . . . and fucked up, but it was my business. It's a free country.

"Why?" I asked Kitten. I questioned whether there were not additional sexual exchanges happening in clubs. "Oh, god, yeah," she explained. "Hand jobs for $20.00. But it's not even that. It's like can't we just forget about all the shit and just have fun and talk about the real thing, burlesque?"

The real burlesque Kitten is referring to is rather intangible. She appears to pine for a romantic (likely fictional time) time when burlesque wasn't dirty or "dying" but when burlesque actually lived. Perhaps for her, acknowledging a more inclusive burlesque history, which involves its intersection with other erotic entertainments, also opens up personal past stories and connotations she would rather omit. For Kitten, who danced in burlesque only briefly in the 1970s, when burlesque was already competing with nude go-go and the golden-age pornography, wants only to talk about the "real" thing.

But perhaps Kitten, as she is among the younger legends in attendance at the Weekender, is simply further along this progression of exotic dance. One of the issues with this constant need for excitement in erotic entertainment and the subsequent pushing of boundaries is that inevitably women will either leave the business, many times feeling the women preceding them "sold their souls to the Devil," or they will stay, often overstepping or transforming the boundaries they originally set for themselves. For those who were financially stable (normally through marriage), more choices were available; but the choices were not there for others performing with (by then) aging bodies, in new entertainment forms pushed forward by the industry. As Kitten described, in her final days of lap dancing,

> The girls are okay with it because that's how they got into it so that's all they
> know. But when you're like me I just didn't accept it. . . . It was awful and
> I didn't need it. It was time for me to move on.

Kitten sat down by the mirror again and examined the same corner of the fake lash atop her shimmery green eyelid. The only sound was the shutter of Matilda's camera. She looked at herself while she drank from a plastic bottle of water, which crackled in her hand. I then pulled out my copy of *Takin' It Off* (1984) that I had purchased at the Burlesque Bazaar the day before. Kitten had told me it was the nudie cutie of which she was most proud. I asked if she'd sign it for me. She wrote:

> To Kaitlyn, Busting with love and good luck.
> *Kitten Natividad*

As she handed back the DVD, she laughed, and said, "From being a star to being just a girl. . . . Yeah. So anyway that was the end for me." She looked in the mirror and examined her face. She then exhaled and looked back at me, "You know" she said softly, "I'm a normal girl, I'm a normal human being under all this glitter and shit."

You know, I'm a normal girl, I'm a normal human being under all this glitter and shit.

GABRIELLA MAZE

ENTERING OUR SMALL, CONSTRUCTED STUDIO space in a room of the Orleans Hotel with a burst of unbridled energy came English-born dancer Gabriella Maze. Gabriella swept her beachy, mermaid-style hair to the side and asked Matilda if she should disrobe. This was the first suggestion of this kind we'd encountered on the project. Matilda considered this offer and proceeded to talk with Gabriella about how she would like to be represented in the portrait. After a brief conversation, the two decided that it would be best to keep bottoms on.

As we began Gabriella's shoot, I casually chatted with the retired dancer as she comfortably posed her tanned body for Matilda's lens. She reflected on some of the tattooing and piercing that often defines the neo-burlesque community, saying, "We were not allowed any of those privileges." Gabriella explained the pressure to look a certain way "or you didn't get work." She continued, "It was a tough life. It was not an easy life. But they [neo-burlesquers] tend to make it seem like everything was glamorous. It [was] not always glamorous. Sometimes you [had] to fight to get your paycheck." Gabriella scrunched her hair on the side of her head, allowed it to fall back toward her shoulders, and recounted what it was like finding work as a dancer in London in 1969:

When I first started dancing, I went from audition to audition to audition. I did work in a couple of sleazy nightclubs, and to be honest with you, I don't remember the names of them in London. And . . . I'm glad I don't remember them because they were bad. They wouldn't even let me dance. They said I could sit and I could be a cocktail waitress because I didn't have any experience working. A friend of mine had torn something out of the Variety newspaper, so I dialed the number and said, "I'm calling about the audition." The woman who answered the phone said, "Oh, I'm sorry, but the audition was yesterday." She must have heard something in my voice, like desperation, and she asked, "Are you in London?" I went to her flat in Holborn and actually auditioned in her kitchen in front of her, her grandmother, and her two daughters. I was standing there and she was writing something on a piece of paper. "We'll call you. Do you have a phone? Do you have an address?" I was a bit of a wild child back then. I never really lived anywhere, so I didn't [have anything permanent]. And then she said, "Do you have a passport...well, you have three weeks to get one. Sign here." And that's how it all started. I signed my first contract actually and went my first time performing on a big stage in a real nightclub; it was in 1970.

Gabriella Maze at the Burlesque Hall of Fame, 2014

I watched Gabriella's remarkably uninhibited shoot with Matilda. Apparently unfazed by our incredibly uninspiring hotel room, in a creative and almost tribal fashion, she undulated for the camera. Though her breasts were bare, she seemed more emotionally naked than physically. And while she moved, she reflected fondly on the British nightclub of the 1970s. Gabriella remembered following variety acts such as magicians, contortionists, musicians, poodle acts, and snake acts, but, she clarified, "they did not take their clothes off. Today all of those people I've mentioned...now take their clothes off. And, to be honest, I think that is what is killing the burlesque of today. There are too many people naked."

I decided against pointing out the potential hypocrisy in her statement—particularly in the context of the current situation. Rather, I asked Gabriella about perseverance. How was she able to persist throughout her career? Whether burlesque was "killed" or is currently being "killed," Gabriella was able to continue in a supposedly "dead" industry for a very long time by shifting in performance form and space. In what I would learn to be her characteristic style, Gabriella was notably open in our first discussion. She articulated these shifts and then, most poignantly, discussed her understanding of empowerment. Though Gabriella battled through great adversity—physical and mental control, and an abduction in early life—she was shielded by a theoretical concept, the term empowerment:

I did what I did and I survived a long time. I worked in a club here in Charleston for many years and I would lie about my age. I would say I was younger than I was so I could get work. When you call up and say "I'm fifty," they say, "Well, don't come for an interview." But I would show up and say I was younger and they would say, "Okay, we'll give you a job." I also worked with the first Dr. Muller's Peep Show in Germany, in Frankfurt, which was the most boring show ever. When it's your turn to get [on the peep show platform]—there would be all these little mirrors around you with little openings, and when somebody puts money in on the other side of that opening, [the door] pops up, it's a peep show. Yeah. Boring. You're on the stage for that five minutes—because it's a peek.

I've done my share of lap dancing, honey, and I'm not ashamed of it. It paid my bills, lessons for my daughter, and everything else that she has. But then it changed—and you get older and the girls keep getting younger. Many a time young girls go ha, how did she make so much money? Because I have the gift of gab, number one, and I'm . . . good at what I do. . . . See, I was abducted at a very young age and I was kept for quite some time and you learn how to survive. And learning how to survive is the biggest lesson in self-discipline I believe as far as having control over yourself. When people control you, it takes a lot. It takes a big, big chunk out of your heart and two out of your soul. If you're not strong enough, it will kill you, even though they didn't kill you.

Taking my clothes off for a living, you hear people say [often] that it gives you power. It actually does give you power. Some people will say it's degrading. . . . But, if you've chosen that path and you've figured out what you've got up there and it's the only job that you're comfortable in because it's the only job [in which] people accept you, it's very, very empowering, it's extremely empowering. So when I'm on that stage, I have the power to cast a spell on everybody. Do you know what I mean? We all have quirks about our own bodies: I don't like my butt or I don't like this, or my nose is too big or my nose is too small, god I wish I had less wrinkles, man where did this come from that wasn't there yesterday. We all have those. But to me, empowerment is not about shape, size, or anything. It's about strength. It owns you. No one can take that from you. And when you have that magical moment on stage where everybody is looking to you, it's almost like you're a god. . . . It's an amazing feeling. So, yeah, that's my answer.

When people control you, . . . it takes a big, big chunk out of your heart and two out of your soul. If you're not strong enough, it will kill you.

Judith Stein at the Burlesque Hall of Fame, 2015

JUDITH STEIN

I N JULY OF 2011, I moved through the foyer of the Gladstone Hotel in Toronto, Canada, to watch the evening performances at the Toronto Burlesque Festival. Toronto, like many cities across North America, holds an annual festival that consists of a series of performances and often brings in a legend to lead workshops, host a Q and A session, perform, and generally enforce the historic legitimacy of the festival by their presence. As I traveled toward my seat, to my left was Judith Stein, "The Great Canadian Beaver," or, as she is known in the community, "Mama Beav." Judith had been brought to Toronto by a local neo-burlesque celebrity and, according to his website, "Toronto's Top Mentalist," Mysterion the Mind Reader.

Mysterion began to introduce the evening's entertainment, and I looked around at the crowded room of neo-burlesquers, and then at Judith. Dressed all in white—the color I would come to associate with her—Judith seemed to be taking it all in. I wondered what was going on behind those perceptive eyes. I wondered what her relationship was to this community. Three years later, by way of a Skype conversation, I got the chance to ask her. This was her response:

> The older legends, the ones that have survived like Toni Elling, they were pretty savvy and they were stars. I think that during the '50s often the strippers were poor white girls that were uneducated. They had nice bodies so somebody dressed them up, showed them a few steps, and put them on stage and away they went. They really didn't have any social skills, let alone education. And they were the ones that taught us our chops. My generation [including] Holiday and Fannie and Kitten Natividad and that whole crew…we were kind of like the hip hippie strippers.

> There were times when it was hilarious and fun and exciting and glamorous, and then other times it was nasty, it was scary. There were times when you were working in a club way out in the middle of, excuse my French, butt-fuck nowhere Texas, staying in a trailer outside. And the club and the bartender would, for a fee of course, tell everyone, everyone, where you were staying.

Judith Stein performs in the Titans of Tease Showcase at the Burlesque Hall of Fame, 2015

And then at three o'clock in the morning, there's some guy banging on your door. Yeah, that kind of stuff or yeah it happened. Basically, if you were a stripper, it wasn't legitimate as this new burlesque movement is. We were like the bad girls, supposedly.

I actually got into a court battle with a fraternity because they invited me to come and do a show for one of their fraternity parties, and it turned into an attempted rape. I took them to court and the judge looked at me and he said, "You're really brave." He said, "A lot of strippers would not have tried this....What are you asking for?" and I said, "I think that these guys' names should be publicized in the university paper and that they should have to take a women's study course for two years."

As in Gabriella's interview, themes of empowerment and personal agency are common threads throughout this project. Judith's narrative puts these principled concepts into practice in a much more tangible way. I wondered what made Judith so—as the judge suggested—"brave." Further, I wondered what would have drawn her to such a progressive sentence for her attackers: education for rehabilitation. I knew Judith was university educated. I knew she was the daughter of middle-class southern Ontario farmers and thus she likely had a different set of options compared to some of her contemporaries. I speculated that it was her strong base that made her brave and asked whether her parents were supportive of her chosen profession. She laughed, and then replied:

I was coming home...I hadn't been home in about three or four years for Christmas. I get back there and Mom said, "Do you want to hang your costume?" because I'd been on the road for about six weeks. They were having friends over; I'd grown up with their kids. And I said, "Okay, what are we going to tell the neighbors?" I said, "Tell you what. We'll tell them I'm a stewardess because I'm traveling a lot," and [Mom and Dad] went "Okay, that's fine." So anyway, the people come around and we're all sitting around and somebody says to me, "So, Judy, what are you doing now?" And my mother says, "She's a stripper!!!!" And she took all these ladies down in the basement [where the costume was hanging] and all these ladies dressed up in my costumes. All the men, all these men, my father's friends are all looking at each other like, "Oh shit."

After we got through that, I thought I needed to have a little chat with my Dad. I took a bottle of whiskey down and two glasses and I said, "Do you want to talk?" And he said, "You're goddamn right I do." "Oooh, okay," I said, "Well from that answer, obviously you know about strippers." He told me a story about a stripper in a bar when he was married to my mom and I was a couple years old. He bought her a bottle of champagne and started talking. He was quite smitten and went to buy her the second bottle of champagne and she said: "You're a young farmer and you're starting out and you have a wife and a child and you don't need to be spending money on champagne for me. . . . [T]his looks really glamorous but I go home and wash my face at the end of the night. I'm just an ordinary person, too."

He said he had never forgotten that and he said, "I know there are some good strippers. Are you any good?" "I am," I said, "I'm making money, I'm traveling." My dad was a farmer and he always wanted to travel and so he handed me a dime and he said, "Call me if you need me."

A couple years later Judith was working in Ontario and received a call from her cousin informing her that her parents would be attending the show. In a panic, she pleaded with the club owner to allow her to remain in a G-string rather than stripping entirely naked. With this permission in hand, Judith performed "Don't Tell Mama" from *Cabaret* to a packed house. Unbeknownst to Judith, and in advance of her parents' arrival, the owner shared the news of the special guests with the audience, resulting in a glowing and supportive standing ovation. In response, Judith picked up the microphone and beamed, "Ladies and gentlemen, thank you very much. It's my honor to introduce the true producers of this show, my parents." Judith's parents also received a standing ovation that evening.

Judith paused. "That's a truly lovely story," I said. "Thank you for sharing that with me." Then, as if seeing me as a young neo-burlesquer in danger of romanticizing the whole thing, Judith sternly clarified:

Look, I know what it's like to be on the road, I know what it's like to be in honkytonks, I know what it's like to have a crappy crowd or to have a good crowd or when it's a job. It's difficult; there are some great neo-burlesquers who I love dearly and I see them putting on good shows and I see them getting it. There's others that have $5,000 worth of costuming on their back. I tell someone, "Honey, this is not the fucking Joffrey Ballet. Okay"?

Judith has since become a pseudo parent and a support for young strippers. She now runs what she calls "a home for wayward strippers" if they are on "the road or if they just need to get away." Below she explains her connection to the "working" kids or the "peelers" in contrast to the neo-burlesque community. She suggested that drawing a distinction between burlesque dancers and strippers rejects women currently involved in the exotic industry and is dismissive of the legends' lived experience. Further, she alluded to class privilege that at times divides neo-burlesque from its historic roots, as she speaks of the cost of neo-burlesque costuming and a push to "educate" legends on politically correct terms:

> It's this neo-burlesquy bullshit. We've just had a whole thing that went down at Burly Con [another burlesque convention] where Bic Carrol, who was one or probably the only male stripper legend, made an oblique reference to Bruce Jenner; all these neo-burlesquers were all over him about learning the proper terms for transgender and they were going to get up a whole crew to "teach all us legends about the terms for new sexuality." I'm going, "Hey wait a minute; the bottom line is back in our day, we didn't care what you had between your legs, you wanted to have between your legs, or did have between your legs. It's what's between your ears that works." The neo-burlesquers were all over him. The working kids [contemporary dancers in strip clubs] don't have time to get involved in that crap like these little hobbyists. That's why I align myself mostly with the peeling kids and peelers.

> And the working strippers get it; burlesque was about the connection with the audience. It wasn't how great or expensive your costume was or what a great dancer you were. It was that you were an entertainer and an entertainer connects…but it's the kids that are working the [strip] clubs that I relate to and I support mostly because I've been there. They know shit happens; whether it gets tough or they just need a break, they can come to Mama Beaver's house and sleep on the couch and I'll take them to the hot springs and feed them chocolate peanut butter balls.

Burlesque was about the connection with the audience.... you were an entertainer and an entertainer connects.

Isis Star at the
Burlesque
Hall of Fame,
2015

ISIS STAR

FOLLOWING THE EVENING'S SHOWCASE, the 2015 Weekender attendees made their way to the nightly after party held in the Mardi Gras Ballroom of the Orleans Hotel. Matilda and I entered the dark space to find bright sparkly people dancing and drinking in an outright celebration of their burly-q lifestyle and community. Situated beside the DJ booth was Isis Star. Isis whipped around her long gray ponytail and transcendentally waved her arms above her head while curving and twisting her lower torso to what seemed to be her own internal rhythm. Seemingly captured by Isis's spell, two female neo-burlesquers began dancing with her. The three women then proceeded to press up against each other in what became an almost tantric dance number, culminating in a passionate kiss between Isis and one of the neo-burlesque enthusiasts.

I thought about this expression of admiration and excitement. I thought about my conversation with Judith. Though the socioeconomic class of members of the neo-burlesque movement can vary, Judith Stein's interview stresses that the lack of emphasis on financial gain is often a distinguishing factor in the resurgence. When the need or striving for survival diminishes, some of the trials experienced by the legends can be omitted from this reimagined burlesque. This de-emphasis on commerce has subsequently allowed for greater freedom; as the community has less concern with commercially viable sex, its members tend to be more focused on sexual exploration and safe space.

Isis very much allies herself with the neo-burlesque movement. She was in essence a revivalist right from the beginning. Later, when I spoke with her, she prefaced our conversation by stating that when she began in the 1960s, "Burlesque was effectively dead, and it was just striptease. The movie *Gypsy* was very instrumental in me wanting to become a stripper, so I always stripped from the burlesque [revival] perspective, but it wasn't always appreciated."

More recently, when neo-burlesque began in the 1990s she exclaimed, "This is great!" As a result, Isis came out of retirement to engage with the neo-burlesque community and in her words, she had "at least a few years to practice from the perspective that I had always worked from anyway. I just really appreciate that the girls are keeping the art alive."

Isis Star performs in the Titans of Tease Showcase at the Burlesque Hall of Fame, 2015

Isis's interview sits in contrast to many others in this project. Fittingly, her performance philosophy also has a rather different perspective, focusing on neo-burlesque ideologies of body acceptance, liberation, and sexual agency, along with her own spiritual practice:

> I think we all, as men, as women, have the God and Goddess in us, and aspects of the God and Goddess in us. Some people connect with it, and are very spiritual and ever-present. Other people are very unconscious. For me it's an act of connection, not only with the Goddess and the Divine Feminine, but with the energy of the audience. I'm giving my energy out. They're giving their energy to me, and it meets in this tantric kiss. . . . [Y]ou have this energy and you can run it through you, and then you give it back to them, and then they give it to you, and you give it back to them. You get this tantric circle of energy going. It's called the fire breath in tantra, and that's what it feels like onstage for me. I'm a real conscious breather. If you see me onstage, I'm really breathing. Number one, you have to breathe to do cape work; otherwise you're going to get very sore muscles. I'm a very conscious

breather onstage, so I'm really taking in and tasting and feeling the audience.

Sex, drugs, and rock 'n' roll—that was before. When I left America things really changed. I always said, "When I get big I'm going to come live in Europe," and when I was twenty-five, I moved to Europe and stayed there for twenty years. It changed the way I perceived myself onstage. Before, I was doing what I thought men wanted me to do to excite them. After that I was doing what I wanted to do, which turned me on and got my energy going. I always danced for myself, but with that knowledge that I was dancing to excite the dead.

Audiences sometimes are really quite shallow and hollow. They are the dead. You have to ignite that spark that's in them, because otherwise they're just going to see you as a sex object or a vagina. I want them to see more of me than just my body. . . .

It's a bit draining sometimes . . . [but] that's why the audience loves me, because they feel me, or they get me in a way. That's what I talk about when I talk about the tantric kiss between the audience and me onstage . . . they feel that. They feel my love for them. For many years I did not love my audience. Now, [this neo-burlesque audience] I love them.

You have to ignite that spark that's in them, because otherwise they're just going to see you as a sex object or a vagina.

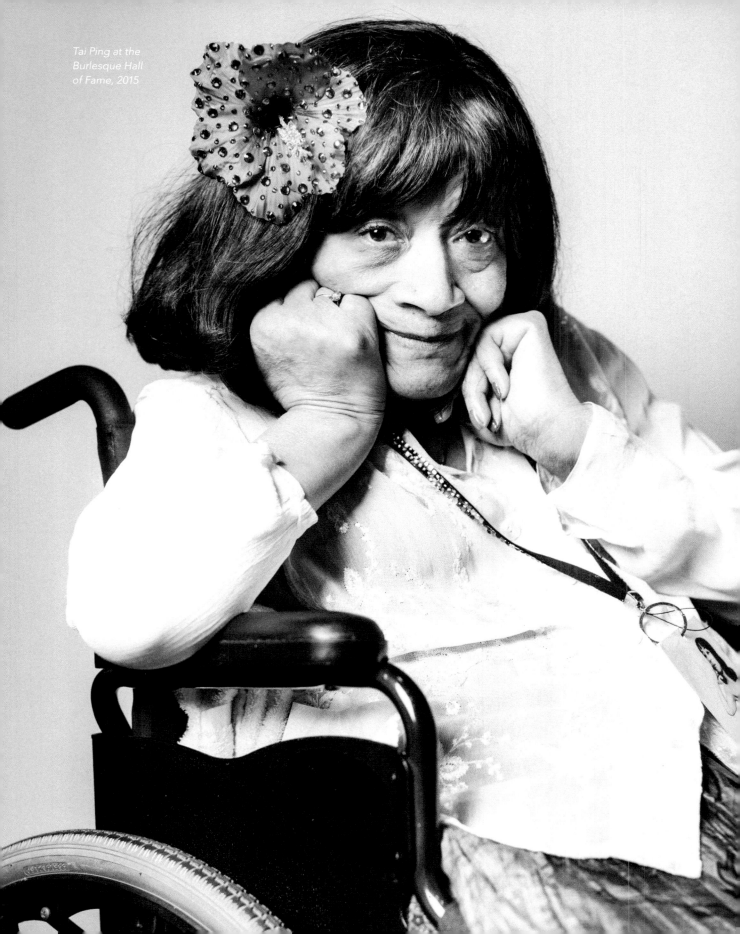

TAI PING

SITUATED IN A LARGE CONFERENCE room of the Orleans Hotel, the Burlesque Bazaar becomes something of a meeting ground over the course of the Weekender. Concessions featuring bespoke, rhinestone nipple tassels; racks of vintage clothing; and legends' vending booths fill the space. In the left corner of the room was burlesque legend Tai Ping. Tai's elbow rested on the arm of her wheelchair as she peacefully leaned her cheek into her hand. I walked over to Tai and examined the past promotional pictures laid out on her table. The images depicted a young Tai in "exotic," "Eastern" wardrobe, complete with a peaked straw hat and a thick line painted across each of her eyelids to accentuate her Asian-ness. I asked Tai about her burlesque persona. "I first worked in Key West [where] I used my middle name, Patricia.... [T]hey told me that [Tai Ping] was too ethnic," she explained. "I felt kind of weird about it when they told me it was too ethnic. I got to California and everybody says your middle name sounds okay, but Tai Ping sounds really pretty.... Tai means peace."

Thus, though her mother was half Native American and half Caucasian, it was her father's Cantonese background that informed her onstage character—a persona that Tai utilized until the end of her career in 1971. I wondered what it was like for Tai to perform her race in such an exaggerated fashion. I wondered what kind of relationship she had to her onstage identity. However, these were not the topics Tai wanted to focus on in her interview. Rather, she wanted to reflect on the beginning of her dance career—so that is what we discussed:

> I asked my mom if I could go to Key West, Florida [where her agent had made a booking for her]. My mom said, "Sure."

> I got to Key West, Florida, and I went on stage and did my number, and then I went to the audience to watch the rest of the show, and the club owner came over and he told me, he said, "That was a pretty nice opening that you did, but where's the rest of your number?" I told him, "That was it." He said, "But where's your panel?" I said, "What's a panel?" He goes, "Well, your gown." I said, "What do I need a gown for?"

He told me to take off things and all that bit, and I told him I couldn't do that. So he says, "Well, I'll call your agent and we'll send you back to Philadelphia." I said, "I can't do that either." Then I said, "I'll try it, but I have to have something to drink." He says, "The customers buy all the performers drinks." I said, "I don't have time to wait for anybody to buy me a drink if you want me to try that for the next show." So he took me over to the bar he says, "What are you drinking?" I say, "VO and coke." He says, "Give her VO and coke." As he walked away, I said, "You better give me a double."

I drank a couple of those and I still wasn't relaxed enough, but I went to the dressing room. Seeing two girls I knew, I said, "That guy out there wants me to take my clothes off, and I don't have anything under my costume to be taking stuff off." They gave me little flesh-toned bikini pants. One girl had pasties, and I said, "But those are too little." She says, "Don't worry about it." She took a string of sequins, and using spirit gum (that stuff we used to put spinny curls in our hair), she wrapped it around and around my boob until it was like I had a strapless bra on. Then she placed some sequins on the bikini pants, to cover my private parts and the seam of my butt in the back, made a little V back there, covered everything. They gave me a skirt to put over it; that's when I found out what a panel was. That was the first time I did stripping, between drinking booze. After that, I was there for a couple of weeks, and that's the first time I became a headliner in burlesque.

It was great fun. You meet people from different clubs that you have run into, and all that bit. It feels like it's still nighttime, but you come out [from a night of work] and you cover your eyes from the sun like a vampire. It's so funny, then you get to the theater, you had to sober up down there. You have time to run in and get a shower and stuff like that, because you had to check in at the theater by 11 o'clock. It was fun. It was tiring, but you really didn't care. You didn't really know it, until you lay down someplace, and, boom, you was gone. It was so busy, busy, hustle, bustle.

One night while traveling from a club, Tai suffered a devastating car accident. The incident required her to remain in intensive care from February to June of that year, during which she was "on a Stryker frame that you turned every two hours." As Tai describes, "They gave me a one in three chance of living." After two years of rehabilitation, Tai was able to go home but her legs were paralyzed. I asked Tai about life as a paraplegic after building a career and, I assume, an identity in dance. She explained the following:

They gave me a one in three chance of living...

I started bugging out. I have been acting when I was a kid, and I said, "Don't anybody go to any plays, or do anything out here?"... they looked at me like I just fell out of a tree or something." Then [I was] introduced to this workshop, it was called PATs, the performing arts of the handicapped.... We would do performances at different functions.

I thanked Tai for sharing her story with me and remarked how much I liked one of the pinup photos that sat in front of her, as I ran my finger along the white border that framed the image. I contemplated Tai's own framing or perhaps reframing of her narrative. Tai, in contrast to many dancers in this project, was never "aged out" of the industry or gained the identity of an "old" dancer. Rather, she found different identities for herself—identities such as Tai the member of PAT, or Tai the student. By contrast, Tai the dancer remained locked in time. She remained eternal in her young, unaltered, free moving body. It seemed, through our conversation, that we silently agreed to leave her there, as a memory in a photo sitting on Tai's vending table. For the Tai before me, in both body and mind, was a different Tai, the new Tai, and that's how she wanted it to be.

Tai Ping and her escort, Kristina Nekyia, during the Walk of Fame in the Titans of Tease Showcase at the Burlesque Hall of Fame, 2013

SUZETTE FONTAINE

A T THE LEGENDS' PANEL IN 2015, a group of about thirty senior strip-teasers sat at a line of tables. One by one, a procession of pensioners each took the microphone, often starting at the beginning of their careers and painting similar narratives. The stories were often of naive young women, with no prior knowledge of stripping, who—driven by promised money and fame—stumbled through an initial routine that was incredibly well received and resulted in striptease stardom.

However, when Suzette Fontaine, seated at the very last table in the very last chair, wrapped her long fingernails around the base of the microphone, she did not start at the beginning but rather, at the end of her career. Suzette discussed her journey to sobriety after she left dancing:

> *I was weak in life and alcohol gave me the strength to face this wall, you know? 'Cause life is not easy. My mother always used to tell me, "You ought to be strong, you ought to be strong," and I was not really that strong. And I paid the price; you pay the price sometimes for many things in life.*

While Suzette was speaking, I thought back to Tai Ping. Tai never told me if alcohol was involved in the cause of her car accident. I never asked that question for in many ways, the cause of the accident is irrelevant. However, in the push to drive and perform at club after club, and (in Tai's case) show up at a theater the following morning and perform again, substance abuse was often encouraged if not pushed upon many dancers; so I always wondered.

Suzette spoke very clearly about the impact of alcohol on her life. On the panel she spoke openly about her fight with substance abuse and further painted a bleak portrait of the industry. By the period in which she was dancing, lap dancing often not only required close physical contact with patrons but also emotional labor,[1] as dancers were asked to be companions to patrons—social and otherwise.

Suzette describes alcohol as a mechanism that mitigated her awareness of and discomfort with her closeness, both physically and emotionally. When we talked later, she referenced the limited options for a poor Hispanic woman and

Suzette Fontaine at the Burlesque Hall of Fame, 2015

pressures from club owners, which forced her to overstep her personal boundaries around sex work for purposes of survival. Explaining to me that she wanted to share her story for the benefit and education of a new generation of dancers, this remarkably brave interview outlines methods of self-preservation that include drug and alcohol abuse, disassociation, and contempt for clients.[2]

Well, I had a few gimmicks; I wore the panel, I wore the pasties, and I was very seductive. Because really, it's men who come to see the show. . . . They expect you to get hot. And sometimes they even masturbated, darling, because they cannot control their masculinity, or whatever. My prop was like a bed; . . . I pretended that I was having sex with somebody, and I'd have multiple orgasms. Yeah, it was wild, honey. To be in burlesque was not to be in a convent. Right, sweetie?

The point is this: never lose your dignity. Even if I lost part of it, it was always something of me. That's why I can tell my story today. . . . There was always some morality in me. . . . I've seen many girls destroy themselves in this career, even commit suicide. Overdose. Overdose, so many of them. I worked in Europe, in Switzerland, for many years. And over there that's what happened. Over there, you're obligated to do consummation. They force you to have consummation with the client. Right. It was a very high-class, beautiful Swiss salon. Here in the United States, you don't have to do that. You just used to do your shows . . . making money, good money—and keep on going to the next town. But when I went to Europe, that's when I got the drinking problem. A lot of champagne. A lot of nice guys, rich men, who buy you nice presents or whatever. When you become so material, eventually you pay the consequence. Because that really didn't fill me up. . . . Because I was really a professional dancer. I like to entertain here in the United States. But Europe, it's all different. Different expectations. And that affected me emotionally. . . . Well, this is personal, but I did it. Yes, I got too involved. It was a lot of pressure, because in those days the Mafia used to be very involved. Many times the [Mafia were the] owners. . . . They approach you about things that you do or you don't do . . . you know? It was up to you. But there was a pressure from the club owners. I paid a high price. I paid my price. I'm being honest with you, that's the truth. . . . But [when] you're young, you know, you're twenty-five, you've got the whole world and you don't have the character, it's hard to handle. You can get lost in that atmosphere. Then, many times, I didn't see. Plus, being Latina, my English was very broken. I didn't have too many choices, really.

I'm not ashamed about it or regret anything, I don't regret the past. But would I do it the same all over again? Oh. Oh, no! No, I wouldn't,

Suzette Fontaine's scrapbook, 2015

sweetheart. I'm going to a program where they teach you twelve steps…the twelve step program. I'm very grateful for that because I almost died. At the end of my career, I was empty when everything went. It's like I dreamed up a castle…a fantasy. And I didn't realize that I was going to get old. I never realized that. Then one guy that used to come in said "Oh, you look like my mother." I'd say, "Well, your mother must be gorgeous." But things like that really started affecting me and it was time to go, darling. Like everything, this career is temporary, it's not for many years. And I thought it was gonna be for all my life, you know?

In Suzette's story "Mother," becomes a measure for age in exotic dance. That is, "you look like my mother" seems to be a way of distinguishing dancers of an appropriate working age from those who are decidedly "old." From this perspective, Suzette very honestly described the emotional impact of growing old in the industry and the toll it took on her identity and sense of self:

At the end of my career I was like forty-seven—and I really didn't have any skills when that happened. I went to psychiatric treatment. I was always

> At the end of
> my career,
> I was
> empty.…It's
> like I dreamed
> up…a fantasy.
> And I didn't
> realize that
> I was going to
> get old.

screaming, crying—because then I had to find out something else to do. Then I did it. I started as a supervisor in a hotel. It was hard to get used to, after you get the applause. All the high-life stuff. . . . Everybody used to say aging is not for sissies. Anyway, we have our moments. You have to be very careful because this career is a risky career.

But honey, I come from a very poor family. I wanted to live a good life. I wanted to be somebody else. Whatever it took, I did it. Sometimes things we do in our life go against our principles. Life keeps going. I had to let go a lot of things. That's why I don't have no regrets. It was a beautiful life, really.

Sometimes I think I chose the wrong career, but I'm not sure about that. . . . What else would I have done? I just didn't have time to go to school to have any skills. I didn't have the support. I was raised by my mother—a single mother—no father. Sometimes you don't have too many choices. You do whatever life offers you.

Suzette
Fontaine at the
Burlesque Hall
of Fame, 2015

at the Roxy Theatre be-
ginning today when Mar-
inka takes center stage
at the E. 9th Street bur-
lesque palace.

MARINKA

MARINKA

MATILDA AND I KNOCKED ON the door of Marinka's condominium in a suburb of Las Vegas and were greeted by a very vocal lapdog, who wore a small ponytail atop her head and whom Marinka referred to as "Baby." The statuesque, and thus appropriately named, Queen of the Amazons led us through her living room, in which were exhibited an idiosyncratic combination of figurines of Catholic deities, semi-nude self-portraits, and an extensive porcelain doll collection. We followed Marinka into her bedroom where a very large renaissance-style painting of the seventy-four-year-old as a young woman hung above the bed. In the painting, Marinka wore a shawl of translucent chiffon, which slid off her shoulders and found a resting place just above her nipples. As I met the eyes of the painted Marinka, who seemed to be referencing a Mary Magdalene figure—although one who had no interest in any kind of redemption—the real-life Marinka explained, "That's me."

I noted Marinka's decision to situate the painting in the present tense, not "that was me" or "that's when I . . ." but "that is me." This situating of old pinup photographs, program clippings, and erotica in the present tense is a common theme among the legends who attend the Burlesque Hall of Fame. That is, for many of the legends involved in this project, their performing self, during the period when their bodies created financial revenue, seems to be their primary and everlasting identity.

As discussed, the neo-burlesque community is in large part founded on the concept of a safe space. The movement often actively promotes difference and body acceptance as it rebels against the narrow view of beauty found in mainstream media. Similarly, this community often depicts mid-twentieth-century burlesque as a place of acceptance, in contrast to contemporary erotic entertainment. The neo-burlesque narrative often places both a body positive and a feminist lens on burlesque history. In this discussion, I would like to focus on one strand of the body positive movement, or one physical difference, which is celebrated by this community: age, specifically in relationship to the display of sexuality. At the gathering at the Burlesque Hall of Fame reunion, aging bodies have been celebrated, but historically this was not the reality for most women interviewed in this project. That is, burlesque has not always been a body positive space. For dancers, rather than aging with this industry, the shift away from staged burlesque meant they were aged out much quicker and much more brutally than had been common even a generation earlier.

Age, Sex, and the Carnivalesque

In her seminal 1972 essay "The Double Standard for Aging," Susan Sontag, suggested that women are viewed as "aged" before their male contemporaries, and from menopause onward, women in Western society are "old."[1] Sontag asserts that men are not judged by their sexual attractiveness in the same way. In this social construction of femininity, a woman is an object that loses its value when it ages. Once aged, if appropriate concealment by way of fashion and behavior is not properly executed, the woman may be seen as guilty of conspicuous display.

This concept of conspicuous display or spectacle has been theorized by Mary Russo, who employs the term "grotesque" when analyzing perceptions of female bodies (particularly aging female bodies). Russo, however, inverts the traditional use of the word, which associates grotesque with something that is low; instead, she repositions it as a "high" level attribute within the discourse of liberation. Recalling a phrase from childhood, "she (the other woman) is making a spectacle out of herself," Russo asserts that making a spectacle of one's self is a specifically female danger.

Russo further suggests that there are particular dangers for marginalized groups in this regard, as these groups evoke the redeployment of taboos surrounding the female form as grotesque, "specifically the pregnant body, the aging body and the irregular body, which are unruly when displayed in the public sphere." In this way, though the legends may have once been the apex of heteronormative display for the sexual satisfaction of men, now the public display of their late life bodies at the BHoF weekender makes them part of the spectacle. Further, the performative nature and the event-style construction of these meetings moves this reunion into the realm of the carnivalesque, which has been defined as "the celebration of the transgressive or unofficial modes of being."[2]

At the Burlesque Hall of Fame reunion, through these carnivalesque presentations of their aging bodies, the legends powerfully confront issues of social denunciation of aging women in performance, as displayed in current popular discourse. In contrast to their previous, potentially (from a historical perspective) anti-feminist stance and conformist performances of sexual norms, these now subversive performances reveal the newfound political possibilities of this aging community.

From this perspective of subversive display, it is understandable that the legends, in their present-day bodies and lifestyle, have been interpreted as feminist icons. However, many narratives in this movement also suggest that the burlesque of the mid-twentieth century shares this ideology. David Owen, describing burlesque in all its historical incarnations, states, "Burlesque not only refers to those normally hidden parts of the body. . . . Through sexual parody, the unspoken assumptions regarding gender, sexual expression, and definitions of beauty are not only exposed but explored."[3] This implies that burlesque of the mid-twentieth century—that is, the commercial stripping of its day—was simultaneously benefiting from financial gain by appeasing (predominantly) male sexual desire while also offering a space to parody assumptions regarding gender and further question and push boundaries surrounding beauty norms. Although meeting this duality as an objective is, of course, possible, doing so seems to have happened rarely.

Most of the women interviewed in this project were performing the mainstream, marketable, and therefore often narrow versions of sexual entertainment as prescribed by the fashions and norms of the time. There was no home video or Internet through which pornography could easily be accessed. The performances of these women were the accessible visual sexual outlets of the day. As a result, framing them as a space to mock cultural fixations surrounding sex or a space that is an alternative to the commodification of the female form does not seem to be supported.

I'd like to reflect on two physical states identified as "unruly" by Mary Russo—age and pregnancy—which force us to confront the intersection between sex and motherhood. These states are of particular relevance to the women interviewed in this project, both having had particular implications for their careers. Jessica Berson has studied Boston's "Combat Zone," a region of the city that remained virtually lawless throughout the 1970s and as a result, this period of Boston's history has became something of a petri dish for new sexual entertainment. Berson suggests that in sexual fantasy "you never want to think about the consequences of sex."[4] In this respect, motherhood represents a reality that sits outside the constructed fantasy of sexual entertainment.[5] Therefore motherhood "is not the fantasy—it's the real world. . . . [Y]ou are confronted with mortality,"[6] life, and subsequently death.

In the strip club setting, motherhood presents the possible implications of sex, confronting patrons with the realities of the dancers' real, functional, and aging bodies. As was noted in Suzette's interview, "Mother" often becomes a descriptive term for women whose sexual attractiveness has diminished or expired in the exotic dance industry. The term "mother," then, comes to represent the grotesque.

Below, Marinka offers an example of this vocabulary when she uses "mother" to describe her progressing age and explain her subsequent decision to leave the industry:

> I said to myself, this is the time; I was fifty years old. I've been lucky that I was for thirty-nine years on that stage. I don't want to go to a place where people will say to me, my mother is younger than you. [All quotations without sources are from Marinka's interviews.]

The concept that one does not wish to view one's mother as a sexual being with sexual desires and would rather ignore the fact that one's very existence is predicated on that sexuality is all too common. However, in the context of erotic entertainment, the issue is often not about one's own mother but rather that a dancer could potentially be older than someone else's mother.

As will be made clear in almost all of the interviews to come, the word "mother" is a term of great significance in exotic dance. With motherhood comes a body that has been used and therefore (even ever so slightly) aged. For women with these connotations of motherhood, in the context of up close and intimate lap dancing, their bodies are often seen to be "too" real and "too" lived in.

Marinka at her home in Las Vegas, 2013

"Performing Magic"

Marinka stretched her long limbs across her silky, champagne-colored bedspread. As she did, the black beads, which hung from her bra, clinked together and made a soft clacking sound; Baby wriggled in my arms and Marinka's life-size portrait and porcelain dolls looked on. As I began talking to Marinka, she described her first job as a featured stripper when she co-featured with then fifty-year-old Yolanda Moreno. I expressed surprise at Yolanda's age and asked if their time performing together was close to the end of Yolanda's career. "No," Marinka corrected me. "Because in those days, I tell you, I worked with ladies who were in their sixties. For example, when I worked with Sally Rand she was around seventy."

Sally Rand is credited with initiating fan dancing (now an iconic staple within the history of burlesque) as a national fad when she first performed her fan routine at Chicago's Century of Progress Exhibition in 1933.[7] Rand is a key figure within the history of burlesque, and, born in 1904, she was likely in her seventies when she worked with Marinka. As has been noted previously, the shift from the theatrical burlesque to lap dancing in the 1970s and 1980s removed a series of theatrical layers that distanced a performer from the spectator. These layers allowed burlesque dancers to achieve a level of fame, an opportunity that is not often afforded to modern-day strippers. In contrast to Marinka, Sally Rand, coming from an earlier generation, was accorded a stardom that allowed her to dance right up until her death.

Marinka situates the following story in the 1980s. As Rand died in 1979, I believe this event likely took place close to the end of Sally Rand's life:

> When I worked with Sally Rand I was booked into a little club in the outskirts of Pittsburgh, Pennsylvania, called Marquee Row. The name of the club was the Go-Go Lounge and I see a very old lady sitting at a little table having a soda. I knew I was going to be working with Sally because my agent had told me but I could never visualize that she was a little old lady. I went to her and I said, "Do you work here," thinking that perhaps she was a cleaning woman. She looked up to me and she said, "You must be Marinka." She extended her hand to me and she said "I'm Sally Rand." I said "OH, Sally, I'm sorry I didn't recognize you." She said, "It's okay; my pictures were taken forty years ago." At this time the manager walked in and said hello. He checked us into the motel. I said "Well, Sally, I guess we have a lot to do" and she said "yes." I went to my room and she went to her room.

> Remember, I saw a little old lady! When 6:00 came, I could not believe it. By now she had all this fabulous makeup, she had this fabulous wig on, she had a lovely dress, and she looked twenty years younger. But that was not enough.... She said to the person who did the lights, to the sound guy, she said, "I want very bright lights and only one spot in magenta on me." I thought, how can she go to work with bright lights? Came the night and I did my show and I hurried up.... They had go-go girls opening the show, then they had me, they had go-go girls, and they had Sally. So Sally came. It was a miracle!... She looked like [she was] thirty-five years old on the stage.

> She did her beautiful fan dance. She had a net from the neck all the way to the feet and to the hands. Her body was covered but it was all brightened up by magenta lights with her pink fan and she did the most lovely fan dance. And that club was full, there were lines outside, lines and lines of people. Every show we packed it in for the week.

Famed burlesque dancers seem to have been able to stay young far later in chronological years than modern strippers and also their contemporaries—burlesque dancers who were not accorded such fame. As is clear within Marinka's description of Sally Rand, the aura of fame thus ameliorates the anti-aging process, and patrons often remain loyal followers of their staged burlesque queen into the dancer's advanced years.

Theatrical burlesque is given a literal and physical frame by the proscenium stage, which, as discussed in Tempest Storm's interview, is then further adorned with the theatrical layers proposed by Barthes. This physical frame and layering also enables the societal framing proposed by Goffman, which, as noted previously, works both aesthetically and socially. The physical changes to Rand camouflaged by her aesthetic framing choices are mentioned twice in Marinka's story: first when Rand exits the hotel with her performance makeup and wig on, apparently lowering her perceived age by twenty years, then further when she is onstage with soft light and a full net costume. The additional frame at play, and potentially the more important one, is the social frame. Sally Rand is known as a famous striptease dancer. As a result, audiences arrive at the theater prepped to perceive her as such. The audience expected to see Sally Rand, they paid to see Sally Rand, and as a result, what they saw was Sally Rand. Through these means, this "little old lady," whom Marinka assumed to be the cleaner, was seen not as a grotesque spectacle but as a dancer revered for her grace and beauty.

By contrast, Marinka had a very different experience. At the end of her career in an early 1990s Berlin strip club, Marinka found herself worried about looking like a mother in such close proximity to her young new generation of patrons. That is, rather than age with the industry, as Rand was able to do, Marinka was aged out.

Lap dancing requires dancers to appear younger in age than staged striptease. This is because the close proximity of dancer to patron in lap dancing allows for fewer opportunities to cover imperfections. When describing the evolution of the exotic dance throughout the course of her career, Marinka suggested that in the days of the burlesque theater, women were able to continue working into a much later age. The strip club, by contrast, required the performer's own personal intimacy that could expose her real, aging body. The need for actual contact, and at least the pretense of their own "real" sexuality, made women much more available and vulnerable, exposing potential cracks in the sexual fantasy with its illusion of youth. Below, Marinka describes her perception of the differences between mid-twentieth-century staged burlesque and the modern strip club format, which she left in the early 1990s:

> When you are on the stage you're performing magic no matter who you are. You don't have to be a magician to do illusions. We were the most illusionist of them all. There were a lot of ways when you can camouflage a lot of things.... Under the light, under a negligee, under stockings, there is magic to be created.... [I]n those days , I tell you, I worked with ladies who were in their sixties.... Today these girls are only sex. And when you sell sex alone and sex is not perfect, it can be boring. Burlesque, I believe, was also a sex industry but we tried to do it to entertain. We did entertain. We had jobs. We had comedy. We had song and we had music and we had sex.

Here, Marinka shares a sentiment similar to those of many of the women interviewed in this project when comparing staged striptease to lap dancing, but her articulation of the point is rather distinctive. Marinka states that "when sex is not perfect, it can be boring," and that although theatrical burlesque was, as she states, a "sex industry," she places sex at the end of a list of other theatrical elements (comedy, song, music). Thus, Marinka is alluding to layers[8] of illusion, suggesting that theatrical elements of stage striptease distance the dancer's real, aging body from her audience. The imperfection of both sex and real (in this case, aging) bodies is masked by theatricality. Lap dancing, as Marinka point outs, requires greater levels of intimacy, and with this physical closeness, layers of theatricality are stripped away so that the age of a dancer becomes exposed and often ultimately judged.

Although scholars have discussed other limiting factors of the profession, minimal work has been done on aging exotic dancers.[9] Carol Rambo Ronai's essay, "Separating Aging from Old Age: The 'Aging' Table Dancer,"[10] published in 1992 examines premature aging in table dancers. Rambo Ronai theorized that table dancers, also known as lap dancers, became "old" much earlier than most members of the population due to the context of their work environment. In contrast to writers of most aging literature, which is generally limited to later life subjects, Rambo Ronai uses aging as a descriptive category as it applies to context and time of life, specifically within the exotic dance industry. Rambo Ronai suggests that "as chronologically young as she might be, she can be old. . . . A dancer's sexual utility and the sincerity of her presentation come into question. The old dancer breaks the tacit rule that women who sell their bodies in one form or another should be selling young, attractive, and cooperative commodities."[11]

Drawing from studies that span the course of the 1970s, which reported a median age of twenty-three for striptease dancers, Rambo Ronai notes that those interviewed for her study conducted in the late 1980s and early 1990s considered the average to be nineteen or twenty. A notable development emerged in the exotic dance industry in the period between the studies Rambo Ronai draws from and her own study: the introduction of lap dancing in 1980. As Marinka stated above, "When you are on the stage you're performing magic," and "you don't have to be a magician to do illusions." However, without such a stage, without such illusions, Marinka suggests that lap dancers sell "sex alone" and under these circumstances, even the very young can be deemed "old."

Ironically, this need for something new and young, which once brought the strip club success, is likely a major factor in its demise. A 2014 report out of Toronto, Canada, found that in 1997, the city issued 2,844 "burlesque entertainer" licenses, a number that has dropped by more than half in the past twenty years. In 2014, 1,284 people in Toronto hold that license, a diminishing trend that can be observed across North America.[12]

Internet sexual entertainment being brought into one's own home or personal space by various chat rooms, groups, and pornography allows for a sense of intimacy that some might be unable to obtain in their offline lives. Although there are questions as to whether this is real intimacy, many Internet users

You don't have to be a magician to do illusions. . . . Under the light, under a negligee, under stockings, there is magic to be created.

believe it to be.[13] The much more public lap dance has given way to the private and personal laptop. In this way, one could theorize that lap dancing is, in and of itself, "old." In the context of Internet-based erotic entertainment, the strip club, like the crumbling burlesque theater before it, has become the old stripper.

The strip club is now the aging performance space, and it will likely "die." However, the performers will, like those before them, live on and continue to move into new spaces and frames—potentially from lap dance to laptop. They too might intersect and influence new forms of sexual entertainment, and it is through these means that they will further disrupt, complicate, and contaminate the commonly believed and simplistic history of striptease.

Retiring Sex: Old Strippers and New Legends

When Matilda finished photographing Marinka, I released Baby and Marinka scooped her up into her arms. As Marinka showed us to the door and Baby bid us a robust farewell, I asked Marinka what she thought was the highlight of her career. She settled on spending time with then elderly Josephine Baker:

> I saw her show once in New York in the Palace Theater. And I saw where she died in Bobino, in Paris. I went to Paris and I went to see her. I came to see her direct. That was the reason for that trip. I went and I sent her a note and reminded her of meeting her in New York. . . . She immediately asked me to come backstage so I went backstage and we talked. And then we went and had something to eat and by now she had lost her house. She was living in a little hotel in Paris.

> That was the last of her shows, Bobino's. She was wonderful, really wonderful. That was '74. . . . She had to be well into her seventies. She died a few months after. She was performing there when she died. She was in the same show that I saw her in at Bobino's in '74 and that was her last show; she died doing that show. . . . She worked until the very end. I think her heart stopped.

Josephine Baker, born in 1906, would have been sixty-six if Marinka saw her perform in 1974. Just as Marinka's memory of working with Sally Rand in the late 1980s was slightly inaccurate (Rand died in 1979), it is also likely through memory and subsequent retelling that the imagined theatrical burlesque was more accepting of difference than it was in reality. The neo-burlesque narrative has often re-remembered and conceptualized burlesque as accepting and inclusive of difference and the legends in turn have, to a certain extent, adhered to this idealization.

When they became "older than mothers," a few of the women involved in this project left the business and were supported through a marriage; often they had children. Others who stayed longer frequently were pushed or aged out of the industry and later, as Marinka did, found "Baby(ies)" and community elsewhere. The Burlesque Hall of Fame provides such a community for many of these dancers. Some who did not have families of their own have found what many of them describe as a "burlesque family." Further, though historical burlesque may not have been body positive, in this niche community with its believed burlesque that embraces late-life sexuality, this ideal is closer to the truth. Here, these now late-life dancers are framed as stars; they are arguably subversive and politically relevant; and here, in this space, being old and sexy is appropriate, socially accepted, and encouraged.

Dusty Summers at the Burlesque Hall of Fame, 2014

DUSTY SUMMERS

WHEN OUR TAXI ARRIVED AT Dusty Summers's house we couldn't actually see it, for in front of the Las Vegas bungalow was an incredibly large motorized home decorated with black and gold decals. Matilda and I unpacked the trunk of the cab, turned the corner around the RV, and balancing backdrops and lighting equipment, made our way to Dusty's door. Dusty waved and excitedly ushered us inside. "We've just got back from a trip," she said pointing at the enormous motor home and introduced us to her husband, Ken, a tall Texan who sat at their kitchen table sporting a large belt buckle and cowboy boots. As Dusty gave us a tour of her home to find the best location for her shoot, Ken offered suggestions from the kitchen. "Don't go in the back yard. Old people don't look good in bright light," Ken pointed out.

While Dusty showed me her dressing room, which showcased multiple head forms with various but very similar blond wigs, Ken asked Matilda to ensure that Dusty's neck appeared elongated. "You need to watch for older people's necks in photos," he advised. Matilda thanked him for the guidance and said she would remember the suggestion. Ken is an immensely keen Burlesque Hall of Fame husband. He attends most BHoF events with Dusty; he helps her sell her photos at the Burlesque Bazaar (often manning the table on his own); and when an usher asked him to put his video camera down while Dusty performed in the Titans of Tease Showcase, he very firmly explained, "That's my wife up there!" and continued filming. As a result, this shoot mattered to Ken. This was clear as he paused, looked at us both, and stated, "I just want her to look her best."

Matilda and I moved into the couple's bedroom, determined by group consensus to have the best light for Dusty. Dusty, self-proclaimed as "Las Vegas's Only Naked Magician," arrived in the room with her signature props, two white doves. As Matilda positioned Dusty, I—in an attempt to be helpful—tried to hold one of the birds, which then proceeded to fly away, but not before relieving itself on me. Dusty laughed at my obvious lack of skill in the area. She then handed me some paper towels so I could clean the dove poo and proceeded to correct my bird-holding form. With the dove now cupped firmly in hand, Dusty told me about her career as a stripping magician:

Maurice Seymour
New York

OUT OF THE MAGICAL HAT OF
Dusty Summers

Dusty Summers

I was working in Fort Walton Beach [Florida]...with a magician named Professor Turban. I eventually married Professor Turban, and I was his assistant. He did birds, doves, and so on, and so I got acquainted with the doves. But, little by little, I added [his magic tricks] to my striptease act.

One time, we were having a big brawl, and he was in Fort Walton Beach. So I took a booking in Fort Lauderdale without him. The owner came up in the dressing room and said we've got a bachelor party, and we need someone that can do something that would have to do with weddings. "Can anyone do anything"? I said, "Well, I've never done it before, but I can probably do my husband's routine," and so I went out there and I did his material and got a hell of an ovation. So I called him on the phone and I said I don't know how you're doing up there in Fort Walton Beach, Turban, but boy, you're going over really good down here in Fort Lauderdale.

In some ways I had the feminine advantage over my former husband [because] there were just tons of male magicians but not female magicians, and certainly not female magicians who took all their clothes off. So the old question of where did you hide that, or where did it go...had a whole new meaning when you're nude, or when you wind up nude. I believe that not only did it open new opportunities for me, but it also extended the length of my career.

Now I perform at the Burlesque Hall of Fame. But I don't want to perform when I have to have help getting on or off that stage. When everything just doesn't look right—don't know a delicate way to say it— when the flap starts flapping more than what I'm actually trying to make it flap...I'm not going to go out there and do it.

Burlesque has been good to me, magic has been good to me, and the world has been good to me. I'll leave it there.

When we had finished our shoot, Dusty, now changed into a matching tracksuit set, very kindly offered to drive Matilda and me back to our hotel in downtown Las Vegas. We said goodbye to Ken, the doves, and the RV, which according to a recent Facebook post, has taken the couple 120,000 miles together. As the three of us drove out of residential Las Vegas, Dusty began telling us about her routine at the BHoF reunion this year. As I listened to Dusty describe a number involving a combination of striptease and magic tricks, I thought about her journeys with Ken, and how by way of the motorized home, Dusty was still touring today.

Dusty and Ken present an interesting paradox. Though she very much wants to maintain the lifestyle of a performer, and though Ken will stop at nothing to film his sixty-five-year-old wife's magic striptease routines, there is fear. There is fear that, as Dusty puts it, the "flap will start flapping," that her

Burlesque has been good to me, magic has been good to me, and the world has been good to me.

neck will show creases, or that when performing her magic "everything doesn't look right."

As was discussed in relationship to Marinka's interview, many women in this industry fear the moment when the theatrical spectacle shifts to the performer making a spectacle of herself. For many, the idea that these bodies could reach their limit of sexual attractiveness is frightening. With this understanding, I remembered that although the Titans of Tease Showcase is often depicted as subversive and political by the neo-burlesque movement, for most of these women, burlesque was about survival. I remembered the need that was once attached to these performances. I remembered that these dancers' bodies were their means of support, often both in terms of revenue and sense of self. And I hoped, very strongly, that Dusty would feel she "look(ed) her best" in her picture.

*Dusty Summers
in her Las Vegas
home, 2014*

Penny Starr Sr. and
Penny Starr Jr. at
the Burlesque Hall
of Fame, 2015

PENNY STARR SR. AND
PENNY STARR JR.

I N A GOLD SEQUINED GOWN, World Famous *BoB* introduced Penny Starr Sr. and Penny Starr Jr. for their act at the 55th annual Titans of Tease Showcase in 2012. "We are coming out now with a grandmother-granddaughter act," *Bob* announced to resounding applause. *BoB* continued:

> The senior of this act is the winner of Miss Bumps and Grinds of 1966 [held] by the Atlantic City Cotton Club, and the junior of this act is the first runner up of Miss Exotic World 2004, and together they will be rubbing their two cents together. The combined age of their boobs is 122 years. Please welcome to the Stage Penny Starr Sr. and Jr!!

The two generations of women scurried on stage. Penny Starr Sr. began posed with her back to the audience, while her granddaughter sensuously unwrapped a sarong to reveal a sequin bra and bottoms. Once undressed, Jr. turned her back to the audience and froze, and Penny Starr Sr. began swaying and grinding her hips. She ran her hands down her black taffeta dress and closed her eyes, as she allowed the music to resonate through her body. She shimmied and the silver stars embroidered on her gown sparkled as they caught the stage lights. The almost eighty-year-old then shuffled around the stage as she slowly zipped off her gown to reveal sparkly silver pasties and a black, beaded skirt. Finally, the grandmother-granddaughter team performed a synchronized cha cha step routine to the crowd's great amusement.

Penny Starr Sr. had raised her granddaughter from a very young age. As a working dancer, she traveled from theater to theater with her granddaughter nestled in a large basket, which she left in the care of other dancers backstage while she was performing. As Penny Starr Sr. describes it:

> The girls would shove a bottle in her mouth while I would go on the stage. [In] her young years…she grew up around the stage all the time. She would play with pasties and all kinds of junk. She wasn't a normal kid. I think when she was three years old she could make a mean martini. She would make martinis for all my friends that used to come and leave then, of course.

She grew up around the stage. She would play with pasties and all kinds of junk. She wasn't a normal kid.

*Penny Starr Sr.
performs in the Titans
of Tease Showcase at
the Burlesque Hall of
Fame, 2014*

Then…we would go out for dinner. She would say let's see, my bubby is having scotch on the rocks, and I'm having on the rocks—because she was teething on ice. Yeah, that was her.

In adulthood, after making a documentary about the Los Angeles–based neo-burlesque troupe Velvet Hammer Burlesque in the 1990s, Penny Starr Jr. began performing. She eventually competed for Miss Exotic World and was crowned first runner up in 2004. She sent a letter with a VHS tape of her winning performance at the goat farm to her grandmother, which Penny Sr. read to me: "Bubby, it had to happen. I am now dancing. Can I take your name?"

More recently, the pair have begun to dance as what Penny Starr Sr. claims is "the only grandmother/granddaughter burlesque troupe in the world." I asked both women what it was like to perform striptease with a relative. They responded respectively:

Penny Starr Sr.:

Oh, it's wonderful, it's really wonderful. I get things wrong though. I miss my cues, and oh my goodness, I do a lot of things wrong, but she overlooks it. I'm not used to working with anybody, and I'm not used to working with CDs. I used to talk to my band, and I had all my music for it that they would go back and play. If I had a good crowd and things were going well, I would say "take me," and they would do another chorus. If the crowd wasn't working with me or it wasn't so good, I would just turn around and say "take me out." But…this, you can't do on a stage. You cannot do this on a CD!!

Penny Starr Jr.:

When we started dancing together, it was very interesting because she never danced with other people, even when she took dance classes as a kid, they were all private, so I said, you're going to teach me your routine and we'll do it together. I bring her to L.A. before Vegas, and you have to understand, she lives in Allentown, and I live in Los Angeles, so any rehearsal time…has been just a few hours before we get to Vegas. We get into a studio and I say, "Okay, you dance it and I'm going to try and learn it," She does it once and I say, "Okay do it again," and then I realize, "Oh, my god, you're not doing it the same way twice!" She's like, "No, why would I do it the same way twice"? I'm like, "Because I have to do it with you!"

Penny Starr Jr. then paused and noted that dancing with her grandmother made her realize something else. Spending time talking about and moving their bodies together made Junior aware of the inherent body image issues that are still very real for her grandmother. Penny Starr Jr. adamantly stated, "Anyone who says that legends don't still have body image issues is lying." She explained that when her grandmother first entered the Burlesque Hall of Fame community as a legend, "she hadn't performed in forty years. She's thinking about her body today versus what it used to look like—and I can tell you, she got a tummy tuck this year. My eighty-year-old grandmother got a tummy tuck this year. Maybe she wouldn't have done that if she wasn't performing."

Issues with body image have been present throughout my meetings with legends. Even within the context of this supposed supportive community of the Burlesque Hall of Fame, for some, performing again has rekindled body consciousness from their past. This reality bumps up against the idealized image of the past often proposed by the neo-burlesque movement, which positions historic burlesque as a place of body acceptance. By contrast, many legends interviewed in this project have often expressed surprise at the variety of body types represented in the neo-burlesque community. Penny Starr Jr. further articulated this point when describing her grandmother's reaction to performers in the independent neo-burlesque shows she produces in Los Angeles:

> This is strictly generational; she has a hard time with girls who aren't traditionally pretty or thin because she has spent her whole life being told that thin is the most important thing. [She says,] "I don't understand how these big girls do it." In her head she's like, "I don't understand why they're just not on diet pills" because that's how she was brought up; I know she was on diet pills. We had a discussion one night where…she's seen me produce [burlesque shows], and she knows how hard I work when I'm producing, for virtually nothing; she's like, ugh, what you girls get paid is terrible. And I said, yeah, but honey, if I were dancing in your day, I'd be too old, and too fat to be doing it. No one would book me and, certainly, no one would let me produce, and she's like, "That's 100% true." What we gained in our freedom, we lost in a certain financial gain.

Here Penny Starr Jr. reveals ways in which the legends community and the neo-burlesque community have come together offering a space of (though at times precarious) liberation and body acceptance. From the context of her "legend" title, there is indeed more bodily freedom present for Penny Starr Sr. For one, she no longer requires diet pills. And though this advance may seem minimal, Penny Sr. is able to make these decisions from the luxury of a safe and un-commercially driven space. Penny Starr Jr. is working to continue this alternative safe space as the neo-burlesque community continues to grow and popularize. From this perspective, she concluded by stating the following:

> I do think it's lovely that from the beginning [of the neo-burlesque movement] we've embraced our elders, so to speak. They have something to offer us, in the sense of history, in the sense of really learning from them, and it's something that we all take for granted. Yes, we honor our legends, but the newbies [to neo-burlesque] don't see it that way. I always feel like there's the first 100 or 200 neo-burlesque performers who were really making it up as we went, and every club you went to you had to explain what burlesque was—[why] were they booking your show, they had no idea.

Whereas the newbies, they didn't have to scrape that out for themselves; they kind of rolled into what we [did,] you know, we planted the flag on the moon and they're, "Yay, we're on the moon." So we have to figure out a way to get those newbies to respect the elders as well, because it's a resource they don't know they are missing. . . . [O]ur legends are not a renewing resource, so we need to embrace what we've got because that's not going to last too much longer.

Camille 2000 performs in the Titans of Tease Showcase at the Burlesque Hall of Fame, 2015

CAMILLE 2000

AT THE MOVERS, SHAKERS, AND Innovators Showcase on the Sunday night of the 2012 Burlesque Hall of Fame Weekender, Camille 2000 took to the stage. Camille wore a studded leather gimp mask and a leather waist cincher that ended at her rib cage revealing her leather pastie-clad breasts. As she rolled and rippled her body across the stage, she carried a leather whip, which she slapped and snapped at her pleasure. I was seated next to April March, who had previously explained to me that she prefers "classic" and therefore "classy" routines, and as a result she winced at each thrust of Camille's pelvis. Camille unzipped and removed her mask, and in doing so, shook out her white hair. She then ran her tongue along the base of the whip, in what appeared to be a simulation of oral sex. At this, the neo-burlesque audience cheered with great enthusiasm, support, and sisterhood.

Camille 2000 is known as the "Girl for Today, Tomorrow and the Future." The name, given to her by famed dancer Rose La Rose in Miami Beach, would prove to be incredibly accurate. In order to combat dwindling burlesque audiences in the 1970s, the forward-looking Camille fused performance art with striptease long before the neo-burlesque movement began. In fact, as a result of her avant-garde striptease style, she is often credited as the "Godmother of Neo-Burlesque." Thus, she attends the Weekender every year and maintains a very close relationship with some of the founding members of the neo-burlesque movement.

Camille was born in Alabama. In her words:

> I'm a southern belle. I was brought up in a very strict religious family. My mother's an ordained minister. . . . I was married for a brief time; that's how I got away, but that didn't work out. . . . At the time [I was] in Georgia and I saw these really pretty girls out on the Valley, they were like dancing in pretty gowns and feathers and had lots of makeup and their hair in a wig. I said, "Oh that looks like fun." They paid pretty good money so I joined the carnival.

On stage, Camille continued to strut, dragging her whip behind her. She then summoned Tigger, a founding member and star of the neo-burlesque scene, and the first ever King of Boylesque. Tigger, dressed in his customary tiger

Camille 2000 at the Burlesque Hall of Fame, 2015

costume, wore a chain leash, which Camille used to pull Tigger around the stage. The routine then came to a climax as Camille used the base of her whip to mimic intercourse with Tigger's backside—a gesture that made the man cat jump with delight.

Later, I asked Camille about her title, the "Godmother of Neo-Burlesque." She had the following to say:

Yes, I think the reason . . . they say that is because when I was in burlesque—[and] I was in Burlesque for twenty years, the first ten years of my career I did gowns and fans and soul music—I guess it would be the traditional classic burlesque. Then, in the last ten years of my career, because we were losing our customers to something called live nude dancing, because we weren't dancing we were losing our audiences. I came up with a number called the Black Widow where I killed myself. I used Alice Cooper's the Black Widow; it was really cool. I had fishnet and rhinestones, and at the end I kill myself and I drop dead. Some people were saying that that was not burlesque, that that was performance art. I'm still a little edgy even at my age now. I got spiked boots on today. . . . It's just me. Some do call me the godmother of neo-burlesque; I'll take that, and I like that.

See, I started doing that before it was popular, . . . because nobody was doing it and they were saying . . . that wasn't burlesque what I was doing; they were calling it performance art.

It is burlesque, and that was burlesque, and I am burlesque. My name was Camille 2000, the Girl for Yesterday, Today, and Tomorrow, and that's true. That was me. While everyone was still in the old school I was killing myself, I was ripping a guy on stage. I also had a Macho Man number I did to the Village People; that was really cool.

I first went to the Burlesque Hall of Fame when it was called Exotic World out in the desert at the goat farm. I went there because I had heard about it and I used to write Dixie Evans when we were friends—we just wrote. We communicated that way. So one year I just went, I went to Vegas, . . . rented a car, . . . and drove out there. I didn't participate, I just went out and checked everything out. No one knew I was there but Dixie. It was nice; it was what it was, a cute little burlesque show out in the middle of a goat farm. I mean, how glamorous can you fucking be at a goat farm?—the wind blowing shit everywhere, the sun, the desert. When I first went, I took my friend Big Fannie with me. When I got out of the car in the middle of the desert, my high heel broke off my shoe as soon as I stepped out in this fucking sand. I was like oh fuck no this ain't going to work.

The goat farm was a mess and not comfortable for a legend to be out there....It was almost suicide. The first time I went was...to see Misty. Another dancer friend Val Don who knew I went to Vegas every year, said check on Misty....After she [Misty] retired from burlesque and got really old, she went out to the goat farm. Dixie was helping her; it was like an old school for old-timers out there....When I saw this ninety-year-old lady come out with the fans and everything, I thought, you know, I should go out one more time. I'm overweight and everything but I went out one more time. It made me feel really good; I like it.

Camille then explained that she was unsure about performing as a "legend" at first, stating "I just wanted to be remembered how I was, and I didn't think it was a good idea going on stage being heavy and older." However, with the help of her adoring community of neo-burlesque "godchildren" she has embraced the role of legend, stating that she's "old" and that's "ok"!

One day the curtains opened and everything and there's just some kind [of] energy that you get from that audience; I guess it's the love that you feel. It's like, wow the drag queens, and really really good. I can't believe how that feels. What I've done all these years, someone really appreciates it.... [W]hen they contacted me many years I thought someone cares about burlesque, I was like shocked, because I had forgot all about it. I had to pull my publicity photos and stuff way out of the closet....[T]hey were way back in the closet. Now they're out in the middle of the floor. I love it. I woke up something inside me that I didn't think could be awake again and I didn't think I could still be this...it's just like being young one more time. It woke up something inside me that I thought was dead; it's been great for me. You know?

It is burlesque, and that was burlesque, and I am burlesque,... the Girl for Yesterday, Today, and Tomorrow.... That was me.

LIZA JOURDAN

WE HAD DONE A SHOOT with Liza Jourdan a year earlier, producing an image that Liza proclaimed to be her favorite picture in the past twenty years. The sixty-six-year-old now floated through the Burlesque Bazaar, grabbing fellow legend friends and recommending that they meet, speak, and shoot with us. This way, Liza became a main source of networking at the 2015 Weekender. With soft skin and a perfectly crafted blond bob, and dressed as though she were about to attend a PTA meeting, Liza is a notable exception to many in the Burlesque Hall of Fame community. A former stripper, Liza became a millionaire via casino construction; she then became a politician and head of the school board in a conservative community in California.

Perhaps most amazingly, when running for politics, Liza was never secretive about her time in burlesque; rather, she spoke of overcoming adversity through the strength of sisterhood. This idea of sisterhood touches on the concept of family, a common sentiment throughout many of the interviews in this project. When I first spoke with Liza she elaborated on this theme of family and more specifically, she talked about her experiences as a second-generation stripper. Her mother (who was only fifteen years older than Liza) stopped performing when Liza began. For some dancers, even the idea that they would dance with, or were contemporaries of, a "mother" was problematic:

Delilah worked with my mother. She was the young girl in my mother's dressing room, and then I was the young girl in her dressing room. And I can remember [after I became a dancer] when I first walked into the dressing room at the Body Shop [and saw Delilah]. I introduced myself, and of course, it can be quite catty in the dressing room, especially for the newcomer. And so I heard her little German accent and I asked her what her name was, and she said Delilah. I said, "Oh, I know you; you worked with my mother." And she gave me this icy look because, of course, my mother could have been seventy years old or something. And I told her that my mother was Caprice. And she realized that my mother was her contemporary.

In keeping with both Suzette's and Marinka's statements in interviews presented earlier, by suggesting that her mother could have been seventy rather than her actual age of thirty-five, Liza positions the term "mother" as synonymous with old. The dancer Delilah assumed the statement "you worked with my mother" to be an insult, as it situated Delilah as being older than Liza and thus potentially of lesser worth.

This having been said, some dancers who were second-generation strippers often joke that they could never compare to their mothers, who danced with the benefit of theatrical framing and much more extensive lighting. For Liza, though her mother stopped dancing when Liza began, her legacy was still present. For one, Liza's mother ran her lights for her; additionally, Liza felt she could never quite surpass the memory of her mother:

> Yes, my mother did the lighting for [me]. So, yeah, she came in and saw me. And then one time Esther Wright—who owned the club, El Rancho, in Los Angeles, which was a very, very long-lasting strip club—came in to see my show with Sally Rand, and after the show, I went down to talk to them. Of course, I was thrilled to meet Sally. And she was wonderful and she complimented me. I had done my bath act, and she said, "Oh, Lily St. Cyr would have loved that show, it's so her," which thrilled me. Then Esther Wright looked over at me and she said, "It's a beautiful show, but your mother had better legs."

Whether Liza's mother's legs were actually better or whether theatrical staging made them seem better, or whether bodies are always smoother, tighter, and younger in memory is unclear. What is clear, in both Liza's account and others throughout this project, is that the intersection between one's mother and sexuality is a space of contention.

Liza danced until she was twenty-eight years old, when she met her husband, a carpenter from Lake Tahoe. When she gave her notice to the club owner he said, "Well, I have a feeling you're the one that's not going to come back, and I hope you'll be happy." Liza smiled and explained it was the best compliment she ever had; "It was nice that I was able to say 'yes,' I didn't come back. I didn't have to." She continued:

It filled that little crack in my armor.

> I was very happy, he was happy. We have two wonderful children. My son is a professor, my daughter is a bartender-server at a really nice restaurant. They had a wonderful life growing up, everything that I didn't have. [By that I don't mean] material because my mother gave me [material things]. . . . I did not want, but [my children] had a mother and father and school, and me able to facilitate their lives, [and this] was extremely fulfilling to me because it filled that little crack in my armor through watching them absorb it. I was very, very lucky, very lucky.

Though for so many dancers, motherhood threated an end to their career, for Liza, motherhood was a beginning. That is, it was a death in a generational chain of dancers and with that death, a new life filling "that little crack in [her] armor."

Eighteen years ago Liza's husband died tragically in a plane crash. This, understandably, was a tremendous blow for Liza and her family. However, making the best of the situation, Liza took their then $20 million construction company and built it to a $30 million company in one year. She further, as mentioned earlier, served on the school board for her California school district. However, it was a trip back to Las Vegas that would be Liza's crowning achievement. That is, against her club owner's now almost forty-year-old prediction, Liza did "come back." She came back to build a large shopping center in Las Vegas for the Howard Hughes Corporation. As she explained to me, "It was kind of interesting to come back to do a job in this beautiful place. I used to be at the other end of the Strip."

Rita Alexander at the Burlesque Hall of Fame, 2014

RITA ALEXANDER

IT WAS THE VIP OPENING night party of the 2014 Burlesque Hall of Fame Weekender. In the Stardust Suite, a brightly colored party room on the top floor of the Orleans Hotel, a group of sponsors, influential neo-burlesquers, and legends sipped cocktails and buzzed with excitement in anticipation of the weekend to come. Standing on the balcony and decidedly detached from the hum of the room was Rita Alexander. Rita had blond hair and wore flowing garments, which caught the light of the Las Vegas skyline, leaving me with the overall impression that she looked like an angel.

Of all the legends that I approached for this project, I felt most nervous speaking to Rita. Whether she was a more private person or simply above it all, Rita, unlike many of the others, didn't seem to want attention, mine or anyone else's. Thus, I approached her quite carefully. I introduced myself and we began with a polite and gentle conversation. Once Rita decided our discussion had legs, she allowed it to move us inside.

We sat down on the 1960s-inspired furniture in the Stardust Suite and Rita leaned closer, putting her hands on either side of one of mine. Like other women in this project, Rita discussed the state of motherhood with me. However, unlike Suzette and Marika, who saw the term as an indicator of age, or Liza, who saw motherhood as a state of growth and fulfillment, Rita equated motherhood with loss, as she had given up a newborn daughter for adoption. It seems that this experience led her to look at the community differently from many women in this project. She had not traveled from theater to theater as other dancers had done; for the most part she remained in New Orleans' French Quarter, the place she called home.

Rita explained that when her pregnancy began to show "the French Quarter took me and [let me hide]." In this way, Rita's support system was not in the female companionship of the industry found in the backstage dressing rooms but in a stable place. In her interview, she outlined her life in the French Quarter, which in her words, "loved her" through many roles—orphan, mother, and star.

The French Quarter saw my life. [New Orleans] saw me from when I was like this little orphan, then she was pregnant. Then she was crying in the corner

Rita Alexander's
scrapbook, 2014

You absolutely
have to
experience
pain and loss
and things
like that…
because then,
when [life is]
awesome, you
truly feel
blessed.

giving up her baby. Then she was working the lights for TT Red. TT was
training me. I got the boobies. And then I was like a star. So they loved me.
They loved me. That whole town loved me because I was theirs. That's how
they felt about it. And I loved them. I was definitely theirs. I just had to be
me. . . . It was because I was theirs. They'd seen me since I was little, running
away from high school from fourteen up. And they'd seen all these tragedies
and these things happen to me and it was like they were happy for me.
It was great. I had a great time. I mean, no good life comes without pain.
You absolutely have to experience pain and loss and things like that to have
a good life because then, when it's awesome, you truly feel blessed. And it
makes you smarter.

I'd love to see my daughter. She'd be fifty or even older. I could be a
grandmother. That brings tears to my eyes. I work with a lot of people that
are adopted and they feel that their parents, or their mother—they blame it
on the mother or whatever—abandoned them. And I say no, that's not
actually true in some cases. In some cases, you were adopted because your
mother loved you enough to know that you deserved a mom and a dad and

somebody with financial means and a chance.... For years, I'd see little girls and I'd think oh, my daughter would be five or ten. Around the time she got to be about twenty-five, I figured well, it's too late now. Whatever's happened has happened. I always prayed for her...

I don't know. One day somebody will come along and they will say to me I think I can find your daughter for you. I pray on these things. I actually pray for what I want and occasionally it happens. Do you want to hear a poem?

> I keep no vows lightly made.
> I see my life as a parade.
> I make no promises.
> I have no debt.
> I pray and work for what I get.
> A strict beginning, a little sinning,
> Hope for a better day in every way.
> A steady calm through every harm,
> God my friend and luck my charm.
> I follow my life as the wind chases trees.
> Sometimes I flicker and sometimes I freeze...

You like that?

Bic Carrol on Fremont
Street, Las Vegas, 2015

BIC CARROL

ON A WARM JUNE EVENING in Las Vegas, Matilda and I walked with Bic Carrol past the doors of the Emergency Arts Center, the former medical service building that is now home to the Beat Coffee House; Feetish Spa Parlour, a fetish-themed nail salon; a travel agency; and the Burlesque Hall of Fame. We continued past the BHoF museum and up Fremont Street toward the El Cortez Hotel and Casino. The El Cortez, which opened in 1941, has been in operation longer than any other hotel in Las Vegas and, as a result, is an institution within the downtown core. Though evening had come, the late day sun still exposed some rust on the hotel's neon signage as well as a missing light bulb on the giant red, rotating high-heeled shoe that framed an advertisement for Prime Rib ($10.95) at the hotel's diner.

Bic gleefully posed in front of the vintage casino while pulling goofy faces for Matilda's camera. The seventy-seven-year-old seemed to have legs of rubber and a face made of putty, which he twisted and turned with great hilarity. "I was always a novelty act," Bic explained:

> I would put the head of a snake into the G-string, holding its body above me. And, as I lowered the snake down in weight, his natural instinct was to go to the floor, and he would pull the G-string down at the same time. So, I would always tell the police I did not touch the G-string. If you're holding a 100-pound boa constrictor...he did it, I didn't do it. I did not do it, I did not touch the G-string, so that [was] always my legal [position]... because the act ended up totally nude at the end, so that was the reason. It was like, oops, didn't mean that to happen.

Bic started his career in burlesque when he arrived in Chicago in the 1950s to build acts for new dancers in supper clubs. Subsequently he would become one of the first male performers in the country. Bic explains that "all my friends were strippers. I didn't know anybody who wasn't. And they all treated me like mothers and big sisters":

I think the legends should put all their memories in a velvet-lined box... because your reputation is like silver. If you take it out too often, it will tarnish.

*The El Cortez Hotel,
Downtown Las Vegas,
2015*

I first started in 1954, and I will tell you the story of how this all started. I was a little farm boy from Illinois who picked up a copy of a magazine called Cabaret, and there was a story in there about a Chinese man in Chicago who taught dance. . . . I always wanted to be a dancer, and it so intrigued me I got on the train and I went to see this man, and he gave me a scholarship. So I went to high school four days a week, and then one day a week [I] took a train to Chicago and took dance classes with him, but his specialty was teaching strippers, and he taught all the big ones. All of a sudden, I knew all these strippers. Well, they were like mothers to me, because I was just seventeen. One day he said to me you're going to go out to Calumet City on Sunday, and you're going to teach classes there. Well, Calumet City was three blocks long of nothing but strip joints, one right after the other. So I go out, and I'd never even seen a stripper on stage, let alone taught one. And the guy says to me "As long as they don't fall off the stage, that's all I care about."

[Promoters] ran ads in the South to be in show business, either $150.00 or $200.00 a week. And [girls] would all sign these contracts, and [the

*Bic Carrol on Fremont
Street, Las Vegas, 2015*

*promoters] would bring them up in busloads. When they got there, they
didn't know what kind of show business it was, and the first thing [the
promoters] would say [was], "Well, all right, you're going to be in the chorus
line, but the chorus line only pays $50.00 a week." They would house these
girls and they would pay for their food, et cetera. When [the girls would] get
their first check, they still owed the promoter money, and then the promoter
for the club would say, "Oh, no, no, no. We didn't say you got all these
freebies. You owe us for the bus fare and the transportation and the food
and the lodging." Then the girls realized, "Okay, we can't go anywhere.
Where are we going to go? We don't have any money," so they kind of fell
into it. They didn't know what they were getting into.*

Later in life, after retiring in Las Vegas, Bic joined the Burlesque Hall of Fame
community. As we walked away from the El Cortez and through the streets
that Sinatra loved and then left, I asked, "What do you think of it all now?
What do you think of BHoF and your present-day community?" I then paused,

Bic Carrol at the Burlesque Hall of Fame, 2014

not sure if Bic—who went from being a choreographer, to dancer, to costume designer, and indeed the only constant male legend at the BHoF Weekender—would feel like this was his community. From many perspectives, he is both an insider and an outsider. So I asked a clarifying question, "Is this your community?" "Yes and no," Bic replied.

See, I will not perform [at the event]. I am going to be seventy-eight years old this year, in June. And, you know what it is? It's interesting. I have scrapbooks coming out my butt. I know who I am and who I was. And, a lot of it I'm not proud of, but I see no necessity in embarrassing myself if I can't be that same person. If I can't show you who I was, then I don't want to get up there and show you a bad version of who I was. Does that make sense?

I think the legends should put all their memories in a velvet-lined box and bring them out just once in a while, and not often, because your reputation is like silver. If you take it out too often, it will tarnish.

Listen, I love burlesque. I love every bit about it. But to glorify it is kind of silly. And I try to explain to people it was a way to make money; it was a job. It wasn't a hobby. To you all now it's a hobby. To us, it was survival.

The lights of Fremont Street flickered behind Bic in a gaudy and spectacular display, which highlighted the uncharacteristic stillness of the seventy-seven-year-old in that moment. Bic was serious about what he was saying. He wanted to be very clear. He was. His words greatly shaped my thinking around this community. They dug into the root questions of this project and seemed to unearth the grit behind the glitter. At the same time, Bic appeared to feel pride in both elements equally—the glitter and the grit. For he was one who survived. And surviving was something to be proud of.

Bic Carrol during the Walk of Fame in the Titans of Tease Showcase at the Burlesque Hall of Fame, 2015

Miss Exotic World, Queen of Burlesque 2013, Lou Lou D'vil performs at the Burlesque Hall of Fame, 2015

Sydni Deveraux competes for the Miss Exotic World, Queen of Burlesque title in the Tournament of Tease, 2014

Neo-burlesque
performers at the
Burlesque Hall of Fame,
2015

Russell Bruner, King of Boylesque, 2012, performs at the Burlesque Hall of Fame, 2014

Attendees at the Burlesque Hall of Fame nightly after-party held at the Orleans Hotel, 2015

Legend Bic Carrol and Best Boylesque winner 2006, Tigger, share a kiss on stage, 2014

CONCLUSION
GLAMOUR OUT OF ADVERSITY

No Shame for Being That

ON THE LAST DAY OF my first Burlesque Hall of Fame Weekender, I sat and watched the Legends' Panel held in a conference room of the Orleans Hotel. Beside a breakfast table of coffee machines, cellophane-wrapped croissants, and Minute Maid orange juice, a line of about twenty legends answered questions posed by the primarily young, female neo-burlesque audience. Outfitted in various forms of 1950s-inspired clothing and many sporting the traditional rebellious body art, at a cursory glance, the keen crowd seemed to physically embody many of the ideals of the neo-burlesque community.[1] I watched as one member of the group raised her hand, stood, and took the microphone. She asked, "Did you ladies consider yourselves feminist?" The panel was silent and the convenor repeated the question. After another pause, one older legend sporting leopard print lounge wear held the microphone and sarcastically rebuffed the question: "Honey, they may have been burning their bras but we were taking them off way before that."

Neo-burlesque grew from the sociopolitical ideologies of performance artists who chose to invert the dated variety show format and reclaim and reinterpret striptease of the mid-twentieth century. On discovering Exotic World in Helendale, California, and thence the Exotic Dancers League, the neo-burlesque community embraced these women as their alternative feminist foremothers. The newcomers considered the EDL members the embodiment of their beliefs about body acceptance and identity. They saw the legends and their lifestyles as subversive in the way these women physically displayed alternative outlooks on aging and sexuality. However, for many of the legends involved in this project, particularly some of the older ones, these ideas seemed alien to their experience of burlesque. Their original performances were based on mainstream ideals of sex, consistent with the time period in which they were dancing, with their main focus being the sexual arousal of men. Further, some dancers, particularly those who had begun performing in the 1950s, felt the women's movement was a negative impact on their careers and thus rejected it. This sentiment was touched on by Marinka when she recounted a protest outside of her theater in Iowa.

> I was in a town called Cedar Rapids, Iowa, and the women's movement was protesting outside. I was not very well received by those people doing the demonstration, some of these college girls outside of the club every day, saying all what they used to say, "burn the bra, equality and this and that and the other." I will say that had a lot to do [with the end of burlesque]. Some college girls were picketing in front of the club where burlesque dancers were performing. I never wanted after that to go back to that town. I didn't like that town at all. But things like that were happening in the '60s.

This sentiment, expressed by Marinka, suggests that not only did she not include herself in the feminist movement—let alone a college-based, anti-sex-work feminist group in Iowa—but also that she saw groups involved in the movement as actually protesting against and threatening both her and her way of life. In addition, she attributes the feminist movement with the end of the burlesque theaters and the further marginalization of burlesque. As Tempest Storm noted, women's patronage is often thought to gentrify and legitimize an entertainment form. Conversely, either the lack of women or the absence of support for women can push entertainments further underground.

I entered this community of exotic dancers with a similar hope of interpreting these legends as the unsung feminists of the twentieth century, perhaps believing they might be depicted as an untold women's movement. Many, however, were uninterested in carrying such a label. Below is an excerpt from my interview with Jo "Boobs" Weldon, the first interview I conducted early in my time with the community. Weldon exposes my preconceived notions and calls for a wider lens for viewing the experiences of these dancers, one that would take into account the hardship in many of these women's lives and the choices available to them:

> The thing that you were saying about feminist icons, when I was young and I saw these women that did burlesque and I could tell that they weren't necessarily having an easy life. But they looked self-invented; they looked like—the phrase I use is that they made glamour out of adversity. Some of them have had seventeen abortions, but they were still proud of carving out their own lives. So they had these really difficult lives; . . . they started when they were teenagers and most of them didn't have ballet training or

whatever, and what I find feminist about them is that they own it [their lives] and they are not ashamed of it. They are, at least financially, empowering themselves, their families, and their communities. I don't necessarily think that stripping is feminist per se, but I think that you can be a stripper and be a feminist. I don't necessarily think that burlesque is feminist per se, or vintage burlesque was feminist per se. But any time I see women making a decision, even if they are forced to it and they are having a hard time, to take things into their own hands and [think], I'm going to control at least this much, that is empowering to see.[2]

Weldon's term "glamour out of adversity" links to a concept expressed by Burlesque Hall of Fame director Dustin Wax. He proposed that many of the new burlesque performers "filtered glamour out of burlesque" when noting that neo-burlesque performers don't say, "I'm going to go into this so I can do this shameful horrible thing, and constantly be subject to physical intimidation and manhandling. It's a personal choice that [these] people have made in sort of reviving this art form.... They [the resurgence] transformed burlesque into primarily a theatrical art, rather than a sort of strictly erotic entertainment in the back room of a seedy bar."[3]

However, Weldon's comment suggests that what some new burlesque performers often choose to filter out is arguably the very thing that might make these women feminist or empowered. The resurgence often separates twentieth-century burlesque from "stripping" and a variety of social issues associated with the sex industries (e.g., abuse, objectification) in order to enjoy burlesque as an empowering, feminist "art form"; however, Weldon states that it is the ability to survive in spite of these issues that is perhaps even more "glamorous."

Lovely Goldmine stated on the Legends' Panel in 2016, "I was a stripper, and you know, I can't understand the young people saying, 'We're not strippers, we're burlesque dancers.'... We were still strippers and there was no shame for being that."[4] This rejection of shame and adoption of pride in their ability to survive has been a recurring sentiment among the participants in this project. From this perspective, if these legends are feminist, they are not feminist because of their sexually overt—and thus liberated—performances in the way that neo-burlesquers are arguably feminists, or in the way that the college-based, anti-sex-work group in Iowa were feminists. In contrast to likely many members of these two groups, they are feminist in spite of social class, educational privilege, or background. They use the very thing many founding members of the second wave women's movement combated, the sexualized female form, to gain their independence and emancipation, which, as several of the interviewees noted, was rarely free or simple. Thus, in engaging with these mid-twentieth-century dancers, be it by way of the resurgence or by academic discourse, rather than attempting to imbue them with ideologies, feminist or otherwise, it is important first to listen to the ways they want their experiences to be framed, told, and remembered.

Framing, a subtheme that has been continuous throughout this project, was observed in relation to both the physical—the literal frame of the theater and the transition from it—and subsequent social framing around burlesque. Defining and framing the legends in the context of contemporary neoliberal discourse is enabled by the prevailing narratives surrounding burlesque and its death. I have suggested that such framings can be problematic in a variety of ways. First, this framing potentially contributes to the stigmatization of other forms of sexual entertainment and subsequently marginalizes the women who did, or currently do, work in such industries. Additionally, presenting twentieth-century burlesque as a safe space can mask the struggle some of the dancers encountered in the industry, as outlined in many of the interviews in this project. Finally, labels such as "feminist" might incorrectly categorize legends into a classification with which they simply do not identify. To label a dancer a sex worker might be offensive or demeaning to their abilities as a dancer. By contrast, labeling them as artists can at times negate some of the hardships or traumas they might have encountered in the industry. I am also aware of our own framing of the members of this community by way of this project. That is, through the use of photographic images and narrative, and by situating these photographs and personal stories and experiences in this very book, we are also potentially contributing to the framing of these individuals and their performances as art. Like the nostalgic death narrative of burlesque, in any telling we, the authors, are always at risk of omission and over-simplicity.

For many of the legends, rather than terms and forms of discourse, the issues at stake seem to come down to space—a space that supported them financially and gave them emotional and physical distance; and a space that now values them in old age. In short, a space that allows them to create glamour out of adversity.

Like Silver

After the panel, I moved down into the Orleans Hotel lobby I stepped on to the boldly patterned carpet, adjusted my eyes to the dim lighting, my nose to cigarette smoke, and my ears to the ring of the slot machines. I made my way past the seemingly constant line for the "all you can eat" buffet toward the Burlesque Bazaar.

Inside the vending space, Bic Carrol also moved through the room to say hello to friends. When I asked Bic in his interview if he felt that he was part of this community, he said both yes and no. From this perspective it might seem odd that I choose to close this project centered on this group, the Exotic Dancers League, with a quote from the (literally) odd man out. However, perhaps by way of his personal distance, Bic Carrol seems to have great clarity when speaking about the ways in which twentieth-century burlesque is "remembered" and "retold." As Bic has proposed, burlesque "wasn't a hobby...."

Titans of Tease Showcase
at the Burlesque Hall of
Fame, 2014

To us, it was survival." As a result, Bic suggests that such stories must be told carefully.

For the neo-burlesque community, there is often a vested interest in omissions as they help to support and strengthen a reading of burlesque that is essential to this new community. This telling of burlesque history that separates it from stripping contributes to the stigmatization of other forms of sexual entertainment and subsequently stigmatizes the women who did, or currently do, work in such industries. As Judith Stein frankly stated in her interview, "If they're denying the stripper roots, that means they're denying us, the legends and all of us that came before them."

However, this is not to suggest that there is not great joy that takes place at the Burlesque Hall of Fame Weekend, which includes intergenerational unity and support systems for aging legends. As Suzette Fontaine explained to me,

This new generation, they really show a lot of respect for us. I'm kind of surprised. Because we are aging, and to see this new generation, the way they admire us—I was not expecting that. When I came to the Hall of Fame,

Titans of Tease Showcase at the Burlesque Hall of Fame, 2015

I was better [sober], but I was completely out of the business. I'd been off of the stage, out of the spotlight, for almost twenty-five years. Then to go back on stage, I was kind of lost, you know what I mean? Because I'd been living in my own cocoon. Yeah, that was the first time in almost twenty-five years. I felt really strange on the stage..., but it was wonderful to be with the hall of fame people—what do you call that? A special place, you know? Yeah. It's lovely. It's lovely. After all, we earned that place,

This well-earned place that Suzette refers to is not just built by the neo-burlesque community but also by the legends themselves. This place involves camaraderie and sisterhood among dancers, qualities that at times stand in place of biological families. Indeed, through adversity came great companionship, which is reflected through their interactions at the present-day Weekender. Liza Jourdan decided to return to the BHoF reunion for simply that: the sisterhood and community that she felt is exemplified by backstage discourse:

What was wonderful was the thought of being in the dressing room together for just one more time, to be able to have that friendship and the laugh as we're putting on makeup and primping. It was more that, for me, than wanting to get on the stage again. Getting on the stage was simply a way of getting entrance into the dressing room. So, the next year, I did my first performance in thirty-seven years. To be able to come back and see the wonderful women who I admire so much, some of these amazing women that have just had amazing lives. And, everybody in the dressing room…because I did work in not a road situation or a theater situation, I worked in nightclubs, [so] the girls would be there for a while. And…working together like that, it became really supportive; when my sister-in-law was pregnant we had a baby shower. And if anybody was short of money that week, you'd chip in and we'd help. It was a very supportive place. You broke up with your boyfriend and you were depressed, everybody would rally around you. Being with women in the dressing room, and the fragrance of makeup and perfume and feathers and rhinestones, it's intoxicating. You know how women have a way of making a comfort out of some little spot, like a little dressing room.

Neo-burlesquer Coco Lectric performs a tribute number to legend Wild Cherry at the Titans of Tease Showcase, 2015

Here, Liza's dressing room exhibits the glamour out of adversity paradigm proposed by Jo Weldon. In Liza's experience, in times of need, dancers supported and cared for each other. It is this support and caring that leads the members of the Exotic Dancers League to continue to meet annually. The members, ranging in age from sixty-five years to eighty-seven, attend for different reasons—some to see friends, some to feel valued, some to perform, or, as for Liza, to relive the dressing room community experience.

In many ways, a new symbolic "dressing room" has been created in collaboration with the young neo-burlesque performers. Together they have formed a supportive place to learn from and simultaneously honor the EDL members.

Host of the Titans of Tease Showcase, World Famous *BoB*, is concerned that the majority of subsidized care facilities for seniors in the United States are backed by religious organizations that often stigmatize members of this community. As a result, through her work with both former sex workers and queer seniors, *BoB* has become an advocate for aging erotic entertainers, dedicated to "creating safe spaces for everyone to age with grace, dignity, and flair." In *BoB*'s words, "I think the closer you are to the finish line, the more people should be cheering for you—not less."

Perhaps it is the redefining and revaluing of these elderly erotica stars—in *BoB*'s advocacy for late-life sex workers, or in Tempest's image tattooed on Lou Lou D'vill's right arm, or in Toni Elling's newfound "BHoF family"—that expresses an arguably unprecedented respect between the young and old. Perhaps, at this Las Vegas hotel—amid the bootie shorts, the sequins, and the so-called smut—there is a support system; a sisterhood, and possibly something that is of great social importance.

When I asked Marinka how she could go from feeling she looked "old" in 1990 (and subsequently leaving the industry) to stripping nearly nude almost thirty years later on the BHoF stage, she explained to me that she was now performing in a very different context for a different audience: "I'm performing now but under 'legend.'...I'm performing as a legend which is a different thing. Already people know that I am one of the older ladies."[5]

This comment made by Marinka is essential to the framing of this Titans of Tease Showcase. In the context of the Legends' Showcase, these once professionals, who mostly performed out of fiscal necessity, are collectively dancing as a leisure activity. A common comment from many of the women I've interviewed in this project is that when they first left the industry, in many cases due to age, they went through a difficult period involving a sense of loss of identity. That is, their professional, physical, and oftentimes their social self (as much socializing as is involved in the industry) depends on perceptions of their sexual attractiveness. If their ability to persuade with their physical attractiveness falters, they are deemed older than one's "mother," or cracks in their perfection are exposed; this is very problematic. As Rambo Ronai states, "Appearing and acting like an old dancer breaks the tacit rule that women who sell their bodies should be selling young, attractive, and cooperative commodities."[6]

The Burlesque Hall of Fame Weekender presents a new entry point for dancers who were aged out of an industry decades earlier. It is not the same context in which they were once young and became old; rather, they are embraced for being old former professionals. Even dancers who were not necessarily famous are treated like stars. As Jo "Boobs" Weldon stated earlier in this project:

> What I think is specifically interesting about the burlesque revival and [regardless of] whether...it's feminist and empowering, is that there isn't any precedent for the way that older women are viewed in the old burlesque revival. Maybe celebrity women, but they aren't really celebrities, they weren't really famous. Tempest was really famous but that is so rare and a lot of women that are coming to the Burlesque Hall of Fame weren't famous like that; most of them weren't.[7]

However, though not all of them were famous at the time, by way of their new, young neo-burlesque admirers they are valued and treated as if they were. Thus, the neo-burlesque community's addition to the reunion has created possibilities for re-remembering history and honoring these old strippers who may not be honored outside of this community. Most of these women were not burlesque queens or celebrities. The neo-burlesque construct has allowed them, for the first time ever, to receive this celebrity status.

This having been said, some legends such as Bic have now begun to push for more criteria when it comes to allowing members into the group. From this perspective, for some of the legends this distinction needs to be made clearer.

Unfortunately, I do have a small beef. Most of the legends, or people that call themselves legends, really aren't. I have asked them repeatedly to just post one newspaper advertisement where you actually got billing, and very few will do it. Myself, Bambi Jones, April March, Tempest Storm, we all do it. We think nothing of it because we are from the theater days. And I think there should be a definition between being a burlesque performer in the theaters and being just a strip joint employee. Because it came to the point that after the theaters closed, then it all went into nightclubs. But they were real nightclubs. You weren't asked to B drink and everything else. So I have kind of a beef with their selection of what they call, quote/unquote, "legends," because some of them aren't, by any stretch of the imagination.[8]

However, Bic's comments regarding the need to keep legends membership exclusive to "stars" continues to be harder and harder to achieve. Though the Exotic Dancers League once had some very big names involved, as neo-burlesque performer Penny Starr Jr. states, "Legends are not a renewing re-source." As time moves further away from framed, theatrical burlesque where stardom was possible, the number of living stars diminishes. As Bic suggests, it would have been very difficult for dancers in their late sixties to have had the opportunity to become stars due to the changing format.

Regardless of former fame, all legends now share in common age and their late life bodies. Unlike the "old" young bodies they had when they were aged out of the industry, their present-day bodies have been greatly changed by time. Rambo Ronai's study suggests that strippers in clubs may be considered "old" as early on as their twenties. With this in mind, when the bodies of this group, which may have been considered "old" for half a century, began to exhibit physical limitations associated with age, the emotional implications could be significant. That is, if you have been "old" for most of your life, what is the impact when you actually enter later life?

Many of the legends are at the edge of their bodily limits. These limits manifest in both visual and physical ways. Some legends have mentioned the exhaustion associated with attending the reunion. They note that the pressure to wear traditional stage makeup means that some dancers need three hours to apply it, due to their limited mobility and issues with dexterity. Additionally, the simple act of attending the events can at times be overwhelming and taxing. In this way, amid the color, costumes, and excitement of the reunion, there are also periods of stillness, where one might find a dancer sitting quietly; for me, stopping to speak or simply to sit during these times were some of the most meaningful moments of this project.

However, this fatigue is not all a result of the physical demands of dancing but often came from the theatrical framing of the event. The social interactions surrounding the legends, even the pressure to appear a certain way, and, regardless of age, the pressure to "turn it on" as women such as Sally Rand and Josephine Baker before them were able to do, might all cause fatigue for these aging performers.

As a result, some of the legends chose not to continue performing in the legend showcase. As Bic Carrol stated in his interview:

> No, I will not perform....I see no necessity in embarrassing myself if I can't be that same person [that I was years ago]. If I can't show you who I was, then I don't want to get up there and show you a bad version of who I was.[9]

Here Bic states that his choice not to continue performing does not stem from a physical inability but rather from fear that his current performance will tarnish his former virtuosity. For some legends, however, there doesn't seem to be a choice in the matter. Holiday O'Hara has severe arthritis, which causes her chronic pain, and, as a result, she believes that every year will be her last year to attend the reunion. When I asked Holiday why she would endure this level of pain simply to attend the event, she explained that she was a performer; that was who she was and thus, performing was what she needed to do. This issue of "need" has also been a thread throughout this project, which often distinguishes the neo-burlesquers from the legends community. Although at the Burlesque Hall of Fame Holiday is no longer making money from her performances, the role of erotic entertainer is her identity.

For many of these dancers, their bodies were their resource and thus, the ability to sell that body underpinned a sense of worth. For some, particularly the older legends, their bodies became a source of financial and subsequently personal agency, which was not a luxury they had enjoyed before. From this perspective, it is hard to imagine that these women, even when performing at the BHoF reunion, can ever completely detach from that reality. As a result, truly liberated safe space is questionable. For even within the context of this supposed safe space, for some legends, performing again has rekindled some body consciousness from their past. As Penny Starr Jr. suggested, "Anyone who says that legends don't still have body image issues is lying....My eighty-year-old grandmother got a tummy tuck this year. Maybe she wouldn't have done that if she wasn't performing."[10]

Further, even inside the sisterhood of the metaphorical dressing room described by Liza, while I was walking through the Burlesque Bazaar it was clear to me that organizers had positioned the dancers' tables very carefully. Still, at times a good half century past their days as dancers, there remains a hierarchy as described by Bic. There are still some dancers who are cold to Kitten Natividad because she overstepped lines and boundaries and moved into pornographic film. Others found Big Fannie Annie's act crude and not "classy" and continue to hold this opinion. In this way, the dancers themselves remain as archives. They are inscribed with past conflicts and differences, not just from external mainstream perceptions of them and their work, or even violence, hardship, and complications, which were common within the industry, but also by differences from each other.

For some of the legends, their understanding of self remains in the past as a historical figure. In fact, for many of these dancers they have been a historical figure for most of their lives. I suppose in this way, though the dancers of mid-twentieth-century burlesque became "old" earlier than dancers a generation before them, in some ways, like Tai Ping, they also remain forever young through the memories and retellings of their time on stage, being admired through frames of distance. Although the staged performance is ephemeral and strip-tease as a framed, theatrical dance form no longer exists, as I looked around at these tables of women—living archives—I realized that by way of their stories, and the neo-burlesquers' stories (however glamorized), there remains a timelessness to mid-twentieth-century burlesque.

This project examined the retelling and reframing of twentieth-century-American burlesque. I sought to complicate what I felt was this overly simplistic narrative in order to show the nuanced experiences of the women involved in this community. Additionally, I observed these women's present-day reality at the reunion, the changes the group encountered over the course of the twentieth century, and the ways in which these changes are told and interpreted.

Over the past five years Matilda and I have had the good fortune to be invited into the backstage dressing rooms, homes, and lives of these aging burlesque dancers as researchers, volunteers, and members of the burlesque community. A range of experiences, from discussing financial need to helping stabilize an eighty-five-year-old as she stepped into a sequined G-string, offered a nuanced lens on both mid-twentieth century-burlesque culture and what it meant to be "aged out" of it.

Bic has suggested that these personal histories—or from the dancers' perspectives, "memories"—are delicate, sensitive, and "like silver." These women and their stories existed in a tension-filled space blurring a multitude of identities, industries, and realities. Thus, their stories need to be told in a manner that honors the multitude of the subjects' identities—star, artist, sex workers, feminist, non-feminist, "mother," or retiree. When the industry supposedly "died," they persisted in living. They were—and continue to be—strippers, "and there was no shame for being that." They are the sparkle and the struggle, the glamour out of the adversity. Ultimately, they are survivors, and that is surely something to be proud of.

Penny Starr Sr. performs in the Titans of Tease Showcase at the Burlesque Hall of Fame, 2014

ACKNOWLEDGMENTS

This project is about community, and it was made for a community, by a community. The support and encouragement of the *Burlesque Hall of Fame*, especially its director, Dustin Wax, was essential to this project's very existence. Additionally, members of *Burlesque Hall of Fame Weekender* team such as Joyce Tang, Miss Kitty Baby, Sweetpea, and David Bishop have over the past five years facilitated interview spaces and photography studios in the hotel rooms of the Orleans; by the footlights of the *Titans of Tease Showcase*; and at the sales booths of the *Burlesque Bazaar*. I would also like to thank librarian Su Kim Chung, who tirelessly helped me to navigate the vast collections of pinup images, programs, posters, and ephemera in the Special Collections of the University of Nevada–Las Vegas library.

While conducting this research I was simultaneously producing a documentary on burlesque queen Tempest Storm, with director Nimisha Mukerji and cinematographer Lindsay George. The image on the cover of this book was taken while shooting this film. This is fitting, as my thoughts on this subject are very much inspired by the strong creative minds of Nimisha, Lindsay, Tempest's manager, Harvey Robins, and, of course, Tempest herself. Further, the concepts in this project have been shaped and influenced by the guidance of my doctoral examiners and supervisors—Sherril Dodds, Bryce Lease, Kélina Gotman, and Mark Turner—and academic mentors Liz Smyth and Dena Taylor, in addition to the immensely constructive working groups led by Kirsten Pullen and Jessica Berson at the *American Society for Theatre Research*. I am also grateful for the gin-fueled support sessions in pubs across London with then fellow graduate student (and now dear friend) Hetty Blades and the Christmas time copyedit conclaves (in which my entire family was involved) at my parents' house in Toronto, Canada.

Matilda Temperley is of course the eyes of this project. As a photographer she has an uncanny ability to compassionately connect with her subjects, without preconceptions or judgment. I believe this is clear throughout this book. What is less clear are the sleepless nights, which turned into sleepless weeks (as she lugged equipment to all-night parties and then to legends' homes suburban Las Vegas early the next morning); the 3 a.m. trips to the Orleans' TGIF Fridays in a desperate search for vegetables; and our five years of shared at-discount, off-strip hotel rooms together. Through these experiences, more than this book could ever reveal, she has been my sounding board, checkpoint, and collaborative counterpart. We would also like to thank Claire and Fred Wigglesworth, who repeatedly put us up (and put up with us), and Helen Mildmay-White, who was of great assistance to Matilda.

I also want to note that our editor, Norm Hirschy, saw the potential of this project from a very early stage. Everyone needs a champion, and he has been just that. For this, Matilda and I are truly grateful. Additionally, we are indebted to the entire production team at OUP, particularly Joellyn Ausanka and Lauralee Yeary, without whom this project may have never come to completion.

And finally, to the legends, thank you for your bravery, thank you for your honesty, and thank you for sharing.

Neo-burlesque performers at the Burlesque Hall of Fame, 2015

The Cheesecake Burlesque Revue at the Burlesque Hall of Fame, 2015

Dirty Martini, Miss Exotic World 2004, at the nightly after-party held at the Orleans Hotel, 2015

NOTES

INTRODUCTION

1. David Hopkins, "Why Dallas Burlesque Owes a Debt to Tammi True," *D Magazine*, February 23, 2011.
2. "Court Calls Them Employees: Says Strip-Tease 'Gift to Theater,'" *Los Angeles Herald-Examiner*, June 15, 1964.
3. In her thesis, "Filthy Publicity: Jennie Lee and the Exotic Dancers League," submitted to California State Polytechnic University in 2011, Kristine Protacio notes that a variety of names have been utilized by the group—"League of Exotic Dancers," "Exotic Dancers League," and "Exotique Dancers League"—representing the different titles by which the group has been registered. However, for the purposes of this project, I will use the second of the three names, "Exotic Dancers League," as it is the title that historically was used most often. Also, Exotic Dancers League is the name used presently by the Burlesque Hall of Fame. For more on the origins of the Exotic Dancers League, see Ben Urish, "Narrative Striptease in the Night Club Era," *Journal of American Culture* 27.2 (2004): 160. Also, for an outline on the Burlesque Hall of Fame's origins, see Michelle Baldwin, *Burlesque and the New Bump-N-Grind* (Golden, CO: Speck Press, 2004).
4. "L.A. Strippers Protest Their Low Take-Off Pay: Burlesque Queens, in Organization Meeting, Threaten 'Cover Up' Strike over Grievances," *Los Angeles Times*, June 19, 1955.
5. Kristine Protacio, "Filthy Publicity: Jennie Lee and the Exotic Dancers League," diss., California State Polytechnic University, 2011.
6. "L.A. Strippers Protest Their Low Take-Off Pay."
7. Michelle Baldwin, *Burlesque and the New Bump-N-Grind* (Golden, CO: Speck Press, 2004), 49.
8. Numerous authors have contributed to the discussions surrounding empowerment versus exploitation for exotic dancers. For further information, see Danielle Egan, *Dancing for Dollars and Praying for Love: The Relationships between Exotic Dancers and Their Regulars* (New York: Palgrave Macmillan, 2006); Katherine Frank, *G-Strings and Sympathy: Strip Club Regulars and Male Desire* (Durham, NC: Duke University Press, 2002); Judith Lynne Hanna, "The Naked Truth," *Exotic Dancer Bulletin* 4.138 (1999); Judith Lynne Hanna, "Exotic Dance Adult Entertainment: Ethnography Challenges False Mythology," *City and Society* 15 (2003); Shelly Manaster, "Treading Water: An Autoethnographic Account(ing) of the Lap Dance," in *Flesh for Fantasy: Producing and Consuming Exotic Dance*, ed. Danielle Egan, Katherine Frank, and Lisa Merri Johnson (New York: Thunder's Mouth Press, 2006); Holly Bell and Lacey Slone, "Exploiter or Exploited: Topless Dancers Reflect on Their Experiences," *Journal of Women and Social Work* 13 (1998); Bernadette Barton, "Dancing on the Mobius Strip: Challenging the Sex War Paradigm," *Gender and Society* 16.5 (2002); Bernadette Barton,

Stripped: Inside the Lives of Exotic Dancers (New York: New York University Press 2006); Bernadette Barton and Constance L. Hardesty, "Spirituality and Stripping: Exotic Dancers Narrate the Body Ekstais," *Symbolic Interaction* 33.2 (2010); Jennifer K. Wesley, "Exotic Dancing and the Negotiation of Identity: The Multiple Uses of Body Technologies," *Journal of Contemporary Ethnography* 32.6 (2000); Jennifer K. Wesley, "Where Am I Going to Stop? Exotic Dancers, Fluid Boundaries, and Effects on Identity," *Deviant Behavior* 24 (2003).

9. Robert Allen, *Horrible Prettiness: Burlesque and American Culture* (Chapel Hill: University of North Carolina Press, 1991).

10. Bernard Sobel, *A Pictorial History of Burlesque* (New York: Bonanza Books, 1956).

11. *The Anatomy of Burlesque*, dir. Linda Lee Tracey, White Pine Productions, 2003.

12. Rachel Shteir, *Striptease: The Untold History of the Girly Show* (New York: Oxford University Press, 2004).

13. For more information and commentary on the burlesque resurgence, see Katharina Bosse, *New Burlesque* (New York: Distributed Art Publishers, 2004); Sherril Dodds, *Dancing on the Canon: Embodiments of Value in Popular Dance* (London: Palgrave, 2011); Debra Ferreday, "'Showing the Girl': The New Burlesque," *Feminist Theory* 9.47 (2008); Lynn Sally, "'It Is the Ugly That Is So Beautiful': Performing the Monster/Beauty Continuum in American Neoburlesque," *Journal of American Drama and Theater* 21.3 (2009); Claire Nally, "Grrrly Hurly Burly: Neo-Burlesque and the Performance of Gender," *Textual Practice* 23.4 (2009); Jacki Willson, *The Happy Stripper: Pleasures and Politics of the New Burlesque* (London: I. B. Tauris, 2008).

14. Lynn Sally, interview, July 22, 2012.

15. Roland Barthes, *Mythologies*, trans. Annette Lavers (Paris: Hill and Wang, 1957).

PART 1: AGING, STAGING, SPARKLE, AND STRUGGLE

1. From World Famous *BoB*'s opening statements while hosting the Titans of Tease Legends of Burlesque Showcase. Performance at the Burlesque Hall of Fame in 2013.

2. World Famous *BoB*'s opening statements.

3. Dustin Wax, talk given at the Burlesque Hall of Fame, Burlesque Hall of Fame Annual Weekender, Orleans Hotel, Las Vegas, NV, June 2013.

4. Dustin Wax, interview, September 9, 2012.

5. Russell Shelnut interview, December 26, 2014.

6. See the documentary film, *Exotic World and the Burlesque Revival*, dir. Red Tremmel, 2012.

7. Titans of Tease Legends of Burlesque Showcase, performed by World Famous *BoB*, Burlesque Hall of Fame, 2013.

8. Titans of Tease Legends of Burlesque Showcase, performed by World Famous *BoB*.

9. Titans of Tease Legends of Burlesque Showcase, performed by World Famous *BoB*.

10. Shelnut, interview, December 26, 2014.

11. Shelnut, interview, December 26, 2014.

12. Big Fannie Annie, interview, July 17, 2014.

13. Wax, talk given at the Burlesque Hall of Fame, Burlesque Hall of Fame Annual Weekender, Orleans Hotel, Las Vegas, NV, June 2013.

14. Wax, talk given at the Burlesque Hall of Fame, June 2013.

15. Dustin Wax, interview, July 1, 2013.

16. Jacques Derrida, *Mal D'archive* (Paris: Editions Galilee, 1995).

17. Peggy Phelan, "The Ontology of Performance. Representation without Reproduction," *Unmarked: The Politics of Performance* (New York: Routledge, 1993).

18. Rebecca Schneider, "Performance Remains," *Performance Research* 6.2 (2001).

19. Dianna Taylor, *The Archive and the Repertoire: Performing Cultural Memory in the Americas* (Durham, NC: Duke University Press, 2003), 33.

20. Jo Weldon, interview, June 23, 2013.

21. Lynn Sally, interview, July 22, 2012.

22. Baldwin, Michelle. *Burlesque and the New Bump-N-Grind* (Golden, CO: Speck Press, 2004).

23. Liepe-Levinson, Katherine. *Strip Show: Performances of Gender and Desire* (London: Routledge, 2002).

24. Liepe-Levinson, *Strip Show*.

25. The Young Vic, "Beauty and the Beast—Matt and Julie's Love Story," performed by Julie Atluz Muz and Matt Fraser, online video clip Youtube, October 12, 2013.

26. Sally, interview, July 22, 2012.

27. The Slipper Room has been the unofficial home of the New York neo-burlesque scene since opening in 1999. It was the first venue to be built specifically to showcase neo-burlesque.

28. Sherril Dodds, "Embodied Transformations in Neo-Burlesque Striptease," *Dance Research Journal* 45.3 (2013): 78.

29. Dodds, "Embodied Transformations."

30. For more on the neo-burlesque community's relationship to feminist discourse and issues surrounding the presentation of sexuality and gender, see Sharon Lamb, "Feminist Ideals for a Healthy Female Adolescent Sexuality: A Critique," *Sex Roles* 62 (2010); Claire Nally,"Grrrly Hurly Burly: Neo-Burlesque and The Performance of Gender," *Textual Practice* 23.4 (2009); Sherril Dodds, *Dancing on the Canon: Embodiments of Value in Popular Dance* (London: Palgrave, 2011); Dodds, "Embodied Transformations."

31. Shteir, Rachel, *Striptease: The Untold History of the Girly Show* (New York: Oxford University Press, 2004).

32. In 1985, a conference entitled Challenging Our Images: The Politics of Pornography and Prostitution brought together sex-positive and anti-porn feminists, and prompted the book of essays *Good Girls/Bad Girls: Feminists and Sex Trade Workers Face to Face* (1987). In the introduction, Laurie Bell states the following:

> It is the definition of feminism that must change in order to include both good girls and bad girls, not they who must conform to a good girl image so as to be considered feminist. Sex trade workers claim, in effect, to be feminists in exile; excluded from a rightful place in the feminist movement, they demand to be recognized as members of the women's community. (p. 17)

For further work on sex-positive feminism, see Annie Sprinkle, *Annie Sprinkle: Post Porn Modernism* (Amsterdam: Torch Books, 1991); Jill Nagle, ed., *Whores and Other Feminists* (New York: Routledge, 1997); Nadine Strossen, *Defending Pornography: Free Speech, Sex, and the Fight for Women's Rights* (London: Abacus, 1995); Tawnya Dudash, "Peepshow Feminism," in *Whores and Other Feminists*, ed. Jill Nagle (New York: Routledge, 1997); Merri Lisa Johnson, *Jane Sexes It Up: True Confessions of Feminist Desire* (New York: Four Walls Eight Windows, 2002); Annie Oakley, *Working Sex: Sex Workers Write about a Changing Industry* (Emeryville, CA: Seal Press, 2007); Jennifer Baumgardner and Amy Richards, "Feminism and Femininity: Or How We Learned to Stop Worrying and Love the Thong," in *All About the Girl: Culture Power and Identity*, ed. A. Harris (New York: Routledge, 2004); Carol Queen and Lynn Comella, "The Necessary Revolution: Sex-Positive Feminism in the Post-Barnard Era," *Communication Review* 11 (2008).

33. Danielle Egan, *Dancing for Dollars and Praying for Love: The Relationships between Exotic Dancers and Their Regulars* (New York: Palgrave Macmillan, 2006); Katherine Frank, *G-Strings and Sympathy: Strip Club Regulars and Male Desire* (Durham, NC: Duke University Press, 2002); Judith Lynne Hanna, "Undressing the First Amendment and Corsetting the Striptease Dancer," *Drama Review* 42.2 (1998): 38–69; Judith Lynne Hanna, "The Naked Truth," *Exotic Dancer Bulletin* 4.138 (1999); Judith Lynne Hanna, "Exotic Dance Adult Entertainment: Ethnography Challenges False Mythology," *City and Society* 15 (2003): 165–193; Shelly Manaster, "Treading Water: An Autoethnographic Account(ing) of the Lap Dance," in *Flesh for Fantasy: Producing and Consuming Exotic Dance*, ed. Danielle Egan, Katherine Frank, and Lisa Merri Johnson (New York: Thunder's Mouth Press, 2006), 3–18; Holly Bell and Lacey Sloan, "Exploiter or Exploited: Topless Dancers Reflect on Their Experiences," *Journal of Women and Social Work* 13 (1998): 352–369; Bernadette Barton, "Dancing on the Möbius Strip: Challenging the Sex War Paradigm," *Gender and Society* 16.5 (2002): 585–602; Bernadette Barton, *Stripped: Inside the Lives of Exotic Dancers* (New York: New York University Press, 2006); Bernadette Barton and Constance L. Hardesty, "Spirituality and Stripping: Exotic Dancers Narrate the Body Ekstasis," *Symbolic Interaction* 33.2 (2010): 280–296; Jennifer K. Wesley, "Exotic Dancing and the Negotiation of Identity: The Multiple Uses of Body Technologies," *Journal of Contemporary Ethnography* 32.6 (2000):

643–669; Jennifer K. Wesley, "Where Am I Going to Stop? Exotic Dancers, Fluid Boundaries, and Effects on Identity," *Deviant Behavior* 24 (2003): 483–503.

34. Marinka, interview, June 3, 2013.

35. Bernadette Barton and Constance L. Hardesty, "Spirituality and Stripping: Exotic Dancers Narrate the Body Ekstasis," *Symbolic Interaction* 33.2 (2010): 280–296.

36. Holiday O'Hara, interview, July 22, 2014.

37. Dodds, "Embodied Transformations."

38. Dodds, "Embodied Transformations."

39. Isis Star, interview, December 19, 2015.

40. Gabriella Maze, interview, October 10, 2014.

41. Judith Stein, interview, December 13, 2015.

42. Beverley Skeggs, *Class, Self, Culture* (London: Routledge, 2004).

43. Toni Bentley, *Sisters of Salome* (New Haven, CT: Yale University Press, 2002).

44. Andrea Stuart, *Showgirls* (London: Random House, 1996); *The Anatomy of Burlesque*, dir. Tracey; Bentley, *Sisters of Salome*.

45. Bentley, *Sisters of Salome*.

46. Anthea Kraut, *Choreographing Copyright: Race, Gender, and Intellectual Property Rights in American Dance* (New York: Oxford University Press, 2016).

47. W. E. B. Du Bois, *Black Reconstruction in America 1860–1880* (New York: Harcourt, Brace, 1935).

48. See Peggy MacIntosh, "White Privilege: Unpacking the Invisible Knapsack," *Independent School* 49.2 (1990); Ruth Frankenberg, *White Women, Race Matters: The Social Construction of Whiteness* (Minneapolis: University of Minnesota Press, 1993); Richard Dyer, *White* (London: Routledge, 1997).

49. Eva Cherniavsky, *Incorporations: Race, Nation, and the Body Politics of Capital* (Minneapolis: University of Minnesota Press, 2006).

50. Susan Manning, *Modern Dance, Negro Dance: Race in Motion* (Minneapolis: University of Minnesota Press, 2004).

51. Manning, *Modern Dance*, xv.

52. Joann Kealiinohomoku, "An Anthropologist Looks at Ballet as a Form of Ethnic Dance," in *Moving History/Dancing Cultures: A Dance Reader*, ed. Ann Cooper Albright and Ann Dils (Middletown, CT: Wesleyan University Press, 2001), 33–43.

53. Toni Elling, interview, June 13, 2014.

54. Siobhan Brooks, "Hypersexualization and the Dark Body: Race and Inequality among Black and Latina Women in the Exotic Dance Industry," *Sexuality Research and Social Policy* 7 (2010).

55. For more information on this exhibition see www.burlesquehall.com/category/exhibitions/pastexhibitions.

56. Margret L. Anderson, "Whitewashing Race: A Critical Perspective on Whiteness," in *WhiteOut: The Continuing Significance of Racism*, ed. Ashley W. Doane and Eduardo Bonilla-Silva (New York: Routledge, 2003), 22.

57. See Merryn Gott, Sharron Hinchliff, and Elisabeth Galena, "General Practitioner Attitudes to Discussing Sexual Health Issues with Older People," *Social Science & Medicine* 58 (2004); Ramzi Hajjar and Hosam Kamel, "Sexuality in the Nursing Home, Part 1: Attitudes and Barriers to Sexual Expression," *Journal of the American Medical Directors Association* (March 2003); K. Saretsky, "The Right to Be Human, How One Facility Cares," *Provider* 12 (1987); G. Szasz, "Sexual Incidents in an Extended Care Unit for Aged Men," *Journal of American Geriatric Society* 31 (1983); M. Wasow and M. Lobe, "Sexuality in Nursing Homes," *Journal of American Geriatric Society* 27 (1979).

58. Joanna Frueh, "The Fear of Flesh That Moves," *High Performance* 14.3 (1991).

59. Kathleen Woodward, "Performing Age, Performing Gender," *National Women's Studies Association Journal* 18.1 (2006).

60. Sebastiano Tempanaro, *On Materialism*, trans. Lawrence Garner (London: Verso, 1970).

61. Carol Rambo Ronai and Rebecca Cross, "Dancing with Identity: Narrative Resistance Strategies of Male and Female Strippers," *Deviant Behavior* 19 (1998): 99–199.

62. Suzette Fontaine, interview, December 19, 2015.

63. Nicholas Ridout, *Passionate Amateurs: Theater, Communism, and Love* (Ann Arbor: University of Michigan Press, 2013), 4.

PART 1: BURLESQUE—DEAD, ALIVE, AND IMAGINED

1. Robert Allen, *Horrible Prettiness: Burlesque and American Culture* (Chapel Hill: University of North Carolina Press, 1991); Kristen Pullen, *Actresses and Whores: On Stage and in Society* (Cambridge: Cambridge University Press, 2005).
2. *The Anatomy of Burlesque*, dir. Linda Lee Tracey, documentary film.
3. Allen, *Horrible Prettiness.*
4. Virginia Keft-Kennedy, "How Does She Do that? Belly Dancing and the Horror of a Flexible Woman," *Women's Studies* 34 (2005): 279–300.
5. *The Anatomy of Burlesque*, dir. Tracey.
6. Allen, *Horrible Prettiness.*
7. Allen, *Horrible Prettiness*; Rachel Shteir, *Striptease: The Untold History of the Girly Show* (New York: Oxford University Press, 2004); Jacki Willson, *The Happy Stripper: Pleasures and Politics of the New Burlesque* (London: I. B. Tauris, 2008); Irving Zeidman, *The American Burlesque Show* (New York: Hawthorn Books, 1967).
8. Allen, *Horrible Prettiness.*
9. Allen, *Horrible Prettiness.*
10. Michelle Baldwin, *Burlesque and the New Bump-N-Grind* (Golden, CO: Speck Press, 2004); Sherril Dodds, *Dancing on the Canon: Embodiments of Value in Popular Dance* (London: Palgrave, 2011); Shteir, *Striptease*; Willson, *The Happy Stripper.*
11. Kristen Pullen, "Dancing Sex, Revolution, and History: The Case of Carol Doda" (Nashville, TN: American Society of Theater Research, November 2012).
12. Pullen, "Dancing Sex, Revolution, and History."
13. David Monaghan, filmmaker and striptease historian, interview, June 26, 2013.
14. Monaghan, interview, June 26, 2013.
15. For an overview of this period in New York and Giuliani's impact on the exotic dance industry, see Kathryn Liepe-Levinson, *Strip Show: Performances of Gender and Desire* (London: Routledge, 2002).
16. Willson, *The Happy Stripper.*
17. Allen, *Horrible Prettiness*; Kristen Pullen, *Actresses and Whores: On Stage and in Society* (Cambridge: Cambridge University Press, 2005); Willson, *The Happy Stripper.*
18. Allen, *Horrible Prettiness*; Willson, *The Happy Stripper.* Irving Zeidman, *The American Burlesque Show* (New York: Hawthorn Books, 1967).
19. Katharina Bosse, *New Burlesque* (New York: Distributed Art Publishers, 2004); Debra Ferreday, "Showing the Girl: The New Burlesque," *Feminist Theory* 9.47 (2008) 47–65; Shteir, *Striptease*; Willson, *The Happy Stripper.*
20. Danielle Egan, *Dancing for Dollars and Praying for Love:The Relationships between Exotic Dancers and Their Regulars* (New York: Palgrave Macmillan, 2006); Katherine Frank, *G-Strings and Sympathy: Strip Club Regulars and Male Desire* (Durham, NC: Duke University Press, 2002); Shelly Manaster, "Treading Water: An Autoethnographic Account(ing) of the Lap Dance," in *Flesh for Fantasy: Producing and Consuming Exotic Dance*, ed. Danielle Egan, Katherine Frank and Lisa Merri Johnson (New York: Thunder's Mouth Press, 2006); Holly Bell and Lacey Slone, "Exploiter or Exploited: Topless Dancers Reflect on Their Experiences," *Journal of Women and Social Work* 13 (1998); Bernadette Barton, "Dancing on the Mobius Strip: Challenging the Sex War Paradigm," *Gender and Society* 16.5 (2002); Bernadette Barton and Constance L. Hardesty, "Spirituality and Stripping: Exotic Dancers Narrate the Body Ekstais," *Symbolic Interaction*, 33.2 (2010); Jennifer K. Wesley, "Where Am I Going to Stop? Exotic Dancers, Fluid Boundaries, and Effects on Identity," *Deviant Behavior* 24 (2003).
21. Sheila Jeffreys, "Keeping Women Down and Out: The Strip Club Boom and the Reinforcement of Male Dominance," *Journal of Women in Culture and Society* 34.1 (2008).
22. Hanna, "First Amendment," 57. This text, much like the majority of Hanna's work on striptease, was groundbreaking for this field in the 1990s.
23. Dahlia Schweitzer, "Striptease: The Art of Spectacle and Transgression," *Journal of Popular Culture* 34.1 (2001): 72.
24. Allen, *Horrible Prettiness*; Shteir, *Striptease*; Becki L. Ross, *Burlesque West: Showgirls, Sex and Sin in Postwar Vancouver* (Toronto: University of Toronto Press, 2009); Neil Miller, *Banned*

in Boston: The Watch and Ward Society's Crusade against Books, Burlesque, and Social Evil (Boston: Beacon Press, 2010); Anne Cheng, "Skin Deep: Josephine Baker and the Colonial Fetish," *Camera Obscura* 23.3 (2008); Toni Bentley, *Sisters of Salome* (New Haven, CT: Yale University Press, 2002); Pullen, *Actresses and Whores*; Kristen Pullen, "Dancing Sex"; Keft-Kennedy, "How Does She Do That?"; Noralee Frankel, *Stripping Gypsy: The Life of Gypsy Rose Lee* (New York: Oxford University Press, 2009); Karen Abbott, *American Rose: A Nation Laid Bare: The Life and Times of Gypsy Rose Lee* (New York: Random House, 2010).

25. Bernard Sobel, *A Pictorial History of Burlesque* (New York: Bonanza Books, 1956).
26. Shteir, *Striptease*, 323.
27. Shteir, *Striptease*, 323.
28. Andrea Stuart, *Showgirls* (London: Random House, 1996).
29. Zeidman, *The American Burlesque Show*, 241–242.
30. Allen, *Horrible Prettiness*, 257.
31. Allen, *Horrible Prettiness*, 257.
32. Ben Urish, "Narrative Striptease in the Night Club Era," *Journal of American Culture* 27.2 (2004): 159.
33. Foley, *Undressed for Success*, 53.
34. Foley, *Undressed for Success*, 53.
35. Foley, *Undressed for Success*, 53.
36. Caitlin Moran, *How to Be a Woman* (London: Ebury Press, 2011).
37. Moran, *How to Be a Woman*, 175–176.
38. Claire Nally, "Grrrly Hurly Burly: Neo-Burlesque and the Performance of Gender," *Textual Practice* 23.4 (2009): 621–643; Ferreday, *Showing the Girl*; Willson, *The Happy Stripper*.
39. Ferreday, *Showing the Girl*.
40. David Owen, "Neo-Burlesque and the Resurgence of Roller Derby: Empowerment, Play, and Community," *Canadian Theater Review* 158 (Spring 2014): 34. This article is part of a special edition of the *Canadian Theater Review* published on burlesque in the spring of 2014.
41. Joanna Mansbridge, "In Search of a Different History: The Remains of Burlesque in Montreal," *Canadian Theater Review* 158 (Spring 2014): 7.
42. Jo Weldon, interview, June 23, 2013.
43. Sherril Dodds, "Embodied Transformations in Neo-Burlesque Striptease," *Dance Research Journal* 45.3 (2013): 78.
44. Baldwin, *Burlesque and the New Bump-N-Grind*, 57.
45. Sherril Dodds, "Embodied Transformations in Neo-Burlesque Striptease," *Dance Research Journal* 45.3 (2013): 75–90.
46. Mansbridge, "In Search of a Different History," 7.
47. Penny Starr Jr., interview, June 12, 2014.
48. Tiffany Carter, interview, October 4, 2012.
49. Judith Stein, interview, December 13, 2015.
50. Lehrer, Kristen. "Dita Von Teese on Burlesque vs. Stripping," *Fox News Magazine*, May 17, 2013.
51. Lehrer, "Dita Von Teese."
52. Lehrer, "Dita Von Teese."
53. Marinka, interview, April 14, 2014.
54. Carol Rambo Ronai and Rebecca Cross, "Dancing with Identity: Narrative Resistance Strategies of Male and Female Strippers," *Deviant Behavior* 19 (1998).
55. Famed burlesque dancer from the 1930s discussed in Marinka's interview, April 14, 2014.
56. Bic Carrol, interview, March 23, 2015.
57. April March, interview, September 19, 2012.
58. Carter, interview, October 4, 2012.
59. Alexandra The Great 48, interview, June 22, 2012.
60. Marinka, interview, June 3, 2013.
61. March, interview, September 19, 2012.
62. Carrol, interview, March 23, 2015.
63. For further expansion on this theory, see Jorn Russen, "The Logic of Historicization: Metahistorical Reflections on the Debate between Friedlander and Broszat," *History and Memory* 9.1/2 (1997).

64. Wax, interview, September 9, 2012.
65. Carrol Dyhouse, *Glamour: Women, History, Feminism* (London; Zed Books, 2011) 2.
66. Dyhouse, *Glamour*.
67. Dyhouse, *Glamour*, 5.
68. Nigel Thrift, "Understanding the Material Practice of Glamour," *Affect Theory Reader*, ed. Melissa Gregg and Gregory J. Seigworth (Durham, NC: Duke University Press, 2010), 297.
69. Thrift, "Understanding the Material Practice of Glamour," 298–299.
70. Weldon, interview, June 23, 2013.
71. Russen, "The Logic of Historicization," 1.
72. Thrift, "Understanding the Material Practice of Glamour."
73. Mansbridge, "In Search of a Different History."
74. Titans of Tease Legends of Burlesque Showcase, performer World Famous *BoB*.
75. Dusty Summers, "Behind the Burly-Q Review," *Facebook*, 2013.
76. Sobel, *A Pictorial History of Burlesque*; Zeidman, *The American Burlesque Show.*
77. Barney Gerard, "Burlesque—Its Rise and Demise," *Variety*, January 4, 1956.
78. Gerard, "Burlesque."
79. Marinka, interview, June 3, 2013.
80. Bambi Jones, interview, March 28, 2015.
81. Sime Silverman, "The Killer of Burlesque," *Variety* 1931.
82. Pat Burnette, "The Good Old Daze," *Cavalcade of Burlesque*, September 1952.
83. March, interview, September 19, 2012.
84. Tiffany Carter, interview, January 25, 2013.
85. O'Hara, interview, July 22, 2014.
86. O'Hara, interview, July 22, 2014.
87. Titans of Tease Legends of Burlesque Showcase, performer Imogen Kelly, Burlesque Hall of Fame, 2013.
88. Russen, "The Logic of Historicization."
89. Titans of Tease Legends of Burlesque Showcase, performer Imogen Kelly.

PART 2

TEMPEST STORM

1. Tempest Storm, interview, January 28, 2013.
2. Bill Boyd, *Tempest Storm: The Lady Is a Vamp* (Atlanta: Peachtree, 1987). This is the only biography of Tempest Storm. Although Tempest says she participated in the writing of the book, she indicates that she is unhappy with the outcome and is currently writing an autobiography biography to rectify this. Other authors who have written about Tempest include Claire Leavey, "Tempest Storm: Burlesque Queen," *Libertine*, August 2013; Rachel Shteir, *Striptease: The Untold History of the Girly Show* (New York: Oxford University Press, 2004).
3. Boyd, *Tempest Storm.*
4. Author's conversation with Harvey Robbins.
5. Roland Barthes, *Mythologies*, trans. Annette Lavers (Paris: Hill and Wang, 1957), 84.
6. Joseph Roach, *It* (Ann Arbor: University of Michigan Press, 2007), 1–4.
7. Elizabeth Rieur, interview, October 24, 2013. Elizabeth Rieur has specifically observed female patronage in burlesque theaters. Rieur positions the middle-class white woman as society's moral compass, protecting the "middle class home from the assaults of the outside world, and…mold[ing] children's moral virtues." As Rieur states, "the middle-class woman is the definition of mainstream in this period."
8. Robert Allen, *Horrible Prettiness: Burlesque and American Culture* (Chapel Hill: University of North Carolina Press, 1991).
9. Allen, *Horrible Prettiness.*
10. Pat Burnette, "The Good Old Daze," *Cavalcade of Burlesque* 1.3 (1952); Bernard Sobel, *A Pictorial History of Burlesque* (New York: Bonanza Books, 1956).
11. Gerard, Barney, "Burlesque: Its Rise and Demise," *Variety*, January 4, 1956.

12. Barney, "Burlesque."
13. Elizabeth Rieur, "The Other Ladies of Burlesque: Female Attendance at Burlesque Shows, 1920–1945," diss., Simmons College, 2013.
14. Allen, *Horrible Prettiness*.
15. Tempest has mentioned this date to me as her tentative date of retirement while also mentioning that, by way of fan events and appearances, in many ways she never actually retired.
16. Roland Barthes, *Mythologies*, trans. Annette Lavers (Paris: Hill and Wang, 1957).
17. Karen Abbott, *American Rose: A Nation Laid Bare: The Life and Times of Gypsy Rose Lee* (New York: Random House, 2010), 304.
18. Boyd, *Tempest Storm*.
19. Storm, interview, January 28, 2013.
20. Author's conversation with Harvey Robbins.

IVY TAM

1. Grant Avenue Follies, "Our Beautiful Ivy," Facebook, 2016.

KITTEN NATIVIDAD

1. Kenneth Turner and Stephan F. Zito, *Sinema: American Pornographic Films and the People Who Make Them* (New York: Praeger, 1974). For some of the foundational work done in the field of pornographic studies, see Linda Williams, *Hard Core: Power, Pleasure, and the "Frenzy of the Visible"* (Berkeley: University of California Press, 1989).
2. Eric Schaefer, "Gauging a Revolution: 16mm Film and the Rise of the Pornographic Feature," in *Porn Studies*, ed. Linda Williams (Durham, NC: Duke University Press, 2003).
3. Schaefer," Gauging a Revolution," 371.
4. Debbie Nathan, *Pornography: A Groundwork Guide* (Toronto: Groundwood Books House of Anansi Press, 2007).
5. Nathan, *Pornography*.
6. Roland Barthes, *Mythologies*, trans. Annette Lavers (Paris: Hill and Wang, 1957).
7. Kristen Pullen, "Dancing Sex, Revolution, and History: The Case of Carol Doda" (Nashville, TN: American Society of Theater Research, November 2012).
8. These "laws" acted more as social guidelines, as bottomless laws in this period (and currently) vacillate jurisdictionally.
9. Barthes, *Mythologies*.
10. Erving Goffman, *Frame Analysis: An Essay on the Organization of Experience* (Boston: Northeastern University Press, 1974), 502.
11. Speaking of unprotected sex in pornographic film, Tim Dean suggests that a feature of bareback porn is "the tactic of persuading viewers that what they are seeing is not performance but the real thing." Dean utilizes the terms "raw and uncensored," which may be interpreted as unprotected. Further, this rawness operates as "part of porn's realism and must be perpetually recreated in order for the action to not register as overly stylized" or theatrical. In this respect, the raw threat of really contracting HIV becomes an indicator of the porn's realness. See Tim Dean, *Unlimited Intimacy: Reflections on the Subculture of Barebacking* (Chicago: University of Chicago Press, 2009), 2.

SUZETTE FONTAINE

1. *Emotional labor* refers to an individual's efforts to regulate the emotions of self and others in order to achieve workplace goals and display rules. For further reading of the consequences of emotional labor, see K. Pugliesi, "The Consequences of Emotional Labor: Effects on Work Stress, Job Satisfaction, and Well-Being," *Motivation and Emotion* 23.2 (1999): 125–154.
2. For more on methods of self-preservation, see Bernadette Barton, "Managing the Toll of the Sex Industry: Boundary Setting among Exotic Dancers," *Journal of Contemporary Ethnography* 36.5 (2007); Bernadette Barton, *Stripped: Inside the Lives of Exotic Dancers* (New York: New

York University Press, 2006); Bernadette Barton and Constance L. Hardesty, "Spirituality and Stripping: Exotic Dancers Narrate the Body Ekstasis," *Symbolic Interaction* 33.2 (2010): 280–296; Jennifer K. Wesley, "Exotic Dancing and the Negotiation of Identity: The Multiple Uses of Body Technologies," *Journal of Contemporary Ethnography* 32.6 (2000): 643–669; Jennifer K. Wesley, "Where Am I Going to Stop? Exotic Dancers, Fluid Boundaries, and Effects on Identity," *Deviant Behavior* 24 (2003): 483–503.

MARINKA

1. Susan Sontag, "The Double Standard of Aging," in *The Other within Us: Feminist Explorations of Women Aging*, ed. Marilyn Pearsall (Boulder, CO: Westview Press, 1972).
2. Justin D. Edwards and Rune Graulund, *Grotesque: The New Critical Idiom* (London: Routledge, 2013), 144.
3. David Owen, "Neo-Burlesque and the Resurgence of Roller Derby: Empowerment, Play, and Community," *Canadian Theatre Review* 158 (Spring 2014): 34–35.
4. Jessica Berson, interview, May 22, 2014.
5. Berson, interview.
6. Berson, interview.
7. Rachel Shteir, *Striptease: The Untold History of the Girly Show* (New York: Oxford University Press, 2004); Carol Rambo Ronai, "Separating Aging from Old Age: The Aging Table Dancer," *Journal of Aging Studies* 6.4 (1992).
8. Roland Barthes has discribed the layers at work in 1950s burlesque dancing in his seminal work: Roland Barthes, *Mythologies*, trans. Annette Lavers (Paris: Hill and Wang, 1957).
9. On the limiting factors of the exotic dance industry and the problems faced by dancers, see Bernadette Barton, "Managing the Toll of the Sex Industry: Boundary Setting among Exotic Dancers," *Journal of Contemporary Ethnography* 36.5 (2007): 571–696; Bernadette Barton, "Dancing on the Möbius Strip: Challenging the Sex War Paradigm," *Gender and Society* 16.5 (2002): 585–602; Bernadette Barton, *Stripped: Inside the Lives of Exotic Dancers* (New York: New York University Press, 2006); Holly Bell and Lacey Sloan, "Exploiter or Exploited: Topless Dancers Reflect on Their Experiences," *Journal of Women and Social Work* 13 (1998): 352–369; Tawnya Dudash, "Peepshow Feminism," in *Whores and Other Feminists*, ed. Jill Nagle (New York: Routledge, 1997); Carol Rambo Ronai and Rebecca Cross, "Dancing with Identity: Narrative Resistance Strategies of Male and Female Strippers," *Deviant Behavior* 19 (1998): 99–199; Sue E. Spivey, "Distancing and Solidarity as Resistance to Sexual Objectification in a Nude Dancing Bar," *Deviant Behavior* 26 (2005): 417–437; Jennifer K. Wesley, "Exotic Dancing and the Negotiation of Identity: The Multiple Uses of Body Technologies," *Journal of Contemporary Ethnography* 32.6 (2000): 643–669; Jennifer K. Wesley, "Where Am I Going to Stop? Exotic Dancers, Fluid Boundaries, and Effects on Identity." *Deviant Behavior* 24 (2003): 483–503.
10. Rambo Ronai, "The Aging Table Dancer."
11. Rambo Ronai, "The Aging Table Dancer," 315.
12. Peter Kuitenbrouwer, "Why Dancing Naked at a Bar Is a Declining Profession in Toronto," *National Post*, May 16, 2014.
13. Christine Rosen, "Electronic Intimacy," *Wilson Quarterly* 36.2 (2012).

CONCLUSION

1. This clothing, emblematic of the neo-burlesque community, is often symbolic of two ideological standpoints. By referencing the 1950s, it might nostalgically harken back to a less serious period before the women's movement, which allowed women to be "fun" and "feminine." Alternately, it is feminist, in that these women believe they are secure in their post-feminist or sex-positive feminist position and subsequently can turn full circle and ironically reclaim and invert pre-women's movement wardrobe. The fact that this clothing might be representative of the very oppression Betty Friedan first combated fifty years earlier is indeed the point. See Betty Friedan, *The Feminine Mystique* (New York: W.W. Norton, 1963).

2. Jo "Boobs" Weldon, interview, June 23, 2013.

3. Dustin Wax, interview, September 9, 2012; July 1, 2013.

4. Lilly Holiday, "Are You a Stripper?" *Facebook*, June 5, 2016.

5. Marinka, interview, June 3, 2013; April 14, 2014.

6. Carol Rambo Ronai, "Separating Aging from Old Age: The Aging Table Dancer," *Journal of Aging Studies* 6.4 (1992): 315.

7. Weldon, interview, June 23, 2013.

8. Bic Carrol, interview, March 23, 2015.

9. Carrol, interview, March 23, 2015.

10. Penny Starr Jr., June 12, 2014.

Neo-burlesque performer in the Titans of Tease Showcase at the Burlesque Hall of Fame, 2015

*Performers at the
Burlesque Hall of Fame,
2014*

Neo-burlesquers perform at the Burlesque Hall of Fame, 2015

A Legend performs at the
Burlesque Hall of Fame,
2015

Victoria DeVille and Laydee Swallowz at the nightly after-party held at the Orleans Hotel, 2015

BIBLIOGRAPHY

Interviews by Author

Note: The asterisk indicates an interview with a performer featured in Part 2 of the book.

*Rita Alexander, September 27, 2014.
Alexandra the Great 48, June 22, 2012.
Jessica Berson, May 22, 2014.
*Big Fannie Annie, July 17, 2014.
*Camille 2000, December 12, 2015.
*Bic Carrol, March 23, 2015.
Tiffany Carter, October 4, 2012; January 25, 2013.
*Toni Elling, June 13, 2014.
*Suzette Fontaine, December 19, 2015.
*Bambi Jones, March 28, 2015.
*Liza Jourdan, March 19, 2015.
*April March, September 19, 2012.
*Marinka, June 3, 2013; April 14, 2014.
*Gabriella Maze, October 10, 2014.
David Monaghan, June 26 2013.
*Kitten Natividad, June 4, 2013; March 20, 2014.
*Ellion Ness, June 13 2014.
*Holiday O'Hara, July 22, 2014.
*Tai Ping, December 19, 2015.
Elizabeth Rieur, October 24, 2013.
Lynn Sally, July 22, 2012.
Russell Shelnut, December 26, 2014.
*Isis Star, December 19, 2015.
*Penny Starr Jr., June 12, 2014.
*Judith Stein, December 13, 2015.
*Tempest Storm, January 28, 2013. Additional information collected by author when assisting Tempest Storm at Viva Las Vegas, March 29–April 1, 2013, and at the Burlesque Hall of Fame Weekend, June 2013.
*Dusty Summers, September 29, 2014.
*Ivy Tam, December 15, 2015.
Dustin Wax, September 9, 2012; July 1, 2013.
Jo Weldon, June 23, 2013.

Published Sources

Abbott, Karen. *American Rose: A Nation Laid Bare: The Life and Times of Gypsy Rose Lee*. New York: Random House, 2010.

Allen, Robert. *Horrible Prettiness: Burlesque and American Culture*. Chapel Hill: University of North Carolina Press, 1991.

Anderson, Margret L. "Whitewashing Race: A Critical Perspective on Whiteness." In *WhiteOut: The Continuing Significance of Racism*, ed. Ashley W. Doane and Eduardo Bonilla-Silva. New York: Routledge, 2003, 22.

Baldwin, Michelle. *Burlesque and the New Bump-N-Grind*. Golden, CO: Speck Press, 2004.

Barthes, Roland. *Mythologies*. Trans. Annette Lavers. Paris: Hill and Wang, 1957.

Barton, Bernadette. "Dancing on the Möbius Strip: Challenging the Sex War Paradigm." *Gender and Society* 16.5 (2002): 585–602.

Barton, Bernadette. "Managing the Toll of the Sex Industry: Boundary Setting among Exotic Dancers." *Journal of Contemporary Ethnography* 36.5 (2007): 571–696.

Barton, Bernadette. *Stripped: Inside the Lives of Exotic Dancers*. New York: New York University Press, 2006.

Barton, Bernadette, and Constance L. Hardesty. "Spirituality and Stripping: Exotic Dancers Narrate the Body Ekstasis." *Symbolic Interaction* 33.2 (2010): 280–296.

Baumgardner, Jennifer, and Amy Richards. "Feminism and Femininity: Or How We Learned to Stop Worrying and Love the Thong." In *All About the Girl: Culture Power and Identity*, ed. A. Harris. New York: Routledge, 2004, 59–67.

Bell, Holly, and Lacey Sloan. "Exploiter or Exploited: Topless Dancers Reflect on Their Experiences." *Journal of Women and Social Work* 13 (1998): 352–369.

Bell, Laurie. *Good Girls/Bad Girls: Feminists and Sex Trade Workers Face to Face*. Seattle: Seal Press, 1987.

Bentley, Toni. *Sisters of Salome*. New Haven, CT: Yale University Press, 2002.

Bosse, Katharina. *New Burlesque*. New York: Distributed Art Publishers, 2004.

Boyd, Bill. *Tempest Storm: The Lady Is a Vamp*. Atlanta: Peachtree Publishers, 1987.

Brooks, Siobhan. "Hypersexualization and the Dark Body: Race and Inequality among Black and Latina Women in the Exotic Dance Industry." *Sexuality Research and Social Policy* 7.2 (2010): 70–80.

Burnette, Pat. "The Good Old Daze." *Cavalcade of Burlesque,* September 1952.

Butler, Judith. "Ageism: Another Form of Bigotry." *Gerontologist* 9.3 (1969): 243–246.

Cherniavsky, Eva. *Incorporations: Race, Nation, and the Body Politics of Capital*. Minneapolis: University of Minnesota Press, 2006.

Corio, Anne, and Joseph DiMona. *This Was Burlesque*. New York: Grosset & Dunlap/Madison Square Press, 1968.

"Court Calls Them Employees: Says Strip-Tease 'Gift to Theater.'" *Los Angeles Herald-Examiner,* June 15, 1964.

Dean, Tim. *Unlimited Intimacy: Reflections on the Subculture of Barebacking*. Chicago: University of Chicago Press, 2009.

Derrida, Jacques. *Mal D'archive*. Paris: Editions Galilee, 1995.

Dodds, Sherril. *Dancing on the Canon: Embodiments of Value in Popular Dance*. London: Palgrave, 2011.

Dodds, Sherril. "Embodied Transformations in Neo-Burlesque Striptease." *Dance Research Journal* 45.3 (2013): 75–90.

Du Bois, W. E. B. *Black Reconstruction in America 1860–1880*. New York: Harcourt, Brace, 1935.

Dudash, Tawnya. "Peepshow Feminism." In *Whores and Other Feminists*, ed. Jill Nagle. New York: Routledge, 1997.

Dyer, Richard. *White*. London: Routledge, 1997.

Dyhouse, Carrol. *Glamour: Women, History, Feminism*. London: Zed Books, 2011.

Edwards, Justin D., and Rune Graulund. *Grotesque: The New Critical Idiom*. London: Routledge, 2013.

Egan, Danielle. *Dancing for Dollars and Praying for Love: The Relationships between Exotic Dancers and Their Regulars*. New York: Palgrave Macmillan, 2006.

Ferreday, Debra. "Adapting Femininities: The New Burlesque." *Journal of Media and Culture* 10.2 (2007).

Ferreday, Debra. "Showing the Girl: The New Burlesque." *Feminist Theory* 9.47 (2008): 47–65.

Foley, Brenda. *Undressed for Success: Beauty Contestants and Exotic Dancers as Merchants of Morality.* New York: Palgrave Macmillan, 2005.

Frank, Katherine. "Exploring the Motivations and Fantasies of Strip Club Customers in Relation to Legal Regulations." *Archives of Sexual Behavior* 34.5 (2005): 487–504.

Frank, Katherine. *G-Strings and Sympathy: Strip Club Regulars and Male Desire.* Durham, NC: Duke University Press, 2002.

Frank, Katherine. "Thinking Critically about Strip Club Research." *Sexualities* 10.4 (2007): 501–517.

Frankel, Noralee. *Stripping Gypsy: The Life of Gypsy Rose Lee.* New York: Oxford University Press, 2009.

Frankenberg, Ruth. *White Women, Race Matters: The Social Construction of Whiteness.* Minneapolis: University of Minnesota Press, 1993.

Friedan, Betty. *The Feminine Mystique.* New York: W.W. Norton, 1963.

Frueh, Joanna. "The Fear of Flesh That Moves." *High Performance* 14.3 (1991): 70–71.

Gander, Kashmira. "New York Nursing Home That Hired Strippers for Elderly Residents Sued by Family." *Independent*, April 19, 2014.

Gerard, Barney. "Burlesque: Its Rise and Demise." *Variety*, January 4, 1956.

Goffman, Erving. *Frame Analysis: An Essay on the Organization of Experience.* Boston: Northeastern University Press, 1974.

Gott, Merryn, Sharron Hinchliff, and Elisabeth Galena. "General Practitioner Attitudes to Discussing Sexual Health Issues with Older People." *Social Science & Medicine* 58 (2004): 2093–2103.

Hajjar, Ramzi R., and Hosam K. Kamel. "Sexuality in the Nursing Home, Part 1: Attitudes and Barriers to Sexual Expression." *Journal of the American Medical Directors Association* 5(2 Suppl) (2004): s4–s7.

Hammond, Doris B. *My Parents Never Had Sex: Myths and Facts of Sexual Aging.* Buffalo, NY: Prometheus Books, 1987.

Hanna, Judith Lynne. "Exotic Dance Adult Entertainment: Ethnography Challenges False Mythology." *City and Society* 15 (2003): 165–193.

Hanna, Judith Lynne. "Undressing the First Amendment and Corsetting the Striptease Dancer." *Drama Review* 42.2 (1998): 38–69.

Holiday, Lilly. "Are You a Stripper?" Facebook, June 5, 2016.

Hopkins, David. "Why Dallas Burlesque Owes a Debt to Tammi True." *D Magazine*, February 23, 2011.

Hurd, Laura, and Alexandra Korotchenko. "Doing Beauty: Women, Ageing and Identity." In *Representing Ageing: Images and Identities*, ed. Ylanne Virpi. Basingstoke, UK: Palgrave Macmillan, 2012.

Jeffreys, Sheila. "Keeping Women Down and Out: The Strip Club Boom and the Reinforcement of Male Dominance." *Journal of Women in Culture and Society* 34.1 (2008): 152–173.

Johnson, Merri Lisa. *Jane Sexes It Up: True Confessions of Feminist Desire.* New York: Four Walls Eight Windows, 2002.

Jordan, Stephanie, and Helen Thomas. "Dance and Gender: Formalism and Semiotics Reconsidered." In *The Routledge Dance Studies Reader*, ed. Alexandra Carter. London: Routledge, 1998.

Kealiinohomoku, Joann. "An Anthropologist Looks at Ballet as a Form of Ethnic Dance." In *Moving History/Dancing Cultures: A Dance Reader*, ed. Ann Cooper Albright and Ann Dils. Middletown, CT: Wesleyan University Press, 2001, 33–43.

Keft-Kennedy, Virginia. "How Does She Do That? Belly Dancing and the Horror of a Flexible Woman." *Women's Studies* 34 (2005): 279–300.

Kraut, Anthea. *Choreographing Copyright: Race, Gender, and Intellectual Property Rights in American Dance.* New York: Oxford University Press, 2016.

Kuitenbrouwer, Peter. "Why Dancing Naked at a Bar Is a Declining Profession in Toronto." *Nation Post*, May 16, 2014.

"L. A. Strippers Protest Their Low Take-Off Pay: Burlesque Queens in Organization Meeting Threaten 'Cover Up' Strike over Grievances." *Los Angeles Times*, June 19, 1955.

Leavey, Claire. "Tempest Storm: Burlesque Queen." *Libertine*, August 2013.

Lehrer, Kristen. "Dita Von Teese on Burlesque vs. Stripping." *Fox News Magazine*, May 17, 2013.

Leslie, Larry Z. *Celebrity in the 21st Century*. Santa Barbara, CA: ABC–CLIO, 2011.

Liepe-Levinson, Katherine. *Strip Show: Performances of Gender and Desire*. London: Routledge, 2002.

MacIntosh, Peggy. "White Privilege: Unpacking the Invisible Knapsack." *Independent School* 49.2 (1990): 31–35.

Manaster, Shelly. "Treading Water: An Autoethnographic Account(ing) of the Lap Dance." In *Flesh for Fantasy: Producing and Consuming Exotic Dance*, ed. Danielle Egan, Katherine Frank, and Lisa Merri Johnson. New York: Thunder's Mouth Press, 2006, 3–18.

Manning, Susan. *Modern Dance, Negro Dance: Race in Motion*. Minneapolis: University of Minnesota Press, 2004.

Mansbridge, Joanna. "In Search of a Different History: The Remains of Burlesque in Montreal." *Canadian Theatre Review* 158 (Spring 2014): 7–12.

Miller, Neil. *Banned in Boston: The Watch and Ward Society's Crusade against Books, Burlesque, and Social Evil*. Boston: Beacon Press, 2010.

Moran, Caitlin. *How to Be a Woman*. London: Ebury Press, 2011.

Mukerji, Nimisha. *Tempest Storm*. Documentary Film, Shotglass Productions, 2016.

Nagle, Jill, ed. *Whores and Other Feminists*. New York: Routledge, 1997.

Nally, Claire. "Grrrly Hurly Burly: Neo-Burlesque and the Performance of Gender." *Textual Practice* 23.4 (2009): 621–643.

Nathan, Debbie. *Pornography: A Groundwork Guide*. Toronto: Groundwood Books/House of Anansi Press, 2007.

Newton, Randi. "What Happens to Strippers When They Age Exposes Society's Harsh Beauty Standards." *Connections.Mic.* February 3, 2015.

Oakley, Annie. *Working Sex: Sex Workers Write about a Changing Industry*. Emeryville, CA: Seal Press, 2007.

Owen, David. "Neo-Burlesque and the Resurgence of Roller Derby: Empowerment, Play, and Community." *Canadian Theatre Review* 158 (Spring 2014): 33–38.

Phelan, Peggy. "The Ontology of Performance. Representation without Reproduction." *Unmarked: The Politics of Performance*. New York: Routledge, 1993.

Preminger, Erik Lee. *Gypsy and Me: At Home and on the Road with Gypsy Rose Lee*. Boston: Little, Brown, 1984.

Protacio, Kristine. "Filthy Publicity: Jennie Lee and the Exotic Dancers League." Unpublished Paper, San Luis Obispo: California Polytechnic State University, 2011.

Pugliesi, K. "The Consequences of Emotional Labor: Effects on Work Stress, Job Satisfaction, and Well-Being." *Motivation and Emotion* 23.2 (1999): 125–154.

Pullen, Kristen. *Actresses and Whores: On Stage and in Society*. Cambridge: Cambridge University Press, 2005.

Pullen, Kristen. "Dancing Sex, Revolution, and History: The Case of Carol Doda." Nashville, TN: American Society of Theater Research, November 2012.

Queen, Carol, and Lynn Comella. "The Necessary Revolution: Sex-Positive Feminism in the Post-Barnard Era." *Communication Review* 11 (2008): 274–291.

Ridout, Nicholas. *Passionate Amateurs: Theatre, Communism, and Love*. Ann Arbor: University of Michigan Press, 2013.

Rieur, Elizabeth. "The Other Ladies of Burlesque: Female Attendance at Burlesque Shows, 1920–1945." Unpublished Paper. Boston: Simmons College, 2013.

Roach, Joseph. *It*. Ann Arbor: University of Michigan Press, 2007.

Ronai, Carol Rambo. "Separating Aging from Old Age: The Aging Table Dancer." *Journal of Aging Studies* 6.4 (1992): 307–317.

Ronai, Carol Rambo, and Rebecca Cross. "Dancing with Identity: Narrative Resistance Strategies of Male and Female Strippers." *Deviant Behavior* 19 (1998): 99–199.

Rosen, Christine. "Electronic Intimacy." *Wilson Quarterly* 36.2 (2012): 48–51.

Ross, Becki L. *Burlesque West: Showgirls, Sex and Sin in Postwar Vancouver*. Toronto: University of Toronto Press, 2009.

Russen, Jorn. "The Logic of Historicization: Metahistorical Reflections on the Debate between Friedlander and Broszat." *History and Memory* 9.1/2 (1997).

Russo, Mary. *The Female Grotesque: Risk, Excess and Modernity*. New York: Routledge, 1994.

Sally, Lynn. "'It Is the Ugly That Is So Beautiful': Performing the Monster/Beauty Continuum in American Neoburlesque." *Journal of American Drama and Theatre* 21.3 (2009): 5–20.

Saretsky, K. "The Right to Be Human: How One Facility Cares." *Provider* 12 (1987): 20–23.

Schaefer, Eric. "Gauging a Revolution: 16mm Film and the Rise of the Pornographic Feature." In *Porn Studies*, ed. Linda Williams. Durham, NC: Duke University Press, 2003.

Schneider, Rebecca. "Archives. Performance Remains." *Performance Research* 6.2 (2001): 100–108.

Schweitzer, Dahlia. "Striptease: The Art of Spectacle and Transgression." *Journal of Popular Culture* 34.1 (2001): 65–75.

Shteir, Rachel. *Striptease: The Untold History of the Girly Show*. New York: Oxford University Press, 2004.

Silverman, Sime. "The Killer of Burlesque." *Variety*, 1931.

Skeggs, Beverley. *Class, Self, Culture*. London: Routledge, 2004.

Sobel, Bernard. *A Pictorial History of Burlesque*. New York: Bonanza Books, 1956.

Sontag, Susan. "The Double Standard of Aging." In *The Other within Us: Feminist Explorations of Women Aging*, ed. Marilyn Pearsall. Colorado: Westview Press, 1972, 19–24.

Spivey, Sue E. "Distancing and Solidarity as Resistance to Sexual Objectification in a Nude Dancing Bar." *Deviant Behavior* 26 (2005): 417–437.

Sprinkle, Annie. *Annie Sprinkle: Post Porn Modernism*. Amsterdam: Torch Books, 1991.

Starr, Bernard. "The Ageism and Sexuality." *Annual Review of Gerontology*, 1985.

Stuart, Andrea. *Showgirls*. London: Random House, 1996.

Szasz, G. "Sexual Incidents in an Extended Care Unit for Aged Men." *Journal of American Geriatric Society* 31 (1983): 407–411.

Tempanaro, Sebastiano. *On Materialism*. Trans. Lawrence Garner. London: Verso, 1970.

Thrift, Nigel. "Understanding the Material Practice of Glamour." In *Affect Theory Reader*, ed. Melissa Gregg and Gregory J. Seigworth. Durham, NC: Duke University Press, 2010.

Tracy, Linda Lee. *The Anatomy of Burlesque*. Documentary Film, White Pines Productions, 2003.

Tremmel, Red. *Exotic World and the Burlesque Revival*. Documentary Film, 2012.

Turner, Kenneth, and Stephan F. Zito. *Sinema: American Pornographic Films and the People Who Make Them*. New York: Praeger, 1974.

Urish, Ben. "Narrative Striptease in the Night Club Era." *Journal of American Culture* 27.2 (2004): 157–165.

Virtanen, Michael. "Lap Dance a Tax-Exempt Art? Night Moves, Albany Strip Club, Takes Nude Dancing Case to New York Court." *Huffington Post*, September 5, 2012.

Vogt, Julie N. "Woman to Woman: Ann Corio and the Rehabilitation of American Burlesque." Unpublished Paper, Madison, University of Wisconsin, 2010.

Wahab, Stephanie, et al. "Exotic Dance Research: A Review of the Literature from 1970 to 2008." *Sexuality and Culture* 15 (2011): 56–79.

Wasow, M., and M. B. Lobe. "Sexuality in Nursing Homes." *Journal of American Geriatric Society* 27 (1979): 73–79.

Wesley, Jennifer K. "Exotic Dancing and the Negotiation of Identity: The Multiple Uses of Body Technologies." *Journal of Contemporary Ethnography* 32.6 (2000): 643–669.

Wesley, Jennifer K. "Where Am I Going to Stop? Exotic Dancers, Fluid Boundaries, and Effects on Identity." *Deviant Behavior* 24 (2003): 483–503.

Williams, Linda. *Hard Core: Power, Pleasure, and the "Frenzy of the Visible."* Berkeley: University of California Press, 1989.

Williams, Linda. *Screening Sex*. Durham, NC: Duke University Press, 2008.

Willson, Jacki. *The Happy Stripper: Pleasures and Politics of the New Burlesque*. London: I. B. Tauris, 2008.

Woodward, Kathleen. "Performing Age, Performing Gender." *NWSA Journal* 18.1 (2006): 162–189.

Zeidman, Irving. *The American Burlesque Show*. New York: Hawthorn Books, 1967.

Leslie Zemeckis. *Behind the Burly Q: The Story of Burlesque in America*. New York: Skyhorse, 2013.

Zemeckis, Leslie. *Behind the Burly Q*. Documentary film. Mistress Inc., 2010.

Performer at the Burlesque Hall of Fame, 2014

Midnight Martini performs her step down number as Miss Exotic World 2014 at the Tournament of Tease, 2015

Performer at the
Tournament of Tease at
the Burlesque Hall of
Fame, 2015

Mr. Gorgeoous performs his title-winning performance in the Tournament of Tease at the Burlesque Hall of Fame, 2014

INDEX

Page numbers in **bold** indicate photographs.

Sobel, Bernard, 74
social framing, 210
soft core pornography, 168
Sontag, Susan, 206
specialty act, 151, 260
spectacle, 206
Spice Girl, 79
stage hands' union, 74
stag films, 167
Star, Isis, 57, **188**, 189, **190**, 191
Stardust Suite, 235
Starr, Bernard, 61
Starr, Blaze, 122, 159
Starr, Penny, Jr., 82–83, **220**, 221–24, 259–60
Starr, Penny, Sr., **220**, **222**, 223–24, 260, **262**
Starr, Rita, **36**
St. Cyr, Lily, 232
Stealers Wheel, 157
Stein, Judith
    attempted rape case, 184
    "B drinking," 86
    class privilege, 57
    dangers of burlesque, 181, 184
    empowerment, 184
    The Great Canadian Beaver, 181, 186
    and her parents, 184–85
    on neo-burlesquers, 83, 189
    pictured (2015), **180**
    as pseudo parent for strippers, 185–86
    on stripping, 255
    Titans of Tease: Legends Showcase (2014), **95**
    Titans of Tease: Legends Showcase (2015),
      182–83, **184**, **187**
stigmatization, 103, 254–55
Stitch n' Bitch, 31
Storm, Tempest
    biography, 53, 275n2
    as burlesque queen, 130–31, 210
    celebrity status, 32, 87, 122, 131, 135–36,
      159, 258, 259
    Christmas cards, 25
    death of burlesque, 168
    and Dita Von Teese, **135**
    Dunes Hotel show, 131
    golden G-string, 25
    on G-strings, 132
    Lou Lou D'vil tattoo, 257
    marriage to Jefferies, 134–35
    meets Lee, 133–34
    and Ness, 117
    online sales, 129
    personal boundaries, 132
    pictured (2013), **126–27**
    pictured (2014), **128**, **135**, **137**
    Regehr as assistant, 11
    retirement of, 133, 276n15

and manager, Harvey Robins, **130**, 134
    romantic relationships, 129
    status of, 11
    "Tempest Storm: The Sexiest Stripper of
      all Time," 135
    Viva Las Vegas car show, 129
    women's patronage of burlesque, 252
strip clubs
    ageism, 62
    "B drinking," 259
    Berlin, 210
    boom times, 70, 73
    and burlesque, 10, 12, 79, 98
    career span of strippers, 259
    death narrative, 211–12
    emancipation, 73
    empowerment, 54
    exploitation in, 73
    Giuliani closing of, 37–38
    hypernormativity, 79
    legends and, 259
    Mafia, 198
    Marinka interview, 210–11
    "motherhood," 207
    neo-burlesque movement, 83, 85
    New York City, 37–38
    patron interaction, 62
    personal boundaries, 210
    scholarship on, 73
    segregation, 59
    substance abuse, 198
    See also strippers
strippers
    abortions, 252
    ageism and, 231–32
    alcoholism, 123–24
    availability of, 132–33
    as "bad girls," 184
    "B drinking," 86–87, 94
    birth control pill and, 52
    and burlesque, 74, 181, 213
    and burlesque dancers, 10, 83, 253
    career span, 197, 212–13, 259
    carnival, 151
    Carrol as trainer, 240
    Chinese, 145, 147
    and chorus girls, 241
    as ecdysiasts, 121
    fiscal independence of, 53–54
    framing of, 11, 131
    The Great Canadian Beaver, 185–86
    hippies strippers, 181
    identity and, 205
    and lap dancing, 76
    median age of, 211
    mid-twentieth-century, 76, 207

Jo "Boobs" Weldon
performs at the Burlesque
Hall of Fame, 2014

Shannon Doah performs in the Titans of Tease Showcase at the Burlesque Hall of Fame, 2015

*Eddie Van Glam performs
in the Tournament of
Tease at the Burlesque
Hall of Fame, 2014*